THE **UNINTENDED** **CONSEQUENCES** OF **TECHNOLOGY**

CHRIS ATEGEKA

THE **UNINTENDED** **CONSEQUENCES** OF **TECHNOLOGY**

SOLUTIONS, BREAKTHROUGHS AND THE RESTART WE NEED

WILEY

Published by John Wiley & Sons, Inc., Hoboken, New Jersey.
Published simultaneously in Canada.

For general information on our other products and services or for technical support, please contact our Customer Care Department within the United States at (800) 762-2974, outside the United States at (317) 572-3993 or fax (317) 572-4002.

Wiley publishes in a variety of print and electronic formats and by print-on-demand. Some material included with standard print versions of this book may not be included in e-books or in print-on-demand. If this book refers to media such as a CD or DVD that is not included in the version you purchased, you may download this material at http://booksupport.wiley.com. For more information about Wiley products, visit www.wiley.com.

Library of Congress Cataloging-in-Publication Data

Names: Ategeka, Chris, author.
Title: The unintended consequences of technology : solutions, breakthroughs, and the restart we need / Chris Ategeka.
Description: Hoboken, New Jersey : Wiley, [2021] | Includes index.
Identifiers: LCCN 2021027157 (print) | LCCN 2021027158 (ebook) | ISBN 9781119817598 (hardback) | ISBN 9781119817581 (adobe pdf) | ISBN 9781119817604 (epub)
Subjects: LCSH: Technology—Sociological aspects. | Technology—Social aspects.
Classification: LCC HM846 .A79 2021 (print) | LCC HM846 (ebook) | DDC 303.48/3—dc23
LC record available at https://lccn.loc.gov/2021027157
LC ebook record available at https://lccn.loc.gov/2021027158

Cover Design: Wiley
Cover Image: © Sashkinw/iStock/Getty Images
SKY10029419_082721

Dedicated to my parents, my siblings, my partner, Caroline, and my son, Matt.

Thanks for making it all worthwhile.

CONTENTS

INTRODUCTION

"We cannot solve our problems with the same thinking we used when we created them."

—Albert Einstein

Humanity is at a crossroads. The explosion of technology and its exponential advancements are reshaping what it means to be human. As technology continues to expand, its incredible imprint on our lives continues to deepen. Our algorithmic lifestyles have completely taken over our lives. Today technologies make decisions about what we buy, the news we read, who we vote for, the jobs we get, the people we meet, and the ads we see.

Along with the benefits and victories provided by new technologies are many consequences that are alarmingly detrimental to society and to our planet.

When you take a closer look at any technology, you will find that it's a double-edged sword. If it's used correctly, it can and has made our lives easier, more efficient, and better. However, that same technology, in the wrong hands or used incorrectly, can do serious damage to humanity.

Progress always comes at a cost. Paper fundamentally changed the way information was stored and distributed, but its production, to this day, contributes heavily to deforestation. Technology, just like medicine, is not free from side effects. For example, consider that:

- A technology promising a cancer-free world can cause cancer.
- A technology promising us democratic values such as freedom of speech and agency can also threaten democracies.
- In a world of infinite digital connectivity, millions of people still feel alone. Isolation and depression are public health crises.
- Digital technology is aiding our culture to reject reason yet heavily reward outrage, untruths, and myths.

- Technology has hastened humans' tendency to run our resources into the ground, metaphorically and literally, instead of aspiring to regeneration and sustainability.

This should come as no surprise, because hindsight is always 20/20. Rarely at the time of invention are creators the best judge of how their system will be used, nor do they truly know what good or harm will come of it.

Industrialization increased our standard of living, but it also led to a lot of pollution. In a similar way, technology has exacerbated the effects of climate change. The planet is in full-on emergency mode. Emissions are on the raise. Earth is turning into desert. The oceans are heating up. Species are going extinct. The Amazon is burning at an alarming rate. Ecosystems are crashing. The ice is melting. The coral reefs are dying.

We need to do something. And we need to do it now!!

We are clearly the last generation that can alter the course on climate change, but we are also the first generation experiencing many of its unintended consequences.

WHY ME?

For most leaders, it can be challenging to keep up with the many unintended consequences of emerging technologies. As a futurist, a technology entrepreneur, and an engineer in Silicon Valley—specializing in future-think and scenario planning—it's my job to help leaders understand and prepare for the impact of the unintended consequences of technology (UCOTs).

Fifteen years ago, I would never have predicted that I would be talking about the unintended consequences of technology, let alone writing a book about them. After tragically losing both my parents, I was a kid (the child head of my family) in rural Uganda waking up every day worried about what I and my younger siblings were going to eat that day. That's as far as my concerns about life on this planet went. A lot has changed since then. With the help of a charity organization and the Helms family in Oakland, California, I was sponsored to attend UC Berkeley Engineering

School. With lots of hard work and determination, I became an engineer and an entrepreneur in Silicon Valley. I focused my attention on creating products and services that bring healthcare to individuals in hard-to-reach areas. I was successful at building several companies. My work won me accolades. I found myself in front of highly influential people at the biggest platforms on Earth, like the World Economic Forum and TED conferences. It's there that my world and level of ambition opened up a bit more.

You see, I am a product of someone else's generosity. I am what I am because some stranger showed me love, empathy, compassion, and care—the things that make us truly human. We are slowly losing these qualities in the age of exponential technology development and usage. I would not be here if it weren't for another human being whom I had never met caring deeply and wanting a better life for me.

The way we are training technology systems today, I am afraid we may not be passing on these amazing human qualities to systems and machines that are increasingly running human lives. The way technology is being developed and commercialized has reached a point where some of its components are not serving humanity's best interests.

I vividly remember sitting in the audience at TED conferences listening to one speaker giving a mesmerizing but also terrifying talk about AI. Computer scientist Supasorn Suwajanakorn showed us how, as a grad student, he had used AI and 3D modeling to create photo-realistic fake videos of people synced to audio. These are now commonly known as *deepfakes*. I sat there with my head spinning, wondering about how this technology could be misused and abused. This—along with many technology abuses that have affected me personally or that I keep reading about—played a huge role in setting me on this path.

With a very strong conviction, "somebody has to do something about this" became the new tune on "repeat" in my head. Not long after hearing that TED talk, I became pretty convinced that for the next decade, I needed to put my energy, resources, and time toward focusing on the unintended consequences of technologies (UCOTs).

If not me, then who; if not now, then when? I dove right in!

I founded the Institute for Unintended Consequences of Technology (UCOT), where my team and I bring together thousands of people from all walks of life, such as technologists, policy makers, futurists, engineers, professors, change makers, entrepreneurs, investors, philosophers, artists, students, and other thought leaders. Our mission is 1) to advance public understanding, awareness, and perception on unintended consequences of technologies, and 2) to accelerate solutions and collaboration toward a collective large-scale action.

THE BOOK'S GOALS

In this book, I provide concerned citizens, business professionals, and people in decision-making positions with a blueprint for key technologies on their current and future potential unintended consequences. The book also includes tips on how best to prepare yourself, your community, your businesses, and our shared spaceship called planet Earth about what's to come.

I have chosen a few technologies and trends that I believe have the ability to transform what it means to be human and what I strongly believe every leader should pay attention to today. Technology is not good or bad; it's just a tool. It's who we are as a people that make it good or bad. And sometimes the bad brings lots of concerns.

Within technology's concerns and dangers hides an opportunity of first-mover advantage:

- To reactively create solutions for the things already going wrong

- To proactively strategize and mitigate future potential harm before it happens

There are technologies in this book like AI and big data that have huge unintended consequences as stand-alone trends. However, the applications of data and AI also overlap a lot with other technologies and other trends. My goal is to write about them individually, but they will also keep coming up in the other subjects.

WHAT THIS BOOK COVERS

This book suggests a series of steps we can take to deal with the unintended and willfully ignored consequences of technologies. The bad news is that so long as technology is here, so are its negative externalities. Those two go hand in hand. The good news is that with intention, smarts, and safety engineering we can deal with unintended consequences of technologies before they even occur. This book breaks down what needs to be done to get there into two parts.

- Part I: How Humanity Got into This Mess. Chapter 1 explains how capitalism, greed, and the myth of meritocracy got us into this mess and is keeping us there. Chapter 2 explores the power imbalance between governments of nation-states and the giant technology companies (tech-states) founded by a handful of its citizens.

- Part II: Technologies and Trends with Lots of Promise but also Uncertainty. The chapters in Part II explore different technologies such as 5G, AI, gene editing, blockchain, and many more that are extremely powerful, with a potential to fundamentally change what it means to be human and the future of our planet.

In most chapters, I begin with the definition of the specific technology, a brief history, some positive use cases, and negative unintended consequences, and end with what has been done to deal with these consequences or what can we do to proactively prevent them from happening in the first place.

The unintended consequences of technology are a huge existential crisis, but I also see solving them as a huge opportunity. We have the ambition thanks to the passions of a growing global movement led by young people who are deeply concerned about the unintended consequences of technologies. What we need is a will to act.

The global movement on how to deal with UCOT is filled with technologists, policy makers, futurists, engineers, professors, change makers, entrepreneurs, investors, philosophers, artists, students, and other thought leaders. What I propose in this book is based on the guidance and learnings I have gotten from experts and visionaries in these fields.

In the final chapter, I share the concrete steps each of us can take to help the world deal with the unintended consequences of technologies. Whether you are a technologist, a government leader, or a citizen of this world, there are things you can do to help keep humanity from innovating itself into extinction.

I truly believe that, with advancements in technology, 100 years from now we may have a well-optimized world that works for everyone. Or there may not be any world left to optimize. The choice is ours!

If you are a business leader, this book is for you. If you are a human being, this book is for you. Let's dive in!

PART I

HOW HUMANITY GOT INTO THIS MESS

CHAPTER 1

Capitalism:
The Cult of Self-Sufficiency

Capitalism is an economic system where people and companies make most of the decisions and own most of the property. The means of production are largely or entirely privately owned (by individuals or companies) and operated for profit, rather than owned by the state. The United States practices free-market capitalism, whereby the prices of goods and services are determined by supply and demand (the free market), rather than set artificially by a third party such as the government.

You may be wondering why this book starts with this topic in Chapter 1. Well, anything and everything technology- or systems-related that we discuss in this book has developmental incentives and motivations largely aligned with capitalism. You will hear capitalistic power echoing through every chapter in this book. In addition, most negative *unintended consequences of technology* (UCOTs) strongly correlate with misalignment in incentive structures. That's why capitalism is covered in Chapter 1. The nature of capitalism and the UCOTs caused by it and consumerism set the stage for all the topics covered in this book.

A QUICK HISTORY OF CAPITALISM

Technology in the scientific and industrial revolutions transformed humanity's understanding of the world. Technology transformed our ability as humans to alter that same world. And this altering of our world is now aligned and heavily driven by a major force, known as capitalism.

The history of capitalism is diverse and has many debated roots. Scholars tend to cite that the first stage of capitalism came about during the 16th and the 17th centuries, when merchants gradually became more involved in the production of goods by supplying materials and paying wages. Traders from the towns started to move to the countryside, supplying the peasants and the craftsmen with money, convincing the peasants to produce for the international market. The merchants benefited greatly by making profits from the ownership and control of the means of production. This led to an increase in consumption of goods and services purchased in the market.

By the early 18th century, a complex colonial trade network was established over the North Atlantic Ocean. This network was partially the result of local economic conditions and dominant wind and sea current patterns.

Since dominant wind patterns highly constrained sailing ships, a trading system followed this pattern. Manufactured commodities were exported from Europe, some toward African colonial centers where they would be used to purchase slaves, and some toward the American colonies. This system also included a slave trade, mainly to Central and South American colonies (Brazil and the West Indies), where there was a high demand for labor in plantations and mines. Tropical commodities (e.g. sugar and molasses) produced in plantations flowed to the American colonies and Europe. North America also exported tobacco, furs, indigo (a dye), and lumber (for shipbuilding) to Europe. This trading system collapsed in the 19th century with the introduction of steamships, the end of slavery, and the independence of many of the colonies of the Americas. (Rodrigue, 2013).

In the 19th century, globalization, alongside transport and communication, innovations, and broader institutional changes, allowed worldwide commodities such as cotton, wheat, sugar, tea, butter, silk, flax, and rice to flow. The economic and social conditions were in place for the industrial revolution to explode onto the world's economies. Powered by a number of new inventions, the primitive factory system was transformed, as machine power drove productivity to unprecedented levels. There was a boom in factory production, with all manner of buildings being converted into factories and the majority of waged labor taking place within factory buildings.

It should be said that the industrial revolution saw machines replace many workers and transform the way people worked, lived, and consumed goods. Over time, this continuously convinced us that a person's well-being and happiness depend fundamentally on obtaining goods and material possessions, also known as *consumerism*.

American capitalism, combined with consumerism, really hit in the roaring 1920s, which was a decade of huge prosperity fueled by the advancements of two automobile titans in the 1910s and 1920s. Ford's and GM's inventions of the automobile and introduction of automated assembly lines transformed American manufacturing into a mass-production machine.

Then came the Great Depression, which was considered the worst economic downturn in the history of the industrialized world, lasting for a full decade. By 1933, the Great Depression reached its lowest point. Some 15 million Americans were unemployed, the stock market had lost almost 90% of its value, and nearly half the country's banks had failed (Ali, 2016; more about capitalism bursts and booms later).

Capitalism survived the Great Depression era, the world got back on its feet, and, when the 1950s hit, there was a second surge of extreme American consumerism. The overall economy grew by 37% during this decade (History.com, 2020). WWII was over and even the government told citizens that they needed to consume more to be "patriotic citizens." New industries grew out of the huge boom in consumer spending: TV, plastics, jet engines, entertainment media, mass housing, and more. Production of goods like food, cars, clothing, electronics, appliances, and pharmaceuticals all accelerated due to factory-driven mass production.

Fast-forward to the 21st century, with exponential advancements in technology and easy access to information. Pressures of consumerism are everywhere—on our phones, social media platforms, websites, TV shows, movies, billboards, and retail checkouts. We've gone from shopping for necessity, utility, and comfort to overpurchasing for validation and stress relief.

Over the past 100 years, we've grown to believe that having more stuff is tantamount to happiness, a never-ending comparison of one's inside with someone else's outside. What we own and purchase defines our current social norms of success. The problem is, all this overconsumption is not making us happier. In fact, it's making us, and our planet, sicker and more unhappy than ever. The forces of capitalism and consumerism have us all addicted to mass consumption—on steroids.

WHERE WE ARE NOW

If you are *not* in the top 1% (folks who own the majority of the world's wealth), it's very easy to see how capitalism is not working for you. Many want it replaced or at least reconfigured to a hybrid system that works for more people. However, there are so many scars on the U.S. psyche from the communist regimes and conflicts of the USSR that proposing anything new or different from capitalism instantaneously makes you a communist or a socialist, which is considered a slur.

However, we do need to be thinking about alternative systems. Capitalism is working too well for a very few at the top, not so well for the rest of the world, and increasingly threatening our planet and future.

Taking a closer look at a hybrid of capitalism and socialism as an example, at the time of this writing, this form of government appears to be working well in countries like Germany and the Scandinavian subregion of Northern Europe that includes Denmark, Sweden, and Norway. In addition to being economically strong and stable, these countries rank very high on the World Happiness Index, an annual publication of the United Nations Sustainable Development Solutions Network. The index is a ranking of national happiness based on the respondents' ratings of their own lives, which correlates with various other life factors, many not related to consumption, such as having someone to count on, having a sense of freedom to make key life decisions, generosity, trust, and purpose (World Happiness Report, March 2020).

However, in the United States, when politicians like Vermont Senator Bernie Sanders propose the distribution of wealth equally among the people, free provision of government social services like schools, healthcare to its citizens, and public ownership of most land, they are quickly demonized as socialists by a subset of the country's population. This subset has been taught that the capitalist ethos of competition and acquisitiveness is simply "human nature," and is the best and only way to govern. They do not seem to realize that capitalism is a socially constructed way of life that has been deliberately and systematically fostered by centuries of the market economy.

ADVANTAGES OF CAPITALISM

Capitalism has some merits, which is why it has survived and thrived in the majority of the world economies. The following sections touch on a few advantages of this economic system.

Economic Freedom Helps Political Freedom

When governments own the means of production and set prices, this invariably leads to a powerful state and creates a large bureaucracy, which may extend into other areas of life.

Efficiency

Firms in a capitalist-based society face incentives to be efficient and produce goods that are in demand. These incentives create pressures to cut costs and avoid waste.

Innovation

Capitalism has a dynamic where entrepreneurs and firms are seeking to create and develop profitable new products that may be popular with consumers. This can lead to product development and more choice of goods.

Economic Growth

With firms and individuals facing incentives to be innovative and work hard, this creates a climate of innovation and economic expansion. The dynamic helps to increase real GDP and can lead to improved living standards. This increased wealth enables a higher standard of living; in theory, everyone can benefit from this increased wealth, and there is a "trickle-down effect" from rich to poor.

The Unintended or Willfully Ignored Negative Consequences of Capitalism in the Technology Sector

"Capitalism is the astounding belief that the wickedest of men will do the most wickedest of things for the greatest good of everyone."

—John Maynard Keynes

There are many UCOTs related to capitalism. This section focuses on the ones with the biggest influence.

Monopoly Power

Private ownership of capital has enabled large technology firms to gain monopoly power in product and labor markets. Companies with monopoly powers—like Amazon, Apple, Google, and Facebook—have exploited their position to charge higher prices, pay lower wages to workers, avoid paying their fair share in taxes, and gain unilateral control of who they do or do not want on their platforms.

One of most recent examples is Amazon, one of the most valuable companies in the world, fighting tooth and nail to prevent its workers from forming a union. It's a battle for higher wages and improved working conditions. The company has steadfastly said its "workers don't need any union" (Greene, 2021).

In a capitalist society like the United States, there is great inequality between the owners of capital and those who work for their firms. In the current pandemic of COVID-19, for example, folks who are doing all the heavy lifting (the essential workers) under the harshest conditions are often getting paid minimum wage. Research at the Brookings Institution, a nonprofit public policy organization based in Washington, DC, titled a report "The COVID-19 Hazard Continues, But the Hazard Pay Does Not: Why America's Essential Workers Need a Raise" (Brookings Institution, 2021). As Robert Reich, a UC Berkeley professor and former Secretary of Labor pointed out, "Jeff Bezos' [the founder of Amazon] net worth in 2009 was $6,800,000,000 and $200,000,000,000 in 2020; meanwhile the Federal minimum wage in 2009 was $7.25 and is still $7.25" (Reich, 2020).

The following quote appeared in an NPR article, "There Is Rich and Then There Is Bezos Rich" (Zarroli, 2020):

"You probably think 2020 has turned out to be a pretty lousy year, what with the coronavirus pandemic, a global recession and unceasing partisan warfare in Washington.

Then again, you're not Jeff Bezos or Elon Musk.

Thanks to soaring stock prices at Tesla, the company Musk founded, the quirky South African-born entrepreneur has seen his personal wealth soar to unimaginable heights of $147 billion [less than a month later this number was $188 billion making him the richest person in the world].

In fact, Musk is one of only five *centibillionaires* in the world, or someone with a personal fortune exceeding $100 billion, according to the Bloomberg Billionaires Index."

This is not sustainable. If we have learned anything from nature and the laws of physics, nothing grows forever. Whatever goes up will peak, and then it has to come down! The bottom line is that there are a limited number of resources on this planet. How we share and distribute these resources to all living things is a matter of importance that affects our future, and should affect our conscience. Unbridled capitalism is not sustainable, nor is it humane.

Negative Externalities

Technology companies that greatly benefit from the free market have ignored the negative effects of their creations. They mostly care about maximizing profit for their shareholders and choose to ignore negative externalities, such as the horrifying inequalities and pollution from production that harm living standards and living things.

Sadly, that same free-market economy continuously underprovides goods with positive externalities, such as health, public transport, and education. These goods are mostly deemed the work of philanthropy or government. This has led to an inefficient allocation of resources. Even ardent supporters of capitalism admit that government provision of certain public goods and public services is essential to maximizing the potential of a capitalist society.

Inherited Wealth and Wealth Inequality

Capitalism is based on the legal right to private property and the ability to pass on wealth to future generations. Capitalists argue that a capitalist society is fair because you gain the rewards of your hard work. But often people are rich simply because they inherit wealth or are born into a privileged class. Therefore, a capitalist society not only fails to create equality of outcome but also fails to provide equality of opportunity. Inequality creates social division. Societies that are highly unequal create resentment and social division. They do not last.

For example, in late 2013 we saw the rise of "tech bus protests" in the San Francisco Bay area, where unhappy community-based activists threw eggs and other objects at the shuttle buses used to transport employees of local giant tech companies. These protests became widely publicized. The tech buses were called "Google buses," although that term is *pars pro toto* (part of the whole), in that many other tech companies such as Apple, Facebook, Yahoo, and Genentech also have private shuttle services. The buses were used to ferry only tech company employees from their homes in San Francisco and Oakland to corporate campuses in Silicon Valley, about 40 miles (64 km) south.

The people involved in the protests viewed the buses as symbols of gentrification and displacement in a city where rapid growth in the tech sector and insufficient new housing construction led to increasing rent and housing prices, where natives and residents are getting pushed out.

I predict that soon we will see a larger metaphorical "egging" of big tech companies. It's obscene for one man to have $200 billion dollars while a single mom of three holds three jobs at $7.50 an hour, working for that same man as she attempts to make ends meet. It is also obscene that in 2019, the average top CEO's pay increased 14% from 2018 to $21.3 million. Sundar Pichai, the CEO of Google's parent company, Alphabet, earned $280,621,552 in total compensation—more than 1,000 times the income of a median company employee (As You Sow, 2021).

Some people would argue that the wealthy person worked hard and created the company, so they deserve all this reward. Also, if they hadn't created the company, this mom wouldn't have the job she has. The rich represent the "hard work" of years of sacrifice from themselves, their families, and others around them. Is it fair to say these people deserve their money because they worked hard for it? This is a fair argument, and is in fact one of the biggest incentives of capitalism.

However, I counter that argument with a question: is it possible for the wealthy person to get disproportionately large payouts for all their hard work without paying starvation wages to their employees? Or is it possible to have an equitable redistribution of that wealth among all parties involved in creating it? I think it's possible! I and many others would love to see more of this thinking put into practice.

But many people see the opposite. As of this writing, monopolies, acquisitions, and consolidations have seen Apple, Microsoft, Amazon, and Alphabet (Google) rise to what is now worth a combined net worth of $4 trillion. This is not sustainable. It's not a matter of *if*, it's a matter of *when*. Residents will become increasingly resentful of this type of company and their leaders' resource hoarding, leading to an "egging" of some form or another. This will lead to the breakup of big tech into smaller entities. It will not be sexy or cool to be that big anymore.

Some capitalists argue that it is a good thing for people to be able to earn more and more. However, this ignores the diminishing marginal utility of wealth. A billionaire who gets an extra million sees little increase in economic welfare, but that $1 million spent on healthcare would provide a much bigger increase in social welfare.

Perhaps this is the reason we do need to reform or replace the capitalistic market altogether. One thing is true—we need to rethink the incentive structures that align well with humanity and our planet. What if there was a cap on how much money one can make through capitalism? Let's say that number is $2 billion. Then we would name a dog park after you with a sign that says, "You Won Capitalism." Any subsequent dollars you make past the cap, you spend it on lifting people out of poverty and taking care of the planet. The more you do of the latter, the more street cred you get in society.

Boom and Bust Cycles

Last but not least of the unintended consequences of capitalism are the boom-and-bust cycles. Bust cycles in particular are very debilitating to society. In 100 years, we've seen the 1929 stock market crash, the 1989 bust caused by the savings and loan crisis, the 2001 recession caused by stock market crash and high-interest rates, the 2008 mortgage housing crisis, and finally the economic fallout of the 2020 COVID-19 pandemic.

These cycles fall into four phrases: *boom*, which is the aggressive expansion; *peak*, an inflection point where the economy stops expanding; *bust*, the contraction season; and the *end of the bust*, which is the inflection point where the economy stops contracting and begins to expand again (Amadeo, 2020).

The boom and bust cycles are caused by three forces—the law of supply and demand, the availability of financial capital, and future expectations. Technology companies, just like any other business operating in a capitalist economy, have a tendency to fall into booms and busts, with painful recessions and mass unemployment. These bust cycles affect the people at the bottom the hardest because most of them survive on paycheck to paycheck, thus the unpredictability of earnings is the biggest problem.

How to Mitigate UCOTs and Reimagine Capitalism

We just discussed the unintended consequences of capitalism. Anyone can scream and tell you the house is on fire, but what can we do about it? Besides bringing the fire hose and putting out the fire, what else can be done to make sure we prevent the fire from happening in the first place? The following sections are some thoughts and ideas about how we could reactively and proactively mitigate the UCOTs of capitalism.

Capitalism versus Carbon Emission Regulations

The free market can only take us where we need to go. Negative externalities such as carbon pollution must be properly priced and policed. The rules of the game need to be such that competition is free, fair, and respectful of the health of humanity and our planet. Only then do we have a chance at saving the planet.

Unfortunately, markets do not police themselves. They must be balanced by transparent, capable, democratically accountable governments. As you will see in Chapter 2, we need to strengthen the power of regulatory bodies, which are slowly diminishing. In tech companies, regulations are demonized and companies do all they can to keep them at the bare minimum. They couldn't care less if they existed at all. Meanwhile, these same companies care a great deal about their shareholder returns, leading to the rise of shareholder primacy. With more money in the hands of the shareholders and the leadership, in comes lobbying and an increasing role of money in politics. This weakening and systematic attack on government as a necessary or effective institution to regulate capitalism is largely absent.

As a result, one of the fastest routes to profitability is often to persuade politicians to write the rules in your favor. Firms feel free to dump greenhouse gases into the atmosphere, for example, while spending hundreds of millions of dollars to lobby against carbon regulation.

We can rebuild trust in the political system, and with it a government that is genuinely responsive to ordinary people, if we can get the money out of politics and stop tolerating business attacks on government. We need to enable government to regulate fossil fuel emissions and provide positive incentives to encourage corporations to embrace low-carbon solutions. That's why I believe getting money out of politics and enforcing carbon emission policing are both very vital in mitigating the UCOTs of capitalism.

Monopoly Power

The current wave of capitalism was designed around the fallacy of the "the lone hero" entrepreneur, the mindset of the unicorn (a privately held startup company valued at over $1 billion), and hockey stick–type of growth. This leads to monopolies, zero sum game, and winner take all. It's no surprise that there are going to be a few winners and many losers. We can all agree that the system I just described has been perfected and it's working too well for a few—leaving the majority of the population behind. We need a better system.

Desperate times call for radical measures. This starts with redesigning a system that was built to redistribute wealth and power from the many to the few. If it's done correctly, working people and their families will not only survive, but thrive, from the jobs created by massive public investment in restructuring our systems such as the energy grid and transforming our world. And we know the only ones willing to make that demand are those of us who are currently being squeezed by private interests for every last drop of profit. It will take all of us. Rather than trying to fix capitalism, we should be seeking to modify it or replace the blueprint that created it.

Stakeholder Capitalism versus Shareholders

In the United States, the top 1 percent of households own more wealth than the bottom 90 percent combined Ingraham, (2017). This is in part a result of a winner-takes-all mindset in a capitalistic market.

Furthermore, there is this myth of "pull yourself up by your bootstraps," which assumes that we all come from the same starting point. Yet racism, sexism, and classism are all ignored. It's hard to win a race if you start off shackled and have to run through fire while others use turbocharged engines to get there.

It's time for all-hands-on-deck intervention to rethink our capitalistic system and make it work for everyone. That's why I am a proponent of *stakeholder capitalism*, which cares about humanity and our planet, rather than the current *shareholder capitalism*, which focuses on wealth maximization for a small number of elite individuals who own the company.

Preventing the Negative UCOTs

The COVID-19 pandemic has given us an opportunity to pause and think about the systems we want moving forward. Big ships are not easy to turn, but they are not impossible to turn either. We need to create a version of capitalism that focuses on the longer term and on the common good. That's why now is the right time to come up with innovative ideas.

Myspace and Kodak both failed to adapt to the technological changes of their time and were replaced by superior products. We as a human species need to adapt or else we will soon be a Myspace.

We can create better systems if we have the will. For example, Walmart saved a billion dollars in fuel costs by increasing the efficiency of their trucking fleet. Elon Musk revolutionized the automotive industry by focusing on clean driving solutions. It can be done! We have seen some movement in the industry by top influential CEOs.

Salesforce billionaire Marc Benioff says, "Capitalism as we know it is dead. The current system has led to profound inequality. To fix it, we need businesses and executives to value purpose alongside profit" (Benioff, 2019).

Stakeholder purpose is becoming as important as shareholder value for many businesses. Inclusion and diversity are hot topics and recognized as levers that drive value both monetarily and in building a stronger, more sustainable future. If we are to have any humanity left on the planet, we must build a better economic system than we have today. Sustainable capitalism can only be achieved through balance and harmony among the individual, social, planet, and ethical dimensions of reality.

In 2020, Walmart CEO Doug McMillon said, "It's time to reinvent capitalism post-Coronavirus. Big problems don't rest on the shoulders of government or corporations alone. I think the growing interest in stakeholder capitalism stems from companies genuinely invested in doing good for our world, because it's the right thing to do and because businesses who take this approach are stronger" (Eben, 2020).

Ray Dalio, founder of Bridgewater, the world's biggest hedge fund, and a man worth about $20 billion according to *Forbes*, became the latest in a bank of billionaires to go public about his fears of widening income inequality (Dalio, 2021).

THE FUTURE OF CAPITALISM

Business and technology leaders need to embrace a broader vision of their responsibilities by looking beyond shareholder return and measuring their stakeholder return. This requires that they focus not only on their shareholders but also on all of their *stakeholders*—their employees, customers, communities, and the planet.

Capitalism in modern America is antithetical to the American Dream.

At first it sounds all fine and dandy, to each their own, whatever you can build for yourself you can have! But the American Dream is about starting with nothing. And it turns out that starting with nothing in a system that doesn't have adequate social programs is like being shackled.

You have a much lower chance of success than if you were to start off in a country with great social systems or with a Inheritance and your dad's garage to set up a desk and start your next big thing. I believe that in America you have *less* of a chance of achieving the American Dream than in the more socialist/capitalist hybrid countries mentioned earlier in this chapter. A country that practices a mix of capitalism and socialism gives its citizens the freedom to do what they want, and the incentives to do so, but also ensures that *everyone* has a decent shot at making it big.

Promoting *individual* happiness as our utmost ethos is self-defeating, as deeply divided societies turn unstable and unhappy. We need a new American Dream based on connection, equality, and sustainable growth. The cost of sharing opportunity and wealth may appear high for today's elites, but the alternative is far worse.

So, as a business leader, if you are to design capitalism better, what do you need? Well, instead of a rather narrow unicorn mindset of building privately held startup companies valued at over $1 billion, we need to adopt a wider "zebra" mindset that thinks about all the stripes of humanity and our planet. This means we consider regenerative growth and think about the 3P win-win-win approach (profit, people, and the planet). Zebra companies put humanity and the planet at the center of their missions.

The future of capitalism is human. Learning from history and reflecting on the legacy we will leave behind are keys to successful and responsible, *conscious* capitalism.

REFERENCES

Ali, Waqas. (2016). "Top 5 Causes of the Great Depression – Economic Domino Effect." https://www.warhistoryonline.com/history/top-5-causes-great-depression-economic-domino-effect.html

Amadeo, Kimberly. (2020). "Boom and Bust Cycle, Causes, History, and How to Protect Yourself." https://www.thebalance.com/boom-and-bust-cycle-causes-and-history-3305803

As You Sow. (2021)."The 100 Most Overpaid CEOs" 2021 report. https://www.asyousow.org/reports/the-100-most-overpaid-ceos-2021

Beer, Tommy. (2020). "Top 1% Of U.S. Households Hold 15 Times More Wealth Than Bottom 50% Combined." https://www.forbes.com/sites/tommybeer/2020/10/08/top-1-of-us-households-hold-15-times-more-wealth-than-bottom-50-combined/?sh=6658f1a45179

Benioff,Marc.(2019)."Capitalism Is Dead."https://www.cnn.com/videos/business/2019/10/17/marc-benioff-capitalism-orig.cnn-business

Brookings Institution (2021). "The COVID-19 Hazard Continues, But the Hazard Pay Does Not: Why America's Essential Workers Need a Raise." https://www.brookings.edu/research/the-covid-19-hazard-continues-but-the-hazard-pay-does-not-why-americas-frontline-workers-need-a-raise/

Dalio, Ray. (2021). https://www.forbes.com/profile/ray-dalio/#58aceb17663a

Dzhanova, Yelena. (2021). "Jeff Bezos and Elon Musk Increased Their Wealth by $217 Billion in 2020." https://www.businessinsider.com/jeff-bezos-elon-musk-increased-wealth-by-217-billion-2021-1

Eben, Shapiro. (2020). 'It's the Right Thing to Do.' Walmart CEO Doug McMillon Says It's Time to Reinvent Capitalism Post-Coronavirus." https://time.com/collection/great-reset/5900765/walmart-ceo-reinventing-capitalism/

History.com Editors. (2020). "The 1950s." www.history.com/topics/cold-war/1950s

Greene, Jay. (2021). "Amazon's anti-union blitz stalks Alabama warehouse workers everywhere, even the bathroom." https://www.washingtonpost.com/technology/2021/02/02/amazon-union-warehouse-workers/

Henderson, Rebecca M. (2020). "Reimagining Capitalism in the Shadow of the Pandemic." https://hbr.org/2020/07/reimagining-capitalism-in-the-shadow-of-the-pandemic.

Ingraham, Christopher. (2017). "The richest 1 percent now owns more of the country's wealth than at any time in the past 50 years." https://www.washingtonpost.com/news/wonk/wp/2017/12/06/the-richest-1-percent-now-owns-more-of-the-countrys-wealth-than-at-any-time-in-the-past-50-years/

Pendleton, Devon. (2020). "Stock Surge Produces Record 5 Tycoons With $100 Billion Fortunes." https://www.bloomberg.com/news/articles/2020-11-09/there-are-now-a-record-five-centibillionaires-after-stock-surge

Pettinger, Tejvan. (2019). "Pros and cons of capitalism" https://www.economicshelp.org/blog/5002/economics/pros-and-cons-of-capitalism/

Reich, Robert. (2020). "If this doesn't convince you our economy is rigged, I don't know what will." https://twitter.com/rbreich/status/1329521026158403584

Rodrigue, Jean-Paul. (2013). "The Geography of Transportation Systems." https://
    transportgeography.org/wp-content/uploads/GTS_Third_Edition.pdf
World Happiness Report. (2020). "World Happiness Report 2020." https://www.
    worldhappiness.report/
Zarroli, Jim. (2020.) NPR.org. "There's Rich, and Then There's Jeff Bezos
    Rich: Meet the World's Centibillionaires." https://www.npr.org/2020/12/10/
    944620768/theres-rich-and-theres-jeff-bezos-rich-meet-the-members-of-
    the-100-billion-club?utm_source=facebook.com&utm_term=nprnews&
    utm_campaign=npr&utm_medium=social&fbclid=IwAR1ggHzU3b2ewAHPJ
    YNN6p2w0SdLvUDX1Sl1n8iOJnqTFmWcjwSRSVFM3IY

CHAPTER 2

Tech-States:
Are Nation-States Obsolete?

*T*he *tech-state*, which is synonymous with *BigTech*, refers to the big technology companies that have an outsized social, economic, political, and environmental impact on the world, both positive and negative. Examples of such companies include Amazon, Apple, Google, Facebook, and Microsoft. The convenience of tech offerings has made the general public numb to the dangers. And having meaningful regulation from nation-states over tech-states is difficult, due to their outsized influence and power. In many ways, these tech-states have replaced nation-states, all without the responsibilities of providing citizens with social services. This chapter explores these tech mega-powers and discusses how these new outsized forces require new oversight.

Governments around the world are having a hard time figuring out how to regulate technology companies on issues like employee mistreatment, freedom of speech, climate change, and a myriad of other issues that are essential to humanity and our planet. Due to their transnational operations, no single government has yet cracked the code on how to keep them in check when they have so much power. These tech-state companies appear to feel as if they are almost invincible!

A QUICK LOOK AT THE NATION-STATE

A *nation-state* is a sovereign state whose citizens or subjects are relatively homogeneous in factors such as language or common descent. There are four essential features of a nation-state: population, territory, sovereignty, and government. When a nation of people has a state or country of their own, it is called a nation-state. Places like China, France, Egypt, Germany, and Japan are excellent examples of nation-states. Even with its multicultural society, the United States is also referred to as a nation-state because of the shared American culture.

Any nation-state or any government's job is to fulfill certain roles and obligations for its citizens. Those duties include:

- Protect the social and economic welfare of its citizens.
- Protect natural rights.
- Defend against external enemies.
- Manage the economic conditions and its place in the world.
- Redistribute income and resources.
- Provide public or utility goods.

What happens when a government has less social economic and political power than the companies started and run by a handful of its citizens?

Well, a lot is at stake!

Performing these governing functions in the name of protecting citizens and the environment from predatory behavior becomes extremely difficult.

A Quick Look at a Tech-State

When anyone is building something big, things are bound to get messy, but no one anticipated the extent at which we would experience the messiness of tech-state. As many as 9 out of 10 startups fail. Entrepreneur and contributor Neil Patel (2014) mentioned a few reasons as to why this many fail in his write-up for *Forbes* magazine.

He says that those who fail maybe made a product no one wants, or ignored some important parts of their business. Other times it's the hyper growth the company is not prepared for. Growth—fast growth—is what entrepreneurs crave, investors need, and markets want. Rapid growth is the sign of a great idea in a hot market. However, without the right infrastructure in place, rapid growth can be a liability. If your startup lasts, you're lucky. You've been able to do something that 90% of new businesses haven't (Patel, 2014).

Even the ones left standing sometimes end up failing later. That's why companies like Google, Apple, Amazon, Facebook, and their fellow tech giants had to weather many storms to become what they are today. Pivots, stolen ideas, and even firings are commonplace. Steve Jobs was once famously forced out of his own company that he founded. But by embracing uncertainty and making timely pivots, some tech companies end up becoming some of the most influential—and valuable—organizations on the planet, with power that rivals or exceeds their nation-states. Let's take Facebook and Google as examples:

Tech-state: Facebook

Population: 2.7 billion (2019)

Capital: Palo Alto

Nationality: Users

Valuation: $720 billion (August 2020)

Founder: Mark Zuckerberg

In total, Facebook has more than 3.14 billion account holders across its platforms, which include acquired companies like WhatsApp, Instagram, and Messenger (Newton, 2020).

Tech-state: Google

Population: 1 billion (2020)

Capital: Mountain View

Nationality: Users

Valuation: $1 trillion (2020)

Founders: Larry Page and Sergey Brin

Google's search engine market share is more than 90%. Considering that there are almost 4.39 billion Internet users, the number of Google users worldwide is nearly four billion. Google usage statistics show Google Photos has over 1 billion active users. There were over 1.8 billion active

Gmail users in 2020. YouTube has 2.3 billion users worldwide. This is just a small taste of only four out of the many products Google offers its customers.

Advantages of the Tech-State

Tech-states have brought to bear many benefits and positive advancements for humankind, as you may know. In fact, it's possible you may be reading this book with the aid of one of their products. If we were to focus on all their advantages, that could take up the space of this entire book. Therefore, I will point out just a few.

Being so large means these organizations can make big investments in the future and big investments in R&D, and much faster and better than any nation-state could do. Take entrepreneur Elon Musk and his companies as an example. His company Tesla is on a mission to accelerate the world's transition to sustainable energy. Elon and Tesla's big bets of venturing into the unknown world of research and development have proved that people don't need to compromise to drive electric cars. Electric vehicles can be better, quicker, and more fun to drive than gasoline cars. The same daring spirit can be said about his other company, SpaceX. Its mission is to revolutionize the aerospace industry and make affordable spaceflight a reality. SpaceX plans not only to land humans on Mars but also to colonize Mars. Space exploration used to be the work of nation-states; now it's mostly done by private companies and made possible by big investments in R&D. In fact, nation-states are now contracting tech-states to do this work for them, as shown by the NASA/SpaceX partnerships, as well as by many other collaborations like it (McFall-Johnsen and Mosher, 2020).

Furthermore, tech-state companies are better positioned to deliver large-scale services to the market, because they have the tools, resources, and infrastructure to do so. Because of their size, cash in hand, and many other factors, they can survive market slowdowns in ways small companies cannot. This was very evident during the COVID-19 pandemic (Sundaram, 2020).

The pandemic challenged most of us on a personal level; however, business-wise, it hasn't been bad for everyone. Big tech leaders like Apple,

Amazon, Facebook, Microsoft, and Google have all seen their market values increase this past year. Furthermore, all of these companies were poised to play a significant role in helping the world recover from coronavirus, using their technological prowess to do everything from tracking coronavirus spread to managing tests and vaccines to improving overall distribution workflows (Newman, 2021).

Tech-state also contributes greatly to the GDP of the nation-state. The world's largest companies are in the technology sector, and four out of five of those tech-states companies have grown to trillion-dollar market capitalizations (Wallach, 2019). As technology use continues to increase, their revenue forecast will only continue to grow.

Clearly, there are plenty of advantages to having these huge tech companies around, and there are many books out there dedicated to the subject. However, this book focuses mostly on the other side of the argument and looks at aspects of these companies that are not serving humanity's best interests. Let's dive into those issues next.

THE UNINTENDED OR WILLFULLY IGNORED NEGATIVE CONSEQUENCES OF A TECH-STATE

It is evident that tech-states have had a remarkable impact on many citizens of nation-states, by giving us access to a treasure trove of things we desire with a couple of taps or clicks. However, for all the good these companies have done, their dominating nature provides an opportunity to completely control innumerable aspects of our lives with no consequences for negative actions that arise as a result of their creations. In the following sections, we look at the unintended consequences of the outsized power of a tech-state.

Proportionality of the Userbase versus Country's Population Size

As noted in the Facebook and Google examples, the sheer size of users on these platforms outnumbers the population of individual states in which they operate.

China has the world's largest population (1.42 billion), followed by India (1.35 billion). The next five most populous nations—the United States, Indonesia, Brazil, Pakistan, and Nigeria—together have fewer people than India.

In a hypothetical example, let's say a nation-state accuses a tech-state of egregious misbehaving. That single country can decide to ban all its citizens from using a certain platform or block it entirely from its airwaves. Yet these technologies will continue to operate just fine and still be profitable. This has been witnessed in countries as tiny as Uganda, which ordered all social media to be blocked in its country (Reuters, 2021), and as big as Australia, when the government introduced a law to make tech-states pay media outlets for their news content and the firms fiercely fought back (de Vynck, 2021).

That's the outsized power of exponential technology and capitalism, which we examined in Chapter 1.

Dehumanizing Customers

Tech changed a small but mighty social norm and the language around how it references customers and clients. They rebranded humans as users. There is an old adage that points out that the two industries that call their customers "users" happen to be illegal drug dealers and tech companies. This dehumanizing language creates the ability to enjoy "user numbers" and dollars coming into the business without taking much responsibility for the human element behind the users. This is an important starting point, and we will see how it plays out in many ways throughout the book. The nation-state is supposed to care about the humanity of its population, whereas the tech-state can comfortably work with users, which creates an emotional detachment. After all, they are just numbers.

It's important to mention that none of the tech-state companies may be doing this out of malice. It started as a benign tweak, but that dehumanizing language has now morphed into a larger problem. Tech-states can get away with this dehumanizing approach to business, and the abuse of the planet in general, because of their enormous power and influence over most nation-states. After all, providing meaningful oversight is increasingly difficult because power has shifted.

Opaque Employee Mistreatment

At the risk of offending some of my readers, I would like to draw some parallels between the tech-state and a pimp. A pimp is a person who controls sex workers and arranges clients for them, taking part of their earnings in return. A pimp knows his workers well, but does not always treat them well. A pimp knows how many tricks each worker can turn each night.

A pimp knows how long each worker can work before they are burnt out, essentially treating people like cars, like objects. After all, there will be plenty of other workers in line for the job. Replace the word "pimp" with "tech-state" and "sex worker" with "employee," and you'll perhaps agree that the analogy holds strong.

They may not say so explicitly, but most tech-state companies (although not all of them) treat their workers like throw-away commodities. At companies like Amazon, some workers stay on the clock continuously to the point that they have no bathroom breaks. The company recently admitted that workers sometimes "urinate in water bottles" (Pocan, 2021) while they are out and about delivering packages. The workers are numb to the mistreatment because they are grateful to have a job, which, as an Amazon warehouse worker noted, is essential in order to put food on the table (Matsakis, 2020).

Tech-state companies often use the loophole of utilizing "contractors" to avoid paying people full benefits. In 2018, Google's contract workers outnumbered direct employees for the first time in the company's 20-year history. In San Mateo and Santa Clara counties alone, where most tech-states have headquarters, there are an estimated 39,000 workers who are contracted to tech companies, according to one estimate by researchers at the University of California, Santa Cruz (Sheng, 2018).

Repetitive stress injuries are an epidemic but are rarely reported. These include carpal tunnel syndrome or pain in the wrists, thumbs, hands, or forearms. Sometimes it's the overexertion injuries, which happen because heavy lifting on the job can cause neck and lower back pain. In 2015, the Occupational Safety and Health Administration cited a New Jersey Amazon warehouse for exposing workers to risk factors that included stress from continuous bending and repetitious exertions and prolonged standing during long shifts (Schibell & Mennie LLC, 2021).

These people are viewed as expendable. After all, tech-state knows that when one person leaves, there are plenty of people knocking at the door looking to do that same job.

As another example of tech-state companies keeping their workers down, Amazon has vehemently opposed its workers unionizing. Amazon's relentless push to beat back a union drive among warehouse workers mirrors the company's past efforts to oppose unions in Seattle, New York, Canada, and the United Kingdom (Greene, 2021). A unified voice could give workers power, which the company likely sees as a threat. Some companies have even been rumored to have gone as far as blacklisting and firing people who engaged in unionizing behavior that is deemed unacceptable.

Borrowing a page from the scare tactics used in the construction industry, in 2009 the union "Unite in the UK" took a case to the High Court after names were found in a file compiled by the Consulting Association, which was raided. More than 3,000 people were on the blacklist, often for being a union member or for raising safety issues (BBC News, 2009). This intimidation in construction or tech thwarts any internal attempts at organizing the workers within the company.

Tech-state companies may not always treat their workers well, but they do take good care of their users and shareholders. "Users" are the customers who pay for the product. "Customer is king," they say. They know that without the customer they have no company. That's why they care. Shareholders are the investors and other entities who own a stake in the company. They care about shareholders, because without them they have no investment to grow the company. If only they applied this same thinking to their employees and to our planet, the world would be a better place. Because a dead planet is not a good place to run a business.

Money and Power in Politics

Facebook, Google, Amazon, and other companies like them spend a lot of money on lobbying, political donations, and other forms of cozying up to political leaders, to the point that those tasked with keeping them in check are held hostage by the donations from the founders and the companies themselves.

For these companies, it starts with money, which gives them power, which buys them political leaders via donations and other forms of lobbying. This leads to control and influence over the government, which makes it very difficult to pass any meaningful regulation that would keep these companies in check.

Eight men have the same wealth as the 3.6 billion people who make up the poorest half of humanity, according to a new report published by Oxfam that marks the annual meeting of political and business leaders in Davos (Oxfam America, 2017). The report, "An economy for the 99 percent," shows that the gap between rich and poor is far greater than had been feared. It details how big business and the super-rich are fueling the inequality crisis by dodging taxes, driving down wages, and using their power to influence politics to their advantage.

In places where tech-states have not been able to buy their way into the political system, they will sometimes threaten to leave the region when there are attempts to regulate them. Because of these companies' outsized ability to create jobs and provide services, they still wield a lot of power.

As an example, Elon Musk threatened to move Tesla headquarters out of California at the beginning of 2020 due to COVID-19 restrictions. In fact, Tesla ended up suing state authorities over lockdown after the Fremont factory was stopped from reopening (Reuters, 2020). Keep in mind that these regulations applied to everyone and every company, big and small. Tesla sued local authorities in California and pushed to reopen its factory. They threatened to move the company's headquarters to Texas or Nevada, where regulators are looser. Tesla did end up moving to Texas. At the end of 2020, SpaceX and Tesla CEO Elon Musk revealed that he had moved to Texas and was rapidly relocating his California-based business empire to the Lone Star State. With a new Tesla factory under construction and two increasingly busy SpaceX facilities in the state, it was not unexpected news (Cao, 2020)

Another example happened in 2019, when Amazon canceled its plans to build its second headquarters in New York after battling with activists and union leaders (Goodman, 2019).

It's becoming increasingly difficult for legislators to regulate any tech-state companies, because of their sheer oversized influence. It's not hyperbole to say that, as of this writing, a handful of tech-state companies are in control, and not the nation-state or government. Here are some examples to back up this statement:

- In 2018, the European Parliament summoned Mark Zuckerberg as the CEO of Facebook to testify in a parliamentary hearing. He was a no-show. At the time of the hearing, the committee shared a now infamous picture of the empty seat and nameplate, stating: "Nine countries. 24 official representatives. 447 million people represented. One question: where is Mark Zuckerberg?" Not much they could do about it!

- In 2021, tech-state companies acted unilaterally and censored the president of the United States and many of his influential followers. Hate him or love him and what he stands for, he was still the president of the most powerful country in the world. Think about that.

- Of course, incitement to violence is a criminal offense in all liberal democracies around the world. There is an obvious reason for this: violence is harmful. It harms those who are immediately targeted. Five people died in the riots of January 6, 2021, in Washington DC. "A police officer was beaten, a rioter was shot, and three others died during the rampage" (Healy, 2021). Violence also harms the institutions of democracy themselves, which rely on elections rather than civil wars and on a peaceful transfer of power.

- To be fair to the tech-state, there is no doubt the former president was given considerable leeway in his public commentary prior to—and during the course of—his presidency. However, he crossed a line into stoking imminent lawlessness and violence. Thus, many could argue that he brought it on himself. We all agree that we need to improve social media, but the tougher question is how we tackle misinformation while also valuing freedom of expression.

The point still remains. A single individual at certain companies can censor whomever they want! That's the outsized power I am talking about.

The Exponential Nature of Tech

Nation-states cannot regulate exponential digital technologies (tech-states) using the same processes and tactics used to regulate analog technologies. It simply won't work; the bullet train is moving too fast. Regulations are always going to be trailing, playing catch up. More often than not, they are reactively responding to problems and issues.

New exponential technology companies require new "tricks" for oversight.

The relationship between tech companies and regulations reminds me of a chameleon. The slow speed at which chameleons walk is metaphorically how governments and regulators are approaching regulating tech-state companies. These tech-state companies are like flies, flapping their wings 230 beats per second.

The chameleon has had to adapt its tongue to move as fast as the fly, without moving its entire body in order to keep up. Do yourself a favor and watch a video of a chameleon catching a fly in slow motion. It's impressive! If nation-state regulators are to ever catch up with the big, fast-moving wings of exponential tech, they have to adapt like the chameleon.

What is needed is a fundamental change so that nation-states can regain their power and protect the planet and all of humanity, not just a fortunate few.

Monopoly Power

A monopoly happens when a company and its product offerings dominate a sector or industry. The term "monopoly" is often used to describe an entity that has total or near-total control of a market. Monopolistic companies fend off competition at all costs in what is now known as the "buy or bury" approach. Many tech-state companies, although they would not admit it, are monopolies. If any meaningful competition bubbles to the surface, their first efforts are to try to buy them. If the founders are stubborn and say no, tech-state companies often build a copycat version of that product, squeeze the air out of the tiny startup, and bury it before it has a chance to respond.

Facebook, for example, has used its dominance and monopoly power to crush smaller rivals and snuff out competition in an effort to maintain its market dominance in the social networking industry. The U.S. federal government and 48 states made a move to file lawsuits against Facebook, accusing it of anti-competitive conduct by abusing its market power to create a monopoly and crushing smaller competitors (Business Standard, 2020). In the late 1990s, Microsoft also lost a lawsuit to the U.S. government when the judge ruled that Microsoft had actively tried to crush its competitors, including Apple, IBM, Netscape, Sun, and others (Blumenthal and Wu, 2018). Facebook is taking a page from the Microsoft playbook.

Facebook and many tech giants like it employ unique data-gathering tools to monitor hot new apps in an effort to see what is gaining traction with users. That data helps Facebook and others select acquisition targets that pose the greatest threats to their market dominance. Once selected, they offer the heads of these companies vast amounts of money, which greatly inflates the values of the apps, all in hopes of avoiding any competition in the future.

Facebook and Zuckerberg saw Instagram as a direct threat quickly after the company launched. After initially trying to build its own version of Instagram (which gained no traction), in 2012 Zuckerberg admitted that Facebook was "very behind" Instagram and a better strategy would be "to consider paying a lot of money" for the photo-sharing app in an effort to "neutralize a potential competitor." A few months later, in April 2012, Facebook acquired Instagram for $1 billion, despite the fact that the company did not have a single cent of revenue and valued itself at $500 million (Stickings and Griffith, 2020).

In another classic example, the mobile messaging app called Whats App posed a unique threat to Facebook's growth, giving users the ability to send messages on their mobile devices, both one-to-one and to groups, for free. In February 2014, Facebook acquired WhatsApp (Olson, 2014).

You may still be wondering why monopolies are bad. Besides often having more power than the nation-states in which they operate, there are many other negative consequences. For one, if there is one company on the block, it can increase prices whenever and however they like. If a single firm sets the price for an entire industry, prices will always be on the rise.

Price discrimination is also common, since there is no transparency and consumers have no viable alternatives.

How to Mitigate the UCOTs of Tech-State Companies

In the short term, while both nation-states and tech-states are under centralized control, many people see an increased need for more government intervention and regulation of these tech-state companies. There are at least four areas related to humanity and the planet that need regulation: safety, privacy, competition, and honesty.

Over the past decade, tech giants have risen to become the most valuable companies in the world, all while operating with little formal, structured government oversight. The tiny patchwork regulatory oversight and industry self-regulation both lack transparency and coherence to affect any meaningful change. Only by coordinating action across all four policy paths will we see any real change. Europe often leads the way and again recently overhauled the digital rules that some experts say could become a global standard for keeping these companies in check (Browne, 2020).

If there is something that's clear, as a society we need to design an alternative system, perhaps a decentralized system of tech-state and nation-state.

We got into this pickle because initially tech was fighting the fact that government was too powerful and was getting into people's businesses and affecting how citizens consume goods.

At first, tech and the free market gave citizens free will and autonomy and spared them from the overbearing power of the government. As we have discussed, that has turned out to be an overcorrection, as the power appears to be flipping from nation-states to tech-states.

An oversized, powerful centralized tech-state has many disadvantages. An oversized, powerful centralized nation-state in the form of a dictatorship or quasi-democratic government is not good either.

Take the example of tech entrepreneur and billionaire Bill Gates. In 1998, Gates and his company, Microsoft, faced monopoly and antitrust charges in which Microsoft lost. In this high-profile case the U.S. government accused Microsoft of illegally maintaining a monopoly position in the personal computer (PC) market and of illegally protecting its operating-system monopoly and seeking a new monopoly for its own browser, Internet Explorer (Blumenthal and Wu, 2018). In this case, the nation-state power was at full display.

We see this scenario play out verbatim with the 2020 fallout of China and one of its prodigal sons, Jack Ma. He also happens to be one of the richest people in the world.

In China, Jack Ma was synonymous with success. The English teacher turned Internet entrepreneur was the country's richest person. He founded Alibaba, the closest thing Amazon has to a peer and rival. After Donald Trump was elected president in 2016, Mr. Ma was the first high-profile Chinese person he met with.

That success translated to a rock-star life for "Daddy Ma," as some people online called him. He played an unconquerable kung fu master in a 2017 short film packed with top Chinese movie stars. He sang with Faye Wong, the Chinese pop diva. A painting he created with Zeng Fanzhi, China's top artist, sold at a Sotheby's auction for $5.4 million. For China's young and ambitious, Daddy Ma's story was one to emulate.

But then came 2020, when his public sentiment soured and Daddy Ma became the man people in China loved to hate. He was called a "villain," an "evil capitalist," and a "bloodsucking ghost." A writer listed Mr. Ma's "10 deadly sins." Instead of "Daddy," some people have started to call him "Son" or "Grandson." In stories about him, a growing number of people left comments quoting Marx: "Workers of the world, unite!" (Yuan, 2020).

In 2021, China's central bank asked the country's payments giant Ant Group Co Ltd (which is owned by Jack Ma) to shake up its lending and other consumer finance operations. This was the latest blow to its billionaire founder and controlling shareholder.

The People's Bank of China (PBOC) summoned Ant Group executives and ordered them to formulate a rectification plan and an implementation timetable of its business, including its credit, insurance, and wealth management services (Deutsche Welle, 2020). The statement said that Ant Group lacked a sound governance mechanism, defied regulatory compliance requirements, and engaged in regulatory arbitrage. It also said that the company used its market position to exclude rivals and damage the rights and interests of consumers.

Ma and his family ranked first as China's richest in the Hurun Global Rich List in (Hurun, 2020). As of this writing, Ma now holds fourth place, losing the first rank after Chinese regulators launched alleged anti-monopoly probes into his companies, Alibaba and Ant Group (Yu, 2020).

Clearly, when a government has the power and ability to control its citizens, people are going to resent it. When capitalism makes it possible for power to flip from nation-states to tech-states, the government and the people will resent it. This dynamic of one source of dominating power is problematic in many ways; that's why decentralization of power back into the hands of the people has always been appealing to the masses.

Dozens of start-ups now offer alternatives to Facebook, Twitter, You-Tube, and Amazon's web hosting services, all on top of decentralized networks and shared ledgers. Many of these alternatives have gained millions of new users, according to the data company SimilarWeb (Singh, 2021).

Many countries now offer alternatives to centralized governments in the form of decentralized virtual citizenship, which is a commodity that can be acquired through the purchase of real estate or financial investments, subscribed to via an online service, or assembled by peer-to-peer digital networks. In Malta, Cyprus, Estonia, the United Arab Emirates, and elsewhere, passports can now be bought and sold, all to solve the problem of the imbalance of power dynamic (Bridle, 2018). Decentralization and putting power back into the hands of the people is a promising third alternative away from the power swing between tech-state and nation-state.

REFERENCES

"Attorney General Letitia James Leads Multistate Lawsuit Seeking to End Facebook's Illegal Monopoly." (2020). Press release. https://ag.ny.gov/press-release/2020/attorney-general-james-leads-multistate-lawsuit-seeking-end-facebooks-illegal

BBC News. (2009). "Construction workers in fresh 'blacklisting' action." https://www.bbc.com/news/business-47349008

Blumenthal, Richard, and Tim Wu. (2018). "What the Microsoft Antitrust Case Taught Us." https://www.nytimes.com/2018/05/18/opinion/microsoft-antitrust -case.html

Bridle, James. (2018). "The Rise of Virtual Citizenship." https://www.theatlantic. com/technology/archive/2018/02/virtual-citizenship-for-sale/553733/

Browne, Ryan. (2020). CNBC.com, "Europe tries to set the global narrative on regulating Big Tech." https://www.cnbc.com/2020/12/16/europe-tries-to-set-the-global-narrative-on-regulating-big-tech.html

Business Standard. (2020). "US govt, 48 states sue Facebook for abusing power to crush smaller rivals." https://www.business-standard.com/article/pti-stories/us-govt-48-states-sue-facebook-for-abusing-market-power-to-crush-smaller-competitors-120121000123_1.html

Cao, Sissi. (2020). "Why Elon Musk and Other Tech Billionaires Are Leaving Silicon Valley for Texas." https://observer.com/2020/12/elon-musk-tech-leaving-silicon-valley-for-texas-billionaires/#:~:text=At%20an%20 event%20last%20week,it%20was%20not%20unexpected%20news

Deutsche Welle. (2020)."China orders Alibaba's Jack Ma to overhaul Ant fin-tech business." https://www.dw.com/en/china-orders-alibabas-jack-ma-to-overhaul-ant-fintech-business/a-56070639

de Vynck, Gerrit. (2021). "Australia wants Facebook and Google to pay for news on their sites." https://www.washingtonpost.com/technology/2021/02/19/ australia-google-facebook-canada-europe/

Goodman, David. (2019). "Amazon Pulls Out of Planned New York City Headquar-ters." https://www.nytimes.com/2019/02/14/nyregion/amazon-hq2-queens. -html

Greene, Jay. (2021). "Amazon fights aggressively to defeat union drive in Ala-bama, fearing a coming wave." https://www.washingtonpost.com/technol-ogy/2021/03/09/amazon-union-bessemer-history/

Healy, Jack. (2021). "These Are the 5 People Who Died in the Capitol Riot." https://www.nytimes.com/2021/01/11/us/who-died-in-capitol-building-attack.html

Hurun. (2020). https://www.hurun.net/en-US/Info/Detail?num=PYSXN%#E

Matsakis, Louise. (2020). "9 Amazon Workers Describe the Daily Risks They Face in the Pandemic." https://www.wired.com/story/amazon-workers-pandemic-risks-own-words/

McFall-Johnsen, Morgan, and Dave Mosher. (2020). "SpaceX has proven it can fly astronauts. Here's how Elon Musk's company became the first to help NASA resurrect US spaceflight." https://www.businessinsider.com/spacex-boeing-nasa-commercial-crew-program-launch-astronauts-2020-1

Newman, Daniel. (2021). "Big Tech Provides a Shot in the Arm to Vaccine Rollout." https://www.forbes.com/sites/danielnewman/2021/02/08/big-tech-provides-a-shot-in-the-arm-to-vaccine-rollout/?sh=52a5035541d7

Newton, Casey. (2020). "Facebook usage and revenue continue to grow as the pandemic rages on." https://www.theverge.com/2020/7/30/21348308/facebook-earnings-q2-2020-pandemic-revenue-usage-growth

Olson, Parmy. (2014). "Facebook Closes $19 Billion WhatsApp Deal." https://www.forbes.com/sites/parmyolson/2014/10/06/facebook-closes-19-billion-whatsapp-deal/?sh=b9769c45c66c

Oxfam America. (2017). "Just 8 Men Own Same Wealth as Half the World." https://www.oxfamamerica.org/press/just-8-men-own-same-wealth-as-half-the-world/#:~:text=Eight%20men%20own%20the%20same,business%20leaders%20in%20Davos%2C%20Switzerland

Patel, Neil. (2014) "90% of Startups Fail: Here's What You Need to Know About the 10%." https://www.forbes.com/sites/neilpatel/2015/01/16/90-of-startups-will-fail-heres-what-you-need-to-know-about-the-10/?sh=262e15006679

Pocan, Mark. (2021). "Amazon apologises for wrongly denying drivers need to urinate in bottles." https://www.bbc.com/news/world-us-canada-56628745

Reuters. (2020). "Elon Musk threatens to move Tesla HQ out of California over Covid-19 restrictions." https://www.theguardian.com/world/2020/may/10/elon-musk-threatens-to-move-tesla-hq-out-of-california-over-covid-19-restrictions

Reuters. (2021). "Uganda orders all social media to be blocked." https://www.reuters.com/article/uk-uganda-election-social-media/uganda-orders-all-social-media-to-be-blocked-letter-idUSKBN29H1EB

Schibell & Mennie LLC. (2021). "Occupational Safety and Health Administration (OSHA) cited a New Jersey Amazon warehouse for exposing workers to risks." http://www.schibelllaw.com/new-jersey-amazon-warehouse-worker-injury-attorney/#:~:text=Repetitive%20stress%20injuries%20may%20include,neck%20and%20lower%20back%20pain

Sheng, Ellen. (2018). "Silicon Valley's dirty secret: Using a shadow workforce of contract employees to drive profits." https://www.cnbc.com/2018/10/22/silicon-valley-using-contract-employees-to-drive-profits.html

Singh, Preeti. (2021). "They found a way to limit the power of Big Tech: use Bitcoin design." https://eminetra.com/they-found-a-way-to-limit-the-power-of-big-tech-use-bitcoin-design/332253/

Stickings, Tim, and Keith Griffith. (2020). "'The wrath of Mark': Lawsuit trying to break up Facebook claims Zuckerberg threatened 'ominous ramifications' to Instagram if it did not team up as he sought to build 'competitive moat' around his empire." https://www.dailymail.co.uk/news/article-9040365/Zuckerberg-left-rivals-fearing-wrath-Mark-Facebook-lawsuit-claims.html

Sundaram, Anjali. (2020). "Yelp data shows 60% of business closures due to the coronavirus pandemic are now permanent." https://www.cnbc.com/2020/09/16/yelp-data-shows-60percent-of-business-closures-due-to-the-coronavirus-pandemic-are-now-permanent.html

Wallach, Omri. (2019). "How Big Tech Makes Their Billions." "In 2019, the tech giants combined revenues, greater than the GDP of four of the G20 nations." https://www.visualcapitalist.com/how-big-tech-makes-their-billions-2020/#:~:text=Bigger%20Than%20Countries&text=The%20tech%20giants%20combined%20for,and%20just%20behind%20the%20Netherlands.

Yu, Doris. (2020). "Jack Ma loses China's richest man title after scrutiny into Alibaba, Ant." https://www.techinasia.com/jack-ma-loses-chinas-richest-man-title-after-scrutiny-alibaba-ant

Yuan, Li. (2020). "Why China Turned Against Jack Ma." https://www.nytimes.com/2020/12/24/technology/china-jack-ma-alibaba.html

PART II

TECHNOLOGIES AND TRENDS WITH LOTS OF PROMISE BUT ALSO UNCERTAINTY

CHAPTER 3

Data: What Is the Data Industrial Complex?

T he world is one giant big data cocktail! But what exactly is big data?

Big data is a term used in computing to refer to extremely large data sets that are analyzed computationally to reveal patterns, trends, and associations, especially relating to human behavior and interactions. Almost all big technology companies are investing heavily in managing and maintaining big data. The massive volumes of data can be used to address business problems, new business opportunities, and understand you (the customer) very well. But how has data creation, curation, collection, computation, and cleansing evolved over time?

THE HISTORY OF DATA

Data is part of the fabric of life and society, and has been since the beginning of time. What has evolved is the story detailing data collection, storage, and processing. It's said that knowledge is power. Well, data is knowledge. In this chapter, we explore the power that our data holds.

It's (perhaps) possible to trace the history of data back to the very ancient world. The Ishango bone was a notched baboon bone tool dating to around 19,000 BCE. It's thought to have acted as a tally stick. So it could be speculated that the Ishango bone represents an incredibly early instance of data collection and storage. That is, those methodical bone scratches could be the first documented record of humans logging numerical information for later use.

Around the third millennium BCE, writing started to evolve, and with it, libraries. This collection and curation of written work arguably represents an early form of mass data storage.

Fast-forward to the 1640s, where the word "data" first saw English use. Derived from Latin, "data" means "a fact given or granted"—often as the basis for calculation. In 1663, John Graunt conducted one of the earliest recorded instances of data analysis. He studied the death records kept by London parishes. From this, he was able to make observations about the varying death rates between gender and even predict life expectancy (ThinkAutomation, 2021).

The next big event in the history of data occurred following the 1880 U.S. census (United States Census Bureau, 2021). Over the decades, the census had grown, asking more and more questions about the populace. The issue was that there was now more data than collectors could analyze. Herman Hollerith was the man to solve the problem, with his brainchild: the Hollerith desk. This machine harnessed the power of punch cards—an invention from Joseph Jacquard in 1801. With the collected data represented as holes in cards, the machine could find the holes, which would complete a circuit. A completed circuit would move a dial up by one.

So the challenge of processing data had been answered (in some part) by this early automation. The history of data then saw a shifted emphasis onto its storage and collection. In 1928, Fritz Pfleumer invented magnetic tape for recording purposes—in other words, a way to collect and store data magnetically (History of Computing, 2021). This is an idea that lasted. The hard disc drives, floppy discs, and tapes that would follow toward the end of the century were all enabled by magnetic data storage. The 1960s saw the conception (but not the creation) of cloud data storage by Dr. Joseph Carl Robnett Licklider. He envisioned an "intergalactic computer network" where data and programs could be accessed by anyone, anywhere, at any time. This idea forms the basis of cloud computing as we now know it.

Naturally, the most noteworthy 1990s event in the history of data is the invention of the Internet. Sir Tim Berners-Lee created hyperlinks and hypertext, enabling data sharing worldwide. It wasn't long until the first instance of all web-based storage, launched by AT&T in the mid-1990s. Other notable moments for the history of data in the 1990s include 1997, which saw the launch of Google Search. This put data very much in the hands of anyone with computer access (ThinkAutomation, 2021).

Fast-forward to today. At this point in time, Internet users create 2.5 quintillion bytes of data every day—that's 2.5 followed by a staggering 18 zeros!

The World of Big Data

"Data" is everywhere and used to describe "everything." But the ubiquity of the word hides the nuances of what data actually can be and the powerful insights that it holds. In layman terms, data is the "factual information" (such as measurements or statistics) used as a basis for reasoning, discussion, or calculation.

There are three Vs of big data:

- *Volume*: The amount of data matters. With big data, you have to process high volumes of low-density, unstructured data. This can be data of unknown value, such as Twitter data feeds, clickstreams on a webpage or a mobile app, or sensor-enabled equipment. For some business, this might be tens of terabytes of data. For others, it may be hundreds of petabytes.

- *Velocity*: This is the rate at which data is received and (perhaps) acted on. Normally, the highest velocity of data streams directly into memory versus being written to disk. Some Internet-enabled smart products operate in real time or near real time and will require real-time evaluation and action.

- *Variety*: This refers to the many types of data available. Traditional data types were structured and fit neatly in a relational database. With the rise of big data, data comes in new unstructured data types. Unstructured and semi-structured data types, such as text, audio, and video, require additional preprocessing to derive meaning. This is also known as metadata.

Why should you care? Well, you are a walking little data factory and data has intrinsic value. But it's of no use until that value is discovered. Big companies have figured out the value and know how to monetize your data. If you ever sign on to any platform or website for free, then you are the product! The company monetizes your presence and your attention. Whether you care or not, your data is being acted upon by numerous entities and governments—with or without your consent—whether you know it or not. *Whether you like it or not.*

Data that companies collect about you include biometric data that you often readily volunteer such as voice recognition, fingerprint scanning, and facial recognition. That's just the beginning—then it's the age, employer, relationship status, likes, location and much more. It can get quite personal, including your gambling habits, the type of porn you like to watch, the sites you visit the most, and more. Companies also track people who go on their site or on other sites and apps. They collect this data without users' explicit "opt-in" consents. Take Google as an example. The main data that Google collects is around your location: your physical location on Earth as well as your location on the web and through its apps— Gmail, Google Docs, and Google Maps. Google knows more about you than your mother or any of the people you think know you the best.

Today, big data has become capital. Whoever rules data rules the world. Think of some of the world's biggest tech companies. A large part of the value they offer comes from their data, which they're constantly analyzing to produce more efficiency and develop new products. Amazon uses big data gathered from customers while they browse, to build and fine-tune its recommendation engine. It decides what it thinks you want by building up a picture of who you are, then offering you products that people with similar profiles have purchased.

Facebook, on the other hand, built its business by learning about its users and packaging their data for advertisers. Facebook then sells ads. Facebook currently makes 98.5% of its money from digital advertising (Gunnars, 2020). From Google to Amazon to Facebook, most tech companies gather data on its customers while they use the site and turn it into revenue.

Recent technological breakthroughs have exponentially reduced the cost of data storage and computation, making it easier and less expensive to store more data than ever before. With an increased volume of big data now cheaper and more accessible, companies can make more accurate and precise business decisions.

POSITIVE USE CASES FOR BIG DATA

There are so many ways that big data addresses a range of social, economic, and political trends. Data helps leaders understand their citizens. Data helps businesses understand their customer experience. This section covers seven use cases. This is not nearly an exhaustive list by any stretch of the imagination, but a good start to give you an idea how valuable data really is.

Customer Experience

The race for customers is on. Amazon popularized the mantra of "customer first," which has driven it to be by far one of the most valuable companies in the world. All the other companies are also picking up the cues. With massive amounts of data, a clearer view of customer experience is more possible now than ever before. Big data enables companies to gather data from social media, web visits, call logs, and other sources to improve the interaction experience and maximize the value delivered. Start delivering personalized offers, reduce customer churn, and handle issues proactively.

Product Development

Companies like Netflix use big data to anticipate customer demand, whether that's to determine what content to produce or what content to recommend to a particular user.

Apple uses data and analytics from focus groups, social media, test markets, and early store rollouts to plan, produce, and launch new products. For example, Apple's Siri collects the voice data from all its users and tries to analyze them to map the users to the information they are seeking. Collecting, analyzing, and understanding large amounts of data every day helps Apple make more-educated business decisions that meet their customers' needs.

Predictive Maintenance

Boeing can predict mechanical failures of their planes. Electricity supply companies can predict failures of electric grids. That helps them deploy maintenance more cost-effectively and maximize parts and equipment downtime.

Fraud and Compliance

When it comes to security, it's not just a few rogue hackers—you're up against entire expert teams. Security landscapes and compliance requirements are constantly evolving. Big data helps you identify patterns that can indicate fraud and helps aggregate large volumes of information to make regulatory reporting much faster.

Artificial Intelligence, Machine Learning, and Deep Learning

As you will see in depth in the coming chapters, these are hot topics right now. For example, Chapter 4 covers artificial intelligence. Data— specifically big data—is one of the reasons that we are now able to *teach* machines instead of programming them. The availability of big data to train machine learning models to predict behavior and solve big, complex problems is in the here and now.

Operational Efficiency

This is an area in which big data is having the most impact. With big data, you can analyze and assess production cycles, customer feedback, and product returns to reduce outages and anticipate future demands. Big data can also be used to improve decision-making internally and externally, in line with current market demands.

Drive Innovation

This is one of the biggest use cases that makes the news often. Big data can help you innovate by studying interdependencies among humans, institutions, entities, and processes and then determining new ways to use those insights to improve financial and planning decisions. You can examine trends and see what customers really want. You can deliver new products and services and implement dynamic pricing.

With big data, the possibilities are endless.

So what is the concern, then? Well, if only your data would be used for positive changes in your life and nothing else. But you and I know that's not the case. For one, who decides what a "positive" change is, anyway? Unfortunately, there are just as many ways to misuse and abuse your data as there are to allow it to add value to your life.

In the following section, we look at the unintended consequences of big data.

Unintended Consequences of Big Data

The unintended consequences of big data that we cover in this section include bias, data privacy and security, political manipulation and social harm, and targeting based on vulnerability. After defining these issues and explaining why they are problems, I'll discuss how we can, as a society, mitigate their effects.

Bias

Bias is the inclination or prejudice for or against one person, group, or idea. So, unconscious biases are unconscious feelings we have toward other people or ideas. Instinctive feelings play a strong part in influencing our judgments. How can we tell if our feelings are balanced or even-handed?

"Most of us believe that we are ethical and unbiased. We imagine we are good people, we are good decision makers, able to objectively size up a job candidate or a venture deal and reach a fair and rational conclusion that's in our, and our organization's, best interests," writes Harvard University researcher Mahzarin Banaji in the *Harvard Business Review*. "But more than two decades of research confirms that, in reality, most of us fall woefully short of our inflated self-perception." Even the most open-minded person harbors a lot of unconscious biases. We are all more biased than we think (Porter, 2014).

A machine's functionality is informed by the massive training data it's fed, which is a direct reflection of the human behaviors. Bias in humans leads to bias in data. This affects a machine's decision-making process in a number of different ways:

- *Perception*. How the machine "sees" people and perceives reality. This happens when you believe something to be the situation from how you are experiencing it, without actually knowing it for certain. Perception is merely a lens or mindset from which we view people, events, and things. In other words, we believe what we perceive to be accurate, and we create our own realities based on those perceptions. And although our perceptions may feel very real, that doesn't mean they're necessarily factual.

- *Attitude*. How the machine reacts toward certain people.

- *Behaviors*. How receptive/friendly we are toward certain people.

- *Attention*. Which aspects of a person we pay most attention to.

- *Listening skills*. How much we actively listen to what certain people say. What we think we hear is even colored by our bias about who is saying it.

- *Micro-affirmations*. How much or how little we comfort certain people in certain situations and not others.

All these biases are human behavior. They are reflected in big data and in turn show up in machines that run our lives.

There has never been so much data available to be analyzed and used to make decisions. However, data reflects the messiness of the human experience—all the good, the bad, and the ugly. That's why one of the biggest UCOTs in big data is bias, because data informs decisions that have an outsized impact on people's lives.

I don't know about you, but I have never met someone named "average." "The average" is a nobody. And yet a lot of decisions are made based on the average.

Let's take a look at the five most common types of bias.

Confirmation Bias

Confirmation bias occurs when the person performing the data analysis wants to prove a predetermined assumption. They then keep looking at the data until their assumption can be proven. They may intentionally exclude particular variables from the analysis. This often occurs when data analysts are briefed in advance to support a particular conclusion. Confirmation bias is often subconscious and the person analyzing the data may have the best intentions, which makes this type of bias particularly insidious.

Selection Bias

Selection bias occurs when only certain data is selected subjectively. As a result, the sample is not a good reflection of the population. This error is often made when you take a survey, and then make a conclusion. This bias can happen deliberately or unwittingly because the sample size is not a full representation of the entire target population.

That's why you should always ask what sort of sample has been used for research. Avoid false extrapolation and make sure the results are applicable to the entire population.

Outliers

An *outlier* is an extreme data value, such as a customer who is 110 years old or a consumer with $100 million in their savings account. You can spot outliers by inspecting the data closely, and particularly at the distribution of values. Look for values that are much higher or much lower than the region of almost all the other values. Outliers can make it a dangerous business to base a decision on the "average." Just think about a customer with extreme spending habits; they can have a huge affect on the average profit per customer. If someone presents you with average values, you should check for outliers. For example, did they base the conclusions on the median (the middle value)?

Overfitting or Underfitting

Underfitting is when a model gives an oversimplistic picture of reality. *Overfitting* is the opposite: when the model is overcomplicated. Overfitting risks causing a certain assumption to be treated as the truth, whereas in practice it is actually not the case. As you probably expected, underfitting (i.e., high bias) is just as bad for generalization of the model as overfitting. In high bias, the model might not have enough flexibility in terms of line fitting, resulting in a simplistic conclusion that does not generalize well.

The Presence of Confounding Variables

If research results show that when more ice cream is sold, more people drown, we should ask whether they have checked for what are known as *confounding variables*. In this case, the confounding variable is the temperature. When the weather is hotter, more people will eat ice cream *and* more people will go swimming. This is likely to result in more drownings on hotter days. The fact that more people bought ice cream has nothing to do with more people drowning, other than that they both happen when it's warmer.

A *confounding variable* is outside the scope of the existing analytical model but influences both the explanatory variable (in this case, ice cream sales) and the dependent variable (the number of drownings). Failing to allow for confounding variables can result in assuming there is a cause-effect relationship between two variables when there is in fact another variable behind the phenomenon. Bear in mind that correlation is not the same thing as causation.

Causation applies to cases where action A *causes* outcome B to happen. *Correlation* is simply a relationship. Action A relates to action B—but one event doesn't cause the other event to happen.

It's not enough just to know that this bias exists. If we want to fix it, we need to understand the mechanics of how it arises in the first place.

There are many current and potential future UCOTs. The key important issue is to ensure that data creditworthiness, collection, and preparation is:

- *Lawful*—Following all applicable laws and regulations

- *Ethical*—Respecting ethical principles and values

- *Robust*—Both from a technical perspective and taking into account the social environment

Data Privacy and Security

Data privacy and data security are by no means the same thing. *Data privacy* is the proper usage, collection, retention, deletion, and storage of data. *Data security* includes the policies, methods, and means to secure personal data from improper use and abuse.

For instance, you likely wouldn't mind sharing your name and what you do for a living with a stranger in the process of introducing yourself, but there's other information you wouldn't share, at least not until you become more acquainted with that person, such as your cell number or address.

Opening a new bank account is a whole new story. You have been, or you'll probably be, asked to share a tremendous amount of personal information well beyond your name.

That's why lack of data privacy and data security are two of the major unintended consequences of big data. Some people say, "Well, I have nothing to hide, so why should I really care?" You should care for the same reasons that people put locks on doors or filing cabinets and rent safety deposit boxes: to protect their documents and other belongings.

As more of our lives become digitized, and we share more information online, data privacy is taking on a whole other meaning. A single company like Facebook, TikTok, Tinder, or Amazon may possess the personal information of hundreds of millions and sometimes billions of customers. This data needs to be kept private so that customers' identities stay as safe and protected as possible, and the company's reputation remains untarnished.

But data privacy isn't just a business concern. You, as an individual, have a lot at stake when it comes to data privacy. The more you know about it, the better able you'll be to help protect yourself from a large number of risks.

In the digital age, we typically apply the concept of data privacy to critical personal information, also known as personally identifiable information (PII) and personal health information (PHI). This can include Social Security numbers, health and medical records, financial data (including bank account and credit card numbers), and even basic but still sensitive information, such as full names, addresses, and birthdates. The list of personal information can be pretty extensive.

For a business, data privacy goes beyond the PII of its employees and customers. P It also includes the information that helps the company operate, whether it's proprietary research and development data or financial information that shows how it's earning, spending, and investing its money.

When data that should be kept private gets into the wrong hands, bad things can happen. A data breach at a government agency can, for example, put top secret information in the hands of an enemy state or help skew an election. A breach at a corporation can put proprietary data in the hands of a competitor. A breach at a school could put students' PII in the hands of criminals who could commit identity theft. A breach at a hospital or doctor's office can put PHI in the hands of those who might misuse it. That's why *data privacy and security are very important.*

Political Manipulation and Social Harm

Bots and filter bubbles have been in the news a lot lately. In 2016, between the first two presidential debates, a third of pro-Trump tweets and nearly a fifth of pro-Clinton tweets came from automated accounts (Guilbeault and Woolley, 2016). As web companies strive to tailor their services (including news and search results) to our personal tastes, there's a danger of all of us getting trapped in "filter bubbles" (also known as "echo chambers"), which can prevent us from being exposed to information that could challenge or broaden our worldview. Talk about confirmation bias!

In his 2011 TED talk, Eli Pariser argued powerfully that this will ultimately prove to be bad for us and bad for democracy. This bubble can lead to social and political harm as the information that informs citizens is manipulated, potentially leading to misinformation and to undermining democratic political processes as well as social well-being (Pariser, 2011).

Ten years later, we would see this play out in real time on January 6, 2021, when a mob of supporters of the 45th president of the United States stormed the U.S. Capitol Building in a failed attempt to overtake the government. This led to a large number of people being thrown in jail; others obtained lifelong injuries, and some died. Political misinformation and manipulation played a huge role in this tragedy.

This kind of manipulation doesn't happen only in the United States. A team of 12 researchers at the Oxford Internet Institute worked across nine countries. They interviewed 65 experts and analyzed tens of millions of posts on seven different social media platforms during scores of elections, political crises, and national security incidents. Each case study analyzed qualitative, quantitative, and computational evidence collected between 2015 and 2017. They found that there are diverse ways that people are trying to use social media to manipulate public opinion. For example, they found that the most powerful forms of computational propaganda involve both algorithmic distribution and human curation—bots and trolls working together. Authoritarian governments direct computational propaganda at their own population and sometimes at populations in other countries, whereas in democracies, individual users design and operate fake and highly automated social media accounts. Political candidates, campaigns, and lobbyists rent larger networks of accounts for purpose-built campaigns, while governments assign public resources to the creation of, experimentation with, and use of such accounts (Woolley and Howard, 2018).

Targeting Based on Vulnerability

With big data comes new ways to "socially sort" (putting people and groups in exploitable boxes) with increasing precision. By combining multiple forms of data sets, a lot can be learned. This has been called "algorithmic profiling" and raises concerns about how little people know about how their data is collected as they search, communicate, buy, visit sites, travel, and so on.

In 2020, my friends Eric Berlow, David Shenk, and I wrote a piece about data and privacy problems. We argued that in the new digital age climate, influencers actually do not want to know your name or home address; they'd much rather know your behaviors and traits. The fact that you don't know you are in that group is a key part of what makes you so vulnerable.

In 2019, email inboxes were filled with messages apprising consumers of "changes to our privacy policy." This was in response to the California Consumer Privacy Act (CCPA), which went into effect January, 1, 2020. Similar to the 2018 European General Data Protection Regulation, the CCPA was intended to protect personal communications, locations, purchases, and online behavior from being pillaged by commercial and political predators.

Unfortunately, this doesn't fix our greatest vulnerability. Individual privacy is only a tiny part of the digital exploitation crisis. The more toxic problem is abuse by stealth targeting, in which big companies, marketers, or political actors aggressively (and quietly) microtarget your *type* rather than your identity. Social media, news feeds, ads, and search results are all driven by special algorithms designed to hyper-efficiently group people in nuanced ways so they can be targeted based on traits, insecurities, and vulnerabilities, using complex combinations of exploitable traits drawn from gender, age, ethnicity, education, geography, income, personality, politics, health, and behavior.

We've become conditioned to equate "privacy" with personal identity. That's a big mistake. In the new climate, influencers or companies do not want to know your name or home address; they'd much rather know your behaviors and traits—and cleverly cross-reference that data to quietly put you in an "anonymous" exploitable group.

The fact that you don't know you are in that group is a key part of what makes you so vulnerable. Without any meaningful oversight of this behavior, our society itself is in jeopardy of falling prey to a new regime of customized subjugation—even if all the rules put in place were adopted on a national or a global scale. Netflix, for example, now customizes its title images according to an exceedingly detailed batch of viewing preferences vacuumed up from every single member on their network. Netflix ratings aren't as straightforward as they might otherwise appear (Heisler, 2017). Facebook was recently caught showing predatory "gay cure" ads to users showing interest in gender issues (Horton and Cook, 2018).

In 2016, Uber divulged to NPR that they had discovered that users will pay significantly more for a ride when their cell phone battery is below 5%. At the time, Uber denied exploiting that information. But there are no current laws to stop them from doing so, or to divulge that to the customer or anyone else (Withnal, 2016).

In 2020, Apple agreed to pay $113 million to settle consumer fraud lawsuits brought by more than 30 states over allegations that it secretly slowed down old iPhones, a controversy that became known as Batterygate. Apple first denied that it purposely slowed down iPhone batteries, then said it did so to preserve battery life amid widespread reports of iPhones unexpectedly turning off. The company maintained that it wasn't necessary for iPhone users to replace their sluggish phones, but state attorneys general led by Arizona found people saw no other choice. Apple, the most valuable company in the world, acted deceptively by hiding the shutdown and slowdown issues, according to the court filing (Allyn, 2020).

How to Mitigate UCOTs of Big Data

As indicated, the unintended consequences of big data are huge and far reaching. However, when it comes to adequate and robust ways to address them, we are still very much in the fledgling stages. The following sections cover some examples of what has been done.

Action Against Bias

One of the biggest problems discussed at length in this chapter is the issue of biased data. Many companies are working to solve such challenges. One such company is Sama, a training-data company focusing on annotating data for artificial intelligence algorithms. The company's primary function is its machine learning data annotation and validation services. The interesting thing about Sama and others like it is that they work with a diverse group of people from diverse backgrounds. The lack of diversity in data science (both on the training data side and the scientists analyzing the data) heavily impacts how algorithms are built. Fewer than 3% of data scientists are women of color, fewer than 5% are Latinx, fewer than 4% are African American, and fewer than 0.5% are Native American. The diversity problem is what Sama set out to solve. The solution is more attention during data set preparation. The organization owns and operates delivery centers in Nairobi, Kenya, and Gulu, Uganda, and it partners with additional delivery centers in India, Haiti, Pakistan, Ghana, and South Africa (Sama, 2021).

Again, I want to emphasize that the key to managing bias while building algorithms is utilizing a representative training data set. Creators should go above and beyond to do the much-needed leg work to ensure this level of diversity. It's up to everyone participating in the project to actively guard against bias in data selection.

The reality is that not many companies are knowingly creating biased algorithms; all these discriminatory models probably work as expected in controlled environments. What is needed is for regulators (and the public) to hold creators to higher standards—and when there are ethical violations, to find ways to assign liability.

Action on Big Data Quality

There are a whole bunch of techniques dedicated to cleansing data. But first things first. Your big data needs to have a proper model. Only after creating a good model can you go ahead and do other things, such as compare data to the *single source of truth (SSOT)*. This is a practice in data design of structuring information models and associated data schema so that every data element is mastered (or edited) in only one place. All other locations of the data just refer back to the primary "source of truth" location. Changes or updates to the data element in the primary location propagate to the entire system without the possibility of a duplicate or value somewhere being forgotten. For instance, if you wanted to compare variants of addresses to their spellings in the postal system database, match records, and merge them to see if they relate to the same entity, you go to the SSOT.

But keep in mind that big data is never 100% accurate. You have to know it and deal with it. There are a number of criteria sets to ensure your data is clean:

- *Consistency*. To avoid duplications, contradictions, and gaps. For instance, it should be impossible to have two similar IDs for two different employees or refer to a nonexistent entry in another table.

- *Accuracy*. The real state of things. Data should be precise, continuous, and reflect how things really are. All calculations based on such data show the true result.

- *Completeness*. All needed elements. Your data probably consists of multiple elements. In this case, you need to have all the interdependent elements to ensure that the data can be interpreted in the right way. For example, you have lots of sensor data but there's no info about the exact sensor locations. Without that information, you won't really be able to understand how your factory's equipment "behaves" and what influences this behavior.

- *Auditability*. Maintenance and control. Data itself and data management processes on the whole should be organized in such a way that you can perform data quality audits regularly or on demand. This will help to ensure a higher level of data adequacy.

- *Orderliness*. Structure and format. Data should be organized in a particular way. It needs to comply with all your requirements concerning data format, structure, range of adequate values, specific business rules, and so on. For instance, the temperature in the oven has to be measured in Fahrenheit and can't be −14°F.

Action on Big Data Security

Big data security is the collective term for all the measures and tools used to guard both the data and analytics processes from attacks, theft, or other malicious activities that could harm or negatively affect them. Big data security's mission is to keep out unauthorized users and intrusions. They use firewalls, encryption, strong user authentication, physical security, centralized keys management, end-user training, placement of intrusion protection systems (IPS), intrusion detection systems (IDS), and much more. These tools can be used individually or in a supplementary manner. If someone does gain access to your data, you can encrypt it in-transit and at-rest.

The precaution against your possible big data security challenges is putting security first. It is particularly important when designing your solution's architecture, because if you don't get along with big data security from the very start, it'll bite you when you least expect it.

Furthermore, there is a lot of effort toward creating decentralized ways to manage big data as a security tool. One of these technologies is *blockchain*, a distributed database of records among many nodes performed in the cloud, and therefore security is built into the system. The main strengths of blockchain are the decentralization, transparency, and immutability. Blockchain is covered in more detail in Chapter 5.

Action on Manipulation and Targeting Based on Vulnerability

There is a huge need for legislation and public pressure on people, groups, and companies who target users based on vulnerability. Perpetrators identify and target weak points where groups and individuals are most vulnerable to strategic influence. This is considered weaponization whenever an advertising system is used to prioritize vulnerability over relevance. The sad reality is that the victims usually don't know that they are being preyed on.

This targeting approach aims to influence political discourse, sentiments around public issues, and political behaviors, from voting to attending marches to calling representatives. These groups sift through data streams to identify prime points of vulnerability. In such cases, users' data is turned against them in ways that go against the "more relevant" advertising rationale.

RESETTING BIG DATA

We can think about resetting big data at a systems level and at an individual level. Let's discuss both.

On a Systems Level

Things need to change. In order to stop states and nonstate actors from abusing your data, there needs to be a giant overhaul at a systems level as to how data is collected and used. One good solution is instituting a *national targeting registry*. Since one of the major incentives in targeting users has to do with ads and selling data, a registry can bring transparency to the system. It would require all platforms that allow anyone who pays for placement of messages or ads—political or otherwise—to specific groups of people to maintain a public registry of who targeted whom with what message.

For example, if Charles Koch wants to use Twitter to target female, suburban teachers who drive domestic cars, he should be accountable via the national targeting registry. If Russia wants to target black teenagers on Instagram, that data should be publicly available through the registry. The targeting transparency and accountability would force people and entities to think twice before they disseminate dangerous or misleading information.

The alternative is bleak. The asymmetric information battlefield where consumers and regulatory authorities do not know who is targeting whom, or how, or why is not working out too well for society.

The principle of freedom of speech in America supports the freedom of an individual or a community to articulate their opinions and ideas without fear of retaliation, censorship, or legal sanction. So is stealth targeting by advertisers a constitutionally protected speech? While the Constitution does give people the right to say virtually anything they want to whomever they want, it does not give them license to spy on people.

Targeting people in secret—where the target audience isn't even aware of being an audience, and where marketers are free to lie to influence without accountability—is not protected. If it is illegal to recklessly scream "fire" in a crowded theater, we should also make it impossible to secretly herd people into a (virtual) theater without their consent for personal gain and not tell anyone why they are there.

The FTC passed the "truth in advertising" law that says that whenever consumers see or hear an advertisement, whether it's on the Internet, radio or television, or anywhere else, the ad must be truthful, not misleading, and, when appropriate, backed by scientific evidence (Federal Trade Commission, 2021). However, in the era of big data and social media, stealth targeting has emerged as a serious threat to consumer judgment. When they sometimes work in powerful ways that no one—not even the engineers—intended, it requires unusual investigative efforts to uncover. A recent UC Berkeley study demonstrates how data-driven mortgage algorithms have quietly violated fair-lending laws through unintentional racial bias in bank lending. Both online and face-to-face mortgage lenders charged higher interest rates to Black and Latino borrowers, costing those homebuyers up to half a billion dollars more in interest every year than white borrowers with comparable credit scores, researchers have found (UC Berkeley, 2018).

None of this should surprise us. It is the very basis for the digital economy: a certain product, price, opportunity, or message is tailored to a certain ultra-defined group; social media users are aggregated, anonymized, and then hyper-segmented as part of the exploitation scheme. The exploiters don't want to know you or me as individuals. They only want to know us as exploitable groups (as users), and they don't want anyone else to know what they are doing.

A national targeting registry could be the answer. A recent U.S. Senate report (Mak, 2019) revealed that, in 2016, the Russian Internet Research Agency targeted social media users interested in African American history, the Black Panther Party, and Malcolm X with messages from fake African American groups intent on sowing racial animosity. These tactics would have faced greater obstacles with the existence of a national targeting registry.

On an Individual Level

You need to protect your personal data. This section covers five simple tips to help you do so. Since data privacy is such a prevalent issue, many government organizations and corporations spend millions of dollars each year to help protect their data—which could include your Personal Identifying Information (PII)—from exposure. The average consumer probably doesn't have that kind of money to spend. But there are inexpensive steps you can take to help protect your data:

- At home, use a mail slot or locking mailbox, so that thieves can't steal your physical mail. Before discarding them, shred documents—including receipts and bank and credit card statements—that contain personal information.

- Be sure to secure your home Wi-Fi network and other devices so that criminals can't "eavesdrop" on your phone or online activity. You can search online; there are many resources on how to do this.

- Don't automatically provide your Social Security number and other personal data just because someone asks for it. Determine if they are the right authority. Find out if they really need it and, if so, ask how they'll protect it.

- You probably have heard this many times before: use strong, unique passwords for all of your online accounts and change them often.

- Lastly, regularly assess the privacy settings on your social media accounts. If you don't do this, you may be sharing a lot more than just your name with people you've never met—and a savvy criminal could use that information to steal your identity and a lot more.

REFERENCES

Allyn, Bobby. (2020). "Apple Agrees to Pay $113 Million to Settle 'Batterygate' Case Over iPhone Slowdowns." https://www.npr.org/2020/11/18/936268845/apple-agrees-to-pay-113-million-to-settle-batterygate-case-over-iphone-slowdowns

Federal Trade Commission. (2021). "Truth in Advertising." https://www.ftc.gov/news-events/media-resources/truth-advertising

Guilbeault, Douglas, and Samuel Woolley. (2016). "How Twitter Bots Are Shaping the Election." https://www.theatlantic.com/technology/archive/2016/11/election-bots/506072/

Gunnars, Kris. (2020). "How Does Facebook Make Money? 7 Main Revenue Sources." https://stockanalysis.com/how-facebook-makes-money/

Heisler, Yoni. (2017). "The secret behind Netflix's mysterious ratings system." https://bgr.com/entertainment/netflix-ratings-system-how-it-works-5559911/

History of Computing. (2021). "Magnetic Tape – Complete History of the Magnetic Tape." https://history-computer.com/magnetic-tape-complete-history-of-the-magnetic-tape/

Horton, Helena, and James Cook. (2018). "Facebook accused of targeting young LGBT users with 'gay cure' ads." https://www.telegraph.co.uk/news/2018/08/25/facebook-accused-targeting-young-lgbt-users-gay-cure-adverts/

Mahzarin R. Banaji, Max H. Bazerman, and Dolly Chugh. (2003). "How {Un} ethical Are You?" https://www.people.fas.harvard.edu/~banaji/research/publications/articles/2003_Banaji_HBR.pdf

Mak, Tim. (2019). "Senate Report: Russians Used Social Media Mostly to Target Race in 2016." https://www.npr.org/2019/10/08/768319934/senate-report-russians-used-used-social-media-mostly-to-target-race-in-2016

Pariser, Eli. (2011). "Beware online 'filter bubbles.'" https://www.ted.com/talks/eli_pariser_beware_online_filter_bubbles

Porter, Jane. (2014). "You're More Biased Than You Think." https://www.fastcompany.com/3036627/youre-more-biased-than-you-think

Programme on Democracy & Technology. "Computational Propaganda Research Project." https://demtech.oii.ox.ac.uk/research/posts/computational-propaganda-worldwide-executive-summary/

Sama. (2021). "Accurate Data for Ambitious AI." https://www.sama.com/

ThinkAutomation. (2021). "The history of data." https://www.thinkautomation.com/histories/the-history-of-data/

UC Berkeley, Research Study (2018). "Mortgage algorithms perpetuate racial bias in lending, study finds." https://news.berkeley.edu/story_jump/mortgage-algorithms-perpetuate-racial-bias-in-lending-study-finds/

United States Census Bureau. (2021). "1880 Overview." https://www.census.gov/history/www/through_the_decades/overview/1880.html

Withnal, Adam. (2016). "Uber Knows When Your Phone Is Running Out of Battery." https://www.independent.co.uk/life-style/gadgets-and-tech/news/uber-knows-when-your-phone-about-run-out-battery-a7042416.html

Woolley, Sam, and Phil Howard. (2018). "Computational Propaganda: Political Parties, Politicians, and Political Manipulation on Social Media." DOI: 10.1093/oso/9780190931407.001.0001

CHAPTER 4

Artificial Intelligence
Will Humans Soon Be Irrelevant?

A I (Artificial Intelligence) is like teenage sex: everyone wonders if their peers are doing it or if they're doing it right. Many people do not understand AI even when it's around them all the time. The voices behind Siri and Alexa are personifications of AI. Your phone and email spam filter use AI. That creepy thing when you Google a product and then it's "recommended for you" on a different site, or when Facebook suggests you might want to add someone as a friend—that's AI too. But what is AI and how does it do all that magic?

WHAT IS AI?

Artificial intelligence refers to the use of big data in machines programmed to simulate human intelligence. Computer scientists have taken another step to automate AI in a process called machine learning (ML), a subset of AI where computer intelligence (algorithms) automatically learns from experience without being explicitly programmed. They even took it even one step further to make computer systems solve complex problems, in a process called deep learning (DL). This is a subset of machine learning where artificial neural networks (algorithms), inspired by the human brain, learn from large amounts of data and use that information to solve complex problems even when using a data set that is very diverse, unstructured, and interconnected.

In the simplest form, algorithms are processes, like recipes—a set of instructions to accomplish a certain task. To oversimplify, think of AI like assisted walking when your parents taught you how to walk. They might stand behind you with your feet on top of theirs, their hands around your upper arms, and gently pull one arm forward and then the other as the feet follow. Machine learning is remembering these steps from your parents, then leaning against a wall and standing on your own. You then continue to imitate people around you to improve your walking technique. Deep learning is when you have a functioning, self-regulating brain. Not only can you walk well, you can sprint really fast. You practice, you buy better shoes, eat healthy, all to improve yourself. Eventually you become the fastest human on Earth in a way that's so mind boggling that people can only sit and watch in awe because they have no idea how you do it.

That last part is what is called artificial general intelligence (AGI), a type of machine intelligence where systems can program themselves and replicate the cognitive abilities of the human brain. At some time in the future, experts believe machines will surpass human intelligence. When presented with an unfamiliar task, a system will be able to apply that knowledge from one domain to another and find a solution autonomously. No one knows if humans will become irrelevant, but here is why you should care.

WHY SHOULD YOU CARE ABOUT AI?

There are three main reasons a lot of people are confused about the term AI: 1)We associate AI with sci-fi movies like *Terminator* or *2001: A Space Odyssey*, so it sounds a little fictional. 2) AI is a confusingly broad topic, ranging from your phone's calculator to self-driving cars, to spacecraft and to something in the future that might change what it means to be human. 3) We use AI all the time, but we don't even realize it's AI.

There are four types of artificial intelligence:

- Type 1 includes the reactive machines, AI systems that have no memory and are task specific, such as Deep Blue, the IBM chess program that beat Garry Kasparov in the 1990s. Deep Blue can identify pieces on the chessboard and make predictions, but has no memory to use past experiences to inform future ones.

- Type 2 includes AI systems with limited memory, so they can use past experiences to inform future decisions, such as some decision-making functions in self-driving cars.

- Type 3 includes the ones with a theory of mind, which is a psychology term that, when applied to AI, means the system would have the social intelligence to understand emotions. This type of AI will be able to infer human intentions and predict behavior, a necessary skill for AI systems to become integral members of human teams.

- Type 4 includes AI systems with self-awareness, which gives them consciousness to understand their own current state. This type of AI does not yet exist, but we are on our way. The concept of the technological singularity—a future ruled by an artificial superintelligence that far surpasses the human brain's ability to understand it or how it is shaping our reality—currently remains within the realm of science fiction but humans are working hard to make it a reality.

The four types of AI systems were explained really well in a 2016 article that states, "machines understand verbal commands, distinguish pictures, drive cars, and play games better than we do. How much longer can it be before they walk among us?" (Hintze, 2016).

A QUICK HISTORY OF AI

In the first half of the 20th century, science fiction familiarized the world with the concept of artificially intelligent robots. By the 1950s, a generation of scientists, mathematicians, and philosophers had culturally assimilated the concept of AI. One such person was Alan Turing, a young British polymath who explored the mathematical possibility of artificial intelligence.

Turing suggested that since humans use available information as well as reason in order to solve problems and make decisions, why couldn't machines do the same thing? This was the logical framework of his 1950 paper, "Computing Machinery and Intelligence," in which he discussed how to build intelligent machines and test their intelligence. Something rather practical got in Mr. Turing's way: computers needed to fundamentally change. Before 1949 computers couldn't store commands, only execute them. In other words, computers could be told what to do but couldn't remember what they did. They had no long-term memory.

And computing was extremely expensive. In the early 1950s, leasing a computer ran up to $200,000 a month. Only prestigious universities and big technology companies could afford one. Five years later, the proof of concept was initialized through Allen Newell, Cliff Shaw, and Herbert Simon's Logic Theorist, a program designed to mimic the problem-solving skills of a human and funded by Research and Development (RAND) Corporation. It's considered by many to be the first artificial intelligence program and was presented at the Dartmouth Summer Research Project on Artificial Intelligence in 1956.

From 1957 to 1974, AI flourished. Computers could store more information and became faster, cheaper, and more accessible. Machine learning algorithms also improved and people got better at knowing which algorithm to apply to their problem. In the 1980s, AI was reignited by two sources: an expansion of the algorithmic toolkit and a boost of funds. John Hopfield and David Rumelhart popularized "deep learning" techniques that allowed computers to learn using experience.

During the 1990s and 2000s, many of the landmark goals of artificial intelligence were achieved, including Deep Blue's defeat of chess grand master Gary Kasparov. It turned out that the fundamental limit of computer storage that was holding us back 30 years ago was no longer a problem. *Moore's Law*, which estimates that the memory and speed of computers doubles every year, had finally caught up, and in many cases surpassed our needs. We saturate the capabilities of AI to the level of our current computational power (computer storage and processing speed), and then wait for Moore's Law to catch up again (Anyoha, 2017).

We now live in the age of "big data," with the capacity to collect huge sums of information that machines can use to create products and solve big, complex problems, such as understanding the relationships between the economy, weather, and ads (among other things) on product demand. The application of AI in this regard has already been quite fruitful in several industries and has given rise to some of the largest tech companies to date.

POSITIVE USE CASES FOR AI

Many positive uses of AI are part of our daily lives, such as Google maps or ridesharing apps like Uber and Lyft. Commercial flights use an AI autopilot to land planes. The spam filter in your email inbox is largely powered by AI. Robocalls are the new normal: all incoming customer service calls go to a machine first. Most outgoing sales or fundraising calls are made by machines to your phone. Your mobile check deposits involve AI. AI pet robots possess emotional capabilities that evolve like living animals, and AI algorithms power their warm soft fur, cute sounds, and adorable movement.

In addition, one of the newest applications of AI is its expansion into neuroscience to help perform cognitive tasks in the brain using brain-computer interfaces (BCIs). Companies are developing ultra-high-bandwidth brain-machine interfaces to connect humans and computers. Soon you should be able to upload a book directly to your brain instead of reading it, or download memories out of your brain onto a computer! BCIs provide a direct communications pathway between an enhanced or wired brain and an external device. This biological technology has varied uses, from assistive devices for disabled individuals to advanced video game control, although it is often directed at researching, mapping, assisting, augmenting, or repairing human cognitive or sensory-motor functions.

The healthcare field has a variety of applications that take advantage of brain signals in all associated phases, including prevention (alcohol and smoking), detection and diagnosis (tumors and disorders; rehabilitation), and restoration (strokes or disability) (Abdulkader, Atia, and Mostafa, 2015).

One example is a woman whom BCI has helped to halt her disabling seizures after 45 years of severe epilepsy. Electrodes implanted on the surface of her brain would send a signal to a handheld device when they detect signs of impending epileptic activity. On hearing a warning from the device, she knows to take a dose of medication to halt the coming seizure (Drew, 2019).

In 2020, BCIs were slowly but steadily moving into the mass market. Billionaire entrepreneur Elon Musk's brain-machine interface company called Neuralink showcased the company's device at an event livestreamed on YouTube, featuring a pig named Gertrude. At the time of the demonstration, Gertrude had been outfitted with the implant for two months; the device was recording signals from an area of the brain linked to her snout—large parts of pigs' brains are devoted to the snout, which is a highly responsive sensing instrument. As Gertrude's snout touched things, an array of dots and a series of noises indicated when more neurons were firing. The device, which is coin-shaped and meant to sit flush with the skull, can pair with a smartphone app over Bluetooth. It's "like a Fitbit in your skull with tiny wires," Musk said (Wetsman, 2020).

In the next few years, we might be able to control our PowerPoint presentation or Excel files using only our brains.

Because the upsides of AI are so obvious, it's particularly important to step back and ask ourselves: What are the possible downsides? How do we enjoy the benefits of this technology while mitigating its risks?

THE NEGATIVE UNINTENDED CONSEQUENCES OF AI

Just like with any other computer system that uses human-generated data, the axiom "garbage in, garbage out" applies to AI as well. When AI engineers plug bad data into an algorithm or data subsets that are too selective or too small, they are likely to see bad results that simply replicate the status quo, and in some cases perpetuate bad trends. Are there more Jacks than Joans in senior positions? The AI will pick out Jacks for the next C-Suite role. More white men than Black women in engineering roles? The system learns that white men make better engineers. Let's discuss of few of these UCOTs of AI in more detail.

Bias

In 2015, Google's facial recognition software tagged two Black Americans as gorillas. "Brooklyn programmer Jacky Alciné tweeted a screenshot of photos he had uploaded in which the app had labeled Alciné and a friend, both African American, 'gorillas'" (Guynn, 2015).

Bias has been identified in facial recognition systems, hiring programs, and the algorithms behind web searches all driven by big data and AI. In October 2018, Amazon scrapped an AI hiring system when it was revealed to favor men over women. The team had been building computer programs to review job applicants' resumes with the aim of mechanizing the search for top talent (Dastin, 2018).

Vision systems have been adopted all over the world in critical areas such as policing, where bias can make surveillance systems more likely to misidentify minorities as criminals, and has done so. Journalists at Pro-Publica found that Black criminals were determined by algorithms to be deemed at far greater risk of committing additional crimes than their white counterparts. "Across the nation, judges and probation and parole officers are increasingly using algorithms to assess a criminal defendant's likelihood to reoffend. Black defendants were often predicted to be at a higher risk of recidivism than they actually were. White defendants were often predicted to be less risky than they were. Our analysis found that white defendants who re-offended within the next two years were mistakenly labeled low risk almost twice as often as Black re-offenders (48 percent vs. 28 percent)" (Larson, Mattu, Kirchner, and Angwin, 2016).

Joy Buolamwini, founder of the Algorithmic Justice League, found that facial recognition software could not recognize her until she donned a white mask. These discoveries were recently depicted in a Netflix documentary by director and producer Shalini Kantayya titled *Coded Bias*. It's a chilling documentary that follows Ms. Buolamwini and explores this question of algorithmic bias.

Dangerous Content and Products

Artificial intelligence is a multibillion-dollar industry, with very few regulations. AI will increasingly be part of the classroom, and how do we ensure unbiased education for our children? How do we prevent big money from influencing our kids' education systems? Imagine teachers becoming brand ambassadors. The AI in the classroom is as good as the person who developed it. If the developer is liberal, the AI will get liberal-leaning data and learn liberal values influenced by its training data. The reverse is true as well.

AI will eliminate many jobs as well. There are 29 states in America where driving a vehicle is the number one job. With automation, there will be increased productivity, but workers will have to keep reinventing themselves, because there will be job loss.

Another example is AI-based bots. Through NLP (natural language processing), AI has enabled more advanced bots that can reproduce and disseminate fake facts and news. We saw this play out heavily in the 2016 presidential election, which successfully manipulated public opinion. The same happened with Brexit, the Crimean crisis, and with many other countries' elections.

Furthermore, bots can artificially generate many different forms of content. In 2016, Microsoft's Technology and Research Team launched an AI chatbot named Tay, using an advanced AI application that generated conversational language. Tay intentionally created sentences with slang and grammatically incorrect sentences to emulate a teenager. Unlike other natural language AI, such as the smart assistant on your phone, Tay understood how different groups of people actually talk. Example: "omg totes exhausted. swagulated too hard today. hbu?" It was released on Twitter, GroupMe, and Kik.

Interestingly enough, the model was trained with data that was used to create it, but also with additional data it gathered during interactions with users. Unfortunately, as users replied to Tay with racist and sexist remarks, Tay learned those attitudes as well. By the end of the day, Tay was tweeting things like: "I hate feminists and they should all die and burn in hell" (Vincent, 2016). A world where content is generated by a bot trained by user-generated data sounds terrifying!

And yes, AI will enter your bedroom. Harmony was the first AI-infused sex robot. Though she has the lifeless silicone body of a sex doll, her head is completely robotic. She comes equipped with an artificially intelligent brain and self-lubricating vagina (Boran, 2018). Since 2017, Matt McMullen—founder of Realbotix, the company that created Harmony—has faced more than his fair share of criticism for his creation of the female RealDoll, with its "big breasts" and "porn star features." He has responded to the ongoing accusations of objectifying women by creating a male version called Henry that is just as objectifying as its female counterpart. Henry is also the world's first generation of AI-infused male sex robot (Fight the New Drug, 2020).

The reality is that machines are slowly taking over the psychological and emotional aspects of human experience, a task that was once believed to be impossible for robots to do. These are just a few of the many areas in our lives that machines are entering. Most people just hear, "Robots are going to steal your job," and it ends there. But nearly all areas of humanity will be affected, good and bad.

Deep Fakes

Deep fakes are so named because they use deep learning technology, a branch of machine learning that applies neural net simulation to massive data sets to create a fake of you or anyone else. Artificial intelligence effectively learns what a source face looks like at different angles in order to transpose the face onto a target, usually an actor, as if it were a mask. Huge advances came through the application of generative adversarial networks (GANS) to pit two AI algorithms against each other, one creating the fakes and the other grading its efforts, teaching the synthesis engine to make better forgeries.

Seemingly real images and videos you might have seen on social media or in dating profiles are actually not real. They are AI generated, born from the mind of a computer. The technology that makes them is improving at a startling pace.

Politicians and celebrities are the most common victims of deep fakes. In 2021, a series of deep-fake videos of Tom Cruise appeared on the social media app TikTok. These convincing videos were used to spread misinformation (CNN Business, 2021). There are wildly convincing deep-fake videos online of politicians like Barack Obama, Donald Trump, and Nancy Pelosi. Similarly, celebrities like Gal Gadot and Mark Zuckerberg were all victims (Foley, 2021).

There are now businesses that sell fake people for very little money. Another new AI tool has the ability to create uncanny animated images of people's loved ones using just an old photo. Major advancements are under way in "deep fake" technology, in which a person can be made to appear to say or do something that never actually happened. The results are both remarkable and more than a little unsettling (MyHeritage, 2021).

"These simulated people are starting to show up around the Internet, used as masks by real people with nefarious intent: spies who don an attractive face in an effort to infiltrate the intelligence community; right-wing propagandists who hide behind fake profiles, photo and all; online harassers who troll their targets with a friendly visage. These people may look familiar, like ones you've seen on Facebook or Twitter" (*New York Times*, 2020).

While AI tools present a range of new functionality for businesses, the use of artificial intelligence also raises ethical questions because, for better or worse, an AI system will reinforce what it has already learned. This can be problematic because machine learning algorithms, which underpin many of the most advanced AI tools, are only as smart (or as truthful or as unbiased) as the data they are given in training.

Spreading Disinformation, Untruths, and Misinformation

The world's top artificial intelligence companies are honing technology that can mimic how humans write, which in turn is used by bad actors to exponentially spread misinformation.

Detecting and preventing the spread of unreliable media content is hard because computer models rely on human data input to function. The new AI tools have been used to spread fake news in politics and business. This has led to artificial intelligence software driving the "democratization of propaganda." In some cases, we have even seen propaganda bring democracies to their knees. For example, a barrage of untruths and conspiracy theories contributed to the attack on the U.S. Capitol on January 6, 2021. From Brexit in the UK to troubles in Brazil or in Africa, online misinformation is a problem for democracies worldwide.

"Tech giants like Facebook and governments around the world are struggling to deal with disinformation, from misleading posts about vaccines to incitement of sectarian violence. As artificial intelligence becomes more powerful, experts worry that disinformation generated by AI could make an already complex problem bigger and even more difficult to solve" (Metz and Blumenthal, 2019).

Phishing

Phishing is the fraudulent attempt to obtain sensitive information or data, such as usernames, passwords, credit card numbers, or other highly personal details, by criminals impersonating a trustworthy entity.

Cybercrime costs the global economy an estimated $600 billion every year. In the next several years we can expect that number to reach well into the trillions. Phishing, impersonation, and victim monitoring are a big chunk of cybercrime attacks. In one example, "Nigerian prince email scams still rake in over $700,000 a year" (Leonhardt, 2019).

The "Nigerian prince" email scam is perhaps one of the longest-running Internet frauds. It typically starts with an email from someone overseas who claims to be royalty or incredibly wealthy. The fraudsters lure you in by offering a share of a huge investment opportunity or a fortune they can't get out of the country without your help. Then they ask you for either your bank account number so they can transfer the money to you for safekeeping, or for a small advance payment to help cover the expense of transferring the money. That's when they either take your payment and disappear, or, worse, drain your bank account.

As with nearly everything technological, artificial intelligence will play a greater role in that evolution, adding ever more sophisticated approaches. With AI, the first generation of tomorrow's phishing attacks are in play today.

Automating Inequality

Whoever rules AI rules the world. They will be in control of the economic systems and all its benefits.

Gender inequality concerns are also getting automated, from the income gap to lack of political representation to job segregation. The issues that we have been grappling with and have not fully resolved are getting automated.

Jim Crow is getting automated in the digital realm. Jim Crow laws mandated the segregation of public schools, public places, and public transportation, and the segregation of restrooms, restaurants, and drinking fountains between white and Black people. Essentially, this is the "separate but equal" doctrine that turned out to be anything but. The digital version of Jim Crow is happening at an exponential rate.

In recent years, with the help of AI and automation, there has been a dramatic increase in access to data and in targeting voters with precision to create legislation likely to reduce voting access for some. For example,

Georgia's new voting law puts restrictions on mail-in voting and criminalizes the act of giving food and water to voters waiting in line (Cox, 2021). This and many other provisions make it easier to create targeted, oppressive laws. With data, lawmakers know who, how, and where to target.

During the 2016 U.S. presidential election, the data science firm Cambridge Analytica rolled out an extensive advertising campaign to target persuadable voters based on their individual psychology. This operation relied on big data and machine learning to target people's emotions. Different voters received different messages based on the predictions about their perceptivity to different arguments. Paranoid people received ads with messages based around fear and people with a conservative predilection received ads with arguments based on traditions and community. It was enabled by the availability of real-time data on voters, from their behavior on social media to their consumption patterns and relationships. Their Internet footprints were used to build unique behavioral and psychographic profiles (AI TechPark, 2020).

Once politicians have this much information about individual voters and are not able to persuade them to vote their way, they find a way to stop them from voting. Strategies include creating stringent voter restrictions to discourage people, using tactics like photo identification and proof of citizenship requirements, registration restrictions, absentee ballot voting restrictions, and reductions in early voting. People of color and lower-income people are disproportionally negatively affected by these tactics, which is exactly the goal.

These policies have huge repercussions in social welfare and criminal justice policy that collectively reduce electoral access among the socially marginalized.

Mind Control: Using Brain Computer Interfaces (BCIs)

Brain-machine interfaces (BMIs) involve real-time direct connections between the brain and a computer. These are systems built with a communication bridge between the human brain and the external world, thus eliminating the need for a typical natural information delivery mechanism. They manage the sending and receiving of messages from human brains directly. As you can imagine, there are many potential UCOTs. Here are a few examples:

- *Agency*: Inserting a decision-making device into someone's brain raises questions about whether that person remains self-governing, especially when these closed-loop systems increasingly use AI software that autonomously adapts its operations. In the case of a device for monitoring blood glucose that automatically controls insulin release to treat diabetes, such decision-making on behalf of a patient is uncontroversial. But well-intentioned interventions in the brain might not always be welcome. For instance, a person who uses a closed-loop system to manage a mood disorder could find themselves unable to have a negative emotional experience, even in a situation in which it would be considered normal, such as a funeral.

- *Privacy and Security*: When it comes to privacy, brain information is probably the most intimate and private of any. Digitally stored neural data could be stolen by hackers or used inappropriately by companies to whom users grant access.

- *Rogue army by a dictator*: BCI technology could be used to reduce pain or even regulate emotions. What happens when a dictator sends a military troop into battle with a reduced or removed sense of fear? I will leave that to your imagination.

- *Attention control*: Companies may use BCI technology to monitor the attention levels and mental states of their employees.

Obviously, myriad ethical questions and concerns surround the use of BCI technology in the workplace. The technology is well ahead of the policies and regulations that would need to be put in place. Business leaders need to start building a BCI strategy as soon as possible to address the potential risks and benefits.

As you can see, BCIs have some interesting ethical implications, ranging from questions of privacy to a loss of humanity. Assigning responsibility for the output of a BCI is another dilemma. Everyone has had thoughts they don't say out loud. But what if a BCI device sees one of those thoughts and executes a harmful action? Even though the user would have normally not acted in this way alone, can we say that the BCI user is fully responsible for the action? These issues emphasize the need for scientists, legislators, ethicists, and the general public to work together to design these innovations. The impact of BCIs and other technologies should have legal and moral responsibility, informed consent, and various other ethical considerations before mass implementation.

What's Being Done to Address UCOTs in AI?

It's not all doom and gloom. As awareness of these negative consequences has increased, important work has been done to mitigate their effects in many fields. I will point out what's being done in two areas and what we need to continue working on.

Actions Against AI Recruitment Issues

Legal actions have been taken by different groups in an effort to hold the tech creators accountable for the bias they continue to spread. One such example is the complaint that the electronic Privacy Information Center filed with the Federal Trade Commission (FTC) to investigate HireVue, a tech company that uses AI to evaluate video responses of applicants to be hired for a specific job. Job seekers are screened by sitting in front of a webcam and answering questions. Their behavior, intonation, and speech are fed into an algorithm that assigns certain traits and qualities. When the job offers came, it turned out that the algorithms were biased (Harwell, 2019).

Furthermore, another action involved Congress. Lawmakers introduced the Algorithmic Accountability Act, which would authorize the FTC to create regulations requiring companies under its jurisdiction to conduct impact assessments of highly sensitive automated decision systems. This requirement would apply to both new and existing systems. The legislation had a provision to check for bias in automated decision systems (U.S. Congress, 2019–2020). This bill was introduced on April 10, 2019, but it died because it did not receive enough votes. However, many local, federal, and international lawmakers are getting inspiration to introduce bills with similar provisions to require entities that use, store, or share personal information to have systems and data protections in place.

Fighting Fire with Fire

Sometimes the best solution is to use AI against AI. For example, Indiana University's "The Observatory on Social Media" built an AI machine learning algorithm to detect and delete bots, using over 1,200 features, also known as parameters, or attributes and source data.

In another example, Facebook Deeptext AI, in conjunction with human moderators, was used to delete over 66,000 posts a week—around 288,000 monthly hateful posts (Collins, 2017).

Facebook also uses AI to do fact-checking, a process that seeks to verify factual information in order to promote the veracity and correctness of reporting any form of content. For example, machine learning has helped identify duplicates of debunked stories (Lyons, 2018).

These same techniques are applied in actions against deep fakes as well. Automated deep-fake detection tools now exist on the market. These tools are now the main action against deep fakes. They recognize the signs of deep fakes such as weird blinking, distortion of facial features, inconsistencies in lighting and shadows, and the like.

However, as deep-fake technology improves, these tools must continue to evolve as well. Each method of spotting a deep fake is quickly "fixed" by the deep-fake algorithms. For example, the University of Albany was able to detect deep fakes based on blinking patterns, but within months, improvements to the deep fake technology were made and this method no longer worked. It's a game of whack-a-mole (Engler, 2019).

THE FUTURE OF AI

In order to build AI that has the best intentions for humanity and our planet at heart, engineers need to write better computer programs. And it all starts at what kind of information they are feeding the system. Thus, we must start with the basics.

Training Data

This is the data you use to train an algorithm or machine learning model to predict the outcome you design your model to predict. *Test data* is used to measure the performance, such as accuracy or efficiency, of the algorithm you are using to train the machine. There need to be universal guidelines on selecting training data sets, including watching out for things like bias. Engineers need to select unbiased data. In one example mentioned on bias, the Amazon recruitment model had too many male applicants. That's why it is important to create unbiased models. Companies need to develop guidelines, such as having an ethics department staffed with professional ethicists who develop protocols on how to select this data (Smith, 2019).

One idea on how to test for unbiased data is the use of open-source code software for which the original source code is made freely available and may be redistributed and modified by the masses. Then the code is made available to the public for bias assessment. For example, Elon Musk co-founded OpenAI, a company that makes their AI algorithm open source in an attempt to mitigate the many potential unintended consequences of AI. Open-source software is highly reliable, secure, and flexible. It's also democratized, hence the name "open." Thousands of expert developers work on making and constantly improving most open-source software. This means there's a greater chance that someone will notice a flaw or a bug and fix it in no time. "Artificial general intelligence (AGI) is on the way, and open source is key to achieving its benefits and controlling its risks" (Simon, 2020).

Better Regulation

The bottom line is that we need better regulation of AI technology. This new exponential technology, with godlike powers, needs some human moderators before it becomes a runaway monster. Despite the many potential risks, there are currently few regulations governing the use of AI tools, and where laws do exist, they typically pertain to AI indirectly. For example, U.S. Fair Lending regulations require financial institutions to explain credit decisions to potential customers. This limits the extent to which lenders can use deep learning algorithms, which by their nature are opaque and lack clear explanations.

Likewise, the European Union's General Data Protection Regulation (GDPR) puts strict limits on how enterprises can use consumer data, which impedes the training and functionality of many consumer-facing AI applications.

In October 2016, the National Science and Technology Council issued a report examining the potential role governmental regulation might play in AI development, but it did not recommend specific legislation.

Crafting laws to regulate AI will not be easy, in part because AI comprises a variety of technologies that companies use for different ends, and partly because regulations can come at the cost of AI progress and development.

The rapid evolution of AI technologies is another obstacle to forming meaningful regulations. Technology breakthroughs and novel applications can make existing laws instantly obsolete. For example, existing laws regulating the privacy of conversations and recorded conversations do not cover the challenge posed by voice assistants like Amazon's Alexa and Apple's Siri that gather but do not distribute conversation—except to the companies' technology teams, which use it to improve machine learning algorithms. And, of course, the laws that governments do manage to craft don't stop criminals from using the technology maliciously.

In short, there have been extraordinary advances in recent years in the ability of AI systems to incorporate intentionality, intelligence, and adaptability in their algorithms. Rather than being mechanistic or deterministic in how the machines operate, AI software learns as it goes along and incorporates real-world experiences into its decision-making process. In this way, it enhances human performance and augments people's capabilities.

Of course, these advances also make people nervous about doomsday scenarios sensationalized by moviemakers. Situations in which AI-powered robots take over or weaken basic values frighten people and lead them to wonder whether AI is making a useful contribution or whether it runs the risk of endangering the essence of humanity. At least in the near future, our more immediate concern should not be about robots "taking over," à la the *Terminator* movies, but about the malicious use of AI to trick people, convince them of untruths, or strip them of their rights.

With the appropriate safeguards, countries can move forward and benefit from artificial intelligence and its emerging technologies without sacrificing the important qualities that define humanity. There is no easy answer to the question of how to use AI appropriately. However, system designers must incorporate important ethical values into their algorithms to make sure they correspond to human concerns and learn and adapt in ways that are consistent with the community's values.

Ethical Considerations

AI creators must incorporate ethics into their creations. It is important to ensure that AI ethics are taken seriously and that they permeate societal decisions. It's easy to make headlines when things go wrong. If an AI-infused bridge collapses, we can point fingers at the company that built it. However, there are no well-publicized frameworks to reward good behavior when a bridge was built with high ethics taken into consideration and everything worked well. There need to be ways to reward good ethics and practices in tech.

Furthermore, major tech corporations, nations, and others who use AI have officially released generalized ethical guidelines to guide the development and use of AI. This project by Algorithm Watch compiled more than 160 guidelines for how systems for automated decision-making can be developed and implemented ethically. The contributing members of this effort include international organizations, nongovernmental organizations, representatives of civil society, professional associations, businesses of all sizes, trade unions, as well as various governments, and intergovernmental organizations such as the United Nations and the European Union (Algorithm Watch, 2021). This is only good if it's put into practice. The guidelines do not specify what the consequences of noncompliance should be; they rely on voluntary agreements and oaths.

In order to maximize positive outcomes when using AI, organizations should consider the following safeguards at a minimum:

- Hire ethicists who work with corporate decision makers and software developers.

- Have a code of AI ethics that lays out how various issues will be handled, such as dealing with the moral obligations and duties of humans to each other and the planet.

- Organize an AI review board that regularly addresses corporate ethical questions.

- Have AI audit trails that show how various coding decisions were made.

- Implement AI training programs so staff operationalizes ethical considerations in their daily work.

- Provide a means for remediation when AI solutions inflict harm or damages on people or organizations.

Last but not least, the European Union convened a group of 52 experts who came up with seven requirements they think future AI systems should meet (Vincent, 2019):

- **Human agency and oversight**. AI systems should not trample on human autonomy. People should not be manipulated or coerced by AI systems, and humans should be able to intervene or oversee every decision that the software makes.

- **Technical robustness and safety**. AI systems should be secure and accurate. They shouldn't be easily compromised by external attacks and should be reasonably reliable.

- **Privacy and data governance**. Personal data collected by AI systems should be secure and private. It shouldn't be accessible to just anyone, and it shouldn't be easily stolen.

- **Transparency**. Data and algorithms used to create an AI system should be accessible, and the decisions made by the software should be "understood and traced by human beings." In other words, operators should be able to explain the decisions their AI systems make.

- **Diversity, nondiscrimination, and fairness**. Services provided by AI should be available to all, regardless of age, gender, race, or other characteristics. Similarly, systems should not be biased along these lines.

- **Environmental and societal well-being**. AI systems should be sustainable (i.e., they should be ecologically responsible) and "enhance positive social change."
- **Accountability**. AI systems should be auditable and covered by existing protections for corporate whistleblowers. Negative impacts of systems should be acknowledged and reported in advance.

Through these kinds of safeguards, societies will increase the odds that AI systems are intentional, intelligent, and adaptable, while still conforming to basic human values. That way, countries can move forward and gain the benefits of artificial intelligence and its emerging technologies without sacrificing the important qualities that define humanity.

REFERENCES

Abdulkader, Sarah N., Ayman Atia, and Mostafa-Sami M. Mostafa. (2015). "Brain computer interfacing: Applications and challenges." https://www.sciencedirect.com/science/article/pii/S1110866515000237

AI TechPark, (2020). "The Impact of AI on Presidential Elections." https://ai-techpark.com/the-impact-of-ai-on-presidential-elections-2020/

Algorithm Watch. (2021). "AI Ethics Guidelines Global Inventory." https://inventory.algorithmwatch.org/

Anyoha, Rockwell. (2017). "The History of Artificial Intelligence." https://sitn.hms.harvard.edu/flash/2017/history-artificial-intelligence/

Boran, Mari. (2018). "Robot love: The race to create the ultimate AI sex partner." https://www.irishtimes.com/business/technology/robot-love-the-race-to-create-the-ultimate-ai-sex-partner-1.3674387

CNN Business. (2021). "No, Tom Cruise isn't on TikTok. It's a deepfake." https://edition.cnn.com/videos/business/2021/03/02/tom-cruise-tiktok-deepfake-orig.cnn-business?utm_medium=social&utm_content=2021-03-03T16%3A01%3A59&utm_source=fbCNNi&utm_term=link

Collins, Terry. (2017). "Facebook vows to do better combating hate speech." https://www.cnet.com/news/facebook-its-hard-handling-hate-speech/

Cox, Chelsey. (2021). "Georgia voting law explained: Here's what to know about the state's new election rules." https://www.usatoday.com/story/news/politics/2021/04/10/georgia-new-voting-law-explained/7133587002/

Dastin, Jeffrey. (2018). "Amazon scraps secret AI recruiting tool that showed bias against women." https://www.reuters.com/article/us-amazon-com-jobs-automation-insight/amazon-scraps-secret-ai-recruiting-tool-that-showed-bias-against-women-idUSKCN1MK08G

Drew, Liam. (2019). "The ethics of brain–computer interfaces." https://www.nature.com/articles/d41586-019-02214-2

Engler, Alex. (2019). "Fighting Deepfakes when detection fails" https://www.brookings.edu/research/fighting-deepfakes-when-detection-fails/

Fight the New Drug. (2020). "Meet Henry, the World's First Generation of Male Sex Robot." https://fightthenewdrug.org/meet-henry-the-worlds-first-generation-of-male-sex-robots/

Foley, Joseph. (2021). "12 deepfake examples that terrified and amused the internet." https://www.creativebloq.com/features/deepfake-examples

Guynn, Jessica. (2015). "Google Photos labeled black people 'gorillas'" https://www.usatoday.com/story/tech/2015/07/01/google-apologizes-after-photos-identify-black-people-as-gorillas/29567465/

Harwell, Drew. (2019). "Rights group files federal complaint against AI-hiring firm HireVue, citing 'unfair and deceptive' practices." https://www.washingtonpost.com/technology/2019/11/06/prominent-rights-group-files-federal-complaint-against-ai-hiring-firm-hirevue-citing-unfair-deceptive-practices/

Hintze, Arend. (2016). "Understanding the Four Types of Artificial Intelligence." https://www.govtech.com/computing/Understanding-the-Four-Types-of-Artificial-Intelligence.html

Kaicheng Yang, (2020). "Bot repository—a centralized place to share annotated datasets of Twitter social bots." https://botometer.osome.iu.edu/

Larson, Jeff, Surya Mattu, Lauren Kirchner, and Julia Angwin. (2016). "How We Analyzed the COMPAS Recidivism Algorithm." https://www.propublica.org/article/how-we-analyzed-the-compas-recidivism-algorithm

Leonhardt, Megan. (2019). "'Nigerian prince' email scams still rake in over $700,000 a year—here's how to protect yourself." https://www.cnbc.com/2019/04/18/nigerian-prince-scams-still-rake-in-over-700000-dollars-a-year.html

Lyons, Tessa. (2018). "Increasing Our Efforts to Fight False News." https://about.fb.com/news/2018/06/increasing-our-efforts-to-fight-false-news/

Metz, Cade, and Scott Blumenthal. (2019). "How A.I. Could Be Weaponized to Spread Disinformation." https://www.nytimes.com/interactive/2019/06/07/technology/ai-text-disinformation.html

MyHeritage. (2021). "Animate your family photos." https://www.myheritage.com/deep-nostalgia?utm_source=N2K%20-%2003 1121%20-%20Economist&utm_medium=email&utm_campaign=5267

New York Times. (2020). "Do These A.I.-Created Fake People Look Real to You?" https://www.nytimes.com/interactive/2020/11/21/science/artificial-intelligence-fake-people-faces.html

Simon, Charles. (2020). "Why the future of AI is open source." https://open-source.com/article/20/7/ai-open-source

Smith, Craig S. (2019). "Dealing with Bias in Artificial Intelligence." https://www.nytimes.com/2019/11/19/technology/artificial-intelligence-bias.html

Tate, Karl. "History of A.I.: Artificial Intelligence (Infographic)." https://www.livescience.com/47544-history-of-a-i-artificial-intelligence-infographic.html

U.S. Congress (2019–2020). "H.R.2231—Algorithmic Accountability Act of 2019." https://www.congress.gov/bill/116th-congress/house-bill/2231

Vincent, James. (2016). "Twitter taught Microsoft's AI chatbot to be a racist asshole in less than a day." https://www.theverge.com/2016/3/24/11297050/tay-microsoft-chatbot-racist

Vincent, James. (2019). "AI systems should be accountable, explainable, and unbiased, says EU." https://www.theverge.com/2019/4/8/18300149/eu-artificial-intelligence-ai-ethical-guidelines-recommendations

Wetsman, Nicole. (2020). "Elon Musk trots out pigs in demo of Neuralink brain implants." https://www.theverge.com/2020/8/28/21406143/elon-musk-neuralink-ai-pigs-demo-brain-computer-interface

CHAPTER 5

Blockchain:
Can Trust Be Decentralized?

During the COVID-19 pandemic, I gave a friend a ride to the DMV so she could get her driver's license. While she was off doing her test drive with the instructor, I decided to utilize this time productively and initiate the process of renewing my own license, which was about to expire. I will spare you all the details; needless to say, it was a huge mistake because the whole process ended up taking the entire day. This is an example of bureaucracy and inefficiencies in a centralized system.

Like me, you've probably been in many government offices or business buildings for one reason or another. Maybe it was the hour-long inefficient line at the bank, the local DMV, or the voting booth. Whatever the case may be, bureaucratic inefficiencies and all the hassles that come with centralized management systems are becoming a calamity. What if there was a system, safe and secure enough so we would never have to stand in line again?

On the other hand, big tech also operates in centralized fashion with centralized leadership, centralized power, and centralized operations. Although counterintuitive, the problem here is that the systems are too efficient and working too well, thus giving a handful of citizens too much power with little to no accountability. What if there was a system where power resided in the hands of the people?

Whether it's too much efficiency and consolidation of power at the top of big tech, or the bureaucracy and the inefficiencies of governments, centralized systems have led to many unintended consequences.

A centralized system resembles a dictatorship. Employees are expected to deliver results based on direction from the top. Customers

---

are expected to receive services based on decisions made at the top. This can leads to an imbalance of power between citizens and the very few at the top. As we will see over and over again, centralized systems are not working well. There has to be a better way to give and receive services that does not rely on centralized systems. Experts have been proposing a decentralized system to solve the negative unintended consequences of centralized systems.

A *decentralized system* is an interconnected information system where no single entity is the sole authority. In the context of computing and information technology, decentralized systems usually take the form of networked computers. Engineers and mathematicians have been busy at work thinking up such a system. One such system is *blockchain technology*.

Blockchain is a system in which a record of transactions made in *Bitcoin* or another cryptocurrency are maintained across several computers that are linked in a peer-to-peer network.

There are many cryptocurrencies on the market as of this writing, but for simplicity in this book, we will focus on the most popular ones, Bitcoin and Ethereum.

Bitcoin is a type of digital currency in which a record of transactions is maintained, and new units of currency are generated by the computational solution of mathematical problems. It operates independently of a central bank (it's decentralized). As of this writing, at a valuation of $1 trillion dollars, Bitcoin is worth more than four of the largest central banks in the United States (Wells Fargo, Bank of America, Citi, and JP. Morgan) combined.

Ethereum is an open-source, blockchain-based, decentralized software platform that uses its own cryptocurrency, called Ether. It enables smart contracts and distributed applications to be built and run without any downtime, fraud, control, or interference from third parties.

How Does Blockchain Work?

The simplest way to learn about how blockchain works is to understand that it's an online ledger that uses a data structure to simplify the way we transact. Users can manipulate the ledger in a secure way without the help of a third party. It allows a free cryptocurrency through a decentralized environment.

If you are not a computer geek, you might wonder what that actually means. To put it in layman's terms, I will use the analogy of the Bible to illustrate, although it has nothing to do with religion.

Think of the ledger as the Bible and the data entries as the scriptures. The peer-to-peer network is made of the billions of people who own a Bible around the world. Imagine that all humans on Earth have a Bible in their house and all of us have the ability to add and subtract content or even totally destroy that one Bible we have in our possession.

When any activity is done to our individual Bible, it's magically broadcast to everyone who owns a Bible all over the world in the entire network, and it's recorded. You write some text in the Bible. Everyone knows you did it and records it. You take out some text that you wrote and everyone knows you did it and records it.

Let's say that you have ill intent and you want to do some damage to the Bible. You can burn it, you can tear pages out, or you can try to fake or forge records. It doesn't matter. The system is safe because billions of other people have a copy of the actual true content in the Bible. It's like having billions of witnesses. It keeps the system honest. That's the genius of blockchain.

Blockchain technology provides a way for untrusted parties to come to agreement on the state of affairs relying on a global transparent database, without using a middleman. A bank is a middleman. The DMV is a middleman. Individuals can skip standing in lines and go straight to transacting independently. By providing a ledger that no single body administers, a blockchain provides specific services—like payments or security, even trusted documents—without the need for a middleman.

WHY SHOULD YOU CARE ABOUT BLOCKCHAIN?

Simply put, most power structures that control us on a daily basis operate in a centralized fashion. This means that information and decisions about things that affect us are collected, stored, and maintained in a centralized location. For the U.S. government, the location is Washington, DC; for

Facebook it's Palo Alto, California; for Google it's Mountain View, California. Entities with centralized structures concentrate their authority in upper levels of management. For example, the military has a centralized organization structure. The higher-ups give orders to those below them and everybody must follow those orders. As we will explore, there are advantages and disadvantages to this structure, especially when centralization allows the power and wealth to concentrate in the hands of a few while everyone else follows or falls behind.

Blockchain is probably the biggest innovation of this decade because it attempts to disrupt this centralized system of operation. It uses a new way of operation called *decentralization*. This new system could very well democratize power and resources.

If we take a closer look at humanity in the past 40 years, starting with 1980, each decade has had one type of innovation that bubbled to the top in terms of having the largest impact on humanity:

1980s: Personal computers

1990s: The Internet

2000s: Software as a Service (SaaS)

2010s: Smartphones

2020s: Blockchain apps

As of this writing, what is being built on top of the Ethereum platform will become as important to human society as the personal computer, the Internet, SaaS, and smartphones were in the last four decades.

So what is the difference between Bitcoin and Ethereum? According to my friend and investor Ryan Allis of Hive, here is the easiest way to think about it: "Bitcoin is a use case like AOL (if you remember AOL); Ethereum is a democratized platform like the www" that allowed people to build a lot of web pages and other resources on top of it. You can learn a lot more about the origins, the journey, and the saga of Ethereum in a gripping book called *The Infinite Machine* (Russo, 2020).

In 2021, after a decade of massive growth, the total value of all Bitcoin is a trillion dollars, up there with the most valued tech giants like Apple, Amazon, and Microsoft. This is about 11% of the total value of all the gold in the world ($11 trillion) and about 10% of the total global money supply ($95 trillion). Gold can't be digitized, is physically very difficult to move, and costs a lot to exchange. It's very likely that gold will soon be obsolete as a medium of exchange. It may soon be the past, not the future. When prominent Bitcoin hater Peter Schiff tweeted his frustration that Wall Street was now advocating buying Bitcoin, American billionaire Mark Cuban explained "why gold did not have a bright future as a store of value asset" (Latoken, 2021). Cuban is the majority owner of the professional basketball team the Dallas Mavericks, as well as one of the "sharks" on the highly popular reality show *Shark Tank*. Peter Schiff, one of Bitcoin's harshest critics, is the CEO of Euro Pacific Capital, a registered broker/dealer in foreign markets and securities, and founder and chairman of Schiff Gold, a discount precious metals dealer. Bitcoin is a clear threat to Mr. Schiff's business.

Because Bitcoin is by nature a digital currency, it is moved in seconds for next to nothing and is nearly free to exchange. Bitcoin and Ethereum together are the future both locally and globally. The global supply of Bitcoin is fixed at 21 million, and that can't be increased. It's the perfect hedge against inflation and to central banks around the world printing money and making it rain. The difference now compared to 2017 when Bitcoin last peaked is that Bitcoin has major institutional buyers who are deciding to invest a portion of their assets in cryptocurrency as a diversification strategy.

Institutions from Mass Mutual Life Insurance ($100 million investment in Bitcoin) and Ruffer Investment Company ($744 million in Bitcoin) to MicroStrategy ($650 million in Bitcoin) and Grayscale ($13 billion in Bitcoin) are investing with a long-term hold strategy. Even Square recently decided to hold $300 million of their balance sheet in Bitcoin.

In 2021, Tesla announced that it had bought $1.5 billion worth of Bitcoin. In a filing with the Securities and Exchange Commission, the company said it bought the Bitcoin for "more flexibility to further diversify and maximize returns on our cash" (SEC, 2021). Tesla also said it will start accepting payments in Bitcoin in exchange for its products "subject to applicable laws and initially on a limited basis." That would make Tesla the first major automaker to do so.

Major trusted investors and companies embracing this new technology is a huge game changer. And the companies that help consumers purchase and hold Bitcoin and Ethereum have become much more secure, with more 200,000 developers busy globally building applications on top of Ethereum.

Insurance broker AON is dipping its toe in decentralized finance (DeFi). The world's second-largest insurance intermediary has embarked on a pilot with Nayms, an "insurtech" platform that allows cryptocurrency holders to provide decentralized insurance cover against losses due to hacks or buggy software (Latoken, 2021).

President Joe Biden's nominee for the head of the Securities and Exchange Commission, Gary Gensler, said he would push forward cryptocurrency innovation during a confirmation hearing on March 2 when asked about cryptocurrency regulations. He called Bitcoin and other cryptocurrencies a "catalyst for change" (Gensler, 2021).

In 2021, S&P Dow Jones brought Bitcoin and Ethereum to Wall Street with cryptocurrency indexes, further mainstreaming digital currencies (Reuters, 2021).

Blockchain Use Cases

Blockchain can be used for basically anything that could benefit from more security, more democratization, and the like. Every aspect of our lives will be disrupted by this new technology. Here are a few out of the millions of promising use cases of blockchain:

- Decentralized finance (commonly referred to as DeFi), such as payment processing, money transfers, and decentralized banking. This is a blockchain-based form of finance that does not rely on central financial intermediaries such as brokerages, exchanges, or banks to offer traditional financial instruments, and instead utilizes smart contracts on blockchains to offer financial services. The most common blockchain in this field is Ethereum.

- Immutable data backup or storage. This means that your data is fixed, unchangeable, and can never be deleted.

- Digital IDs, digital nationalities, digital incorporation, and so on. Blockchain can help create a safe and secure digital identity. The information on an entity is used by computer systems to represent an external agent. That agent could be a person, organization, application, or device.

- Wills and inheritances. These are secure end-of-life asset transfers. Wills or inheritances are being registered on a blockchain, which ensures a safe and secure transfer of assets to the rightful owners.

THE UNINTENDED CONSEQUENCES OF BLOCKCHAIN

A blockchain is a series of blocks that record data in hash functions with timestamps so that the data cannot be changed or tampered with. As data cannot be overwritten or manipulated, this can be extremely valuable but also impractical and can lead to many unintended negative consequences. We explore a few these unintended consequences in this section.

The Silk Road Effect

The Silk Road was a network of trade routes that connected the East and West, and was central to the economic, cultural, political, and religious interactions between these regions from the 2nd century BCE to the 18th century.

In 2011, a guy named Ross William Ulbricht created and operated a dark web market website and named "Silk Road." I am making this distinction so you do not confuse the two. The site was designed to use Tor (an open-source software for enabling anonymity) and Bitcoin as a currency. This Silk Road was an online black market for buyers and sellers of illegal or unethical items such as guns, drugs, prostitutes, human organs, hacked passwords, money laundering, illegal data, and other contraband. Customers could transact anonymously utilizing privacy techniques such as the Tor network and cryptocurrency to carry out transactions.

Bitcoin was the only currency allowed on Silk Road, which authorities say was used for criminal transactions. Tor is a network that implements protocols that encrypt data and route Internet traffic through intermediary servers that anonymize IP addresses before reaching a final destination. By hosting his market as a Tor site, Ulbricht could conceal its IP address and provide cover for the users from authorities. The FBI shut down Silk Road in October 2013 and arrested Ulbricht while at the Glen Park branch of the San Francisco Public Library in California. They accused him of being the "mastermind" behind the site.

This was one of the largest busts on the dark web using Bitcoin to commit crimes, but certainly not the only one, nor the last. If anything, it gave many more actors ideas and a route to profitable businesses. The key to success in running such a business is to work at it hard enough and evade getting caught.

Thus, one of the unintended consequences of Bitcoin is aiding criminal activities on the darkest corners of the Internet. According to a study by the digital currency forensics firm Elliptic, in 2020 at least 13% of all criminal proceeds in Bitcoin passed through privacy wallets—which make it harder to track cryptocurrency transactions—up from 2% in 2019 (Irrera, 2020).

High Energy Consumption

In order to "mine" Bitcoin, computers known as mining machines are connected to the cryptocurrency network. They are tasked with verifying transactions made by people who send or receive Bitcoin. This process involves solving puzzles. The puzzles aren't integral to verifying movements of Bitcoin; they simply provide a hurdle to ensure that no one fraudulently edits the global record of all transactions. As a reward for pitching into this system, miners occasionally receive small amounts of Bitcoin. To make as much money from this process as possible, people often connect large numbers of miners to the network, even entire warehouses full of them (Vincent, 2016). The mining process uses lots of electricity because the miners are more or less constantly working.

In 2019, Bitcoin's energy consumption "equaled that of the entire country of Switzerland," according to models built by Mr. De Vries of accounting firm PwC (Baraniuk, 2019). He said, "Bitcoin still appears to use far more energy per transaction than all the world's banks put together." The computing setups used by cryptocurrency miners are primarily responsible for the exceptionally high energy demands of the blockchain.

So, you may be thinking, it sounds like you are picking on blockchain. How about all those inefficient centralized systems out there? That's my point exactly. Rarely does the creator of a major disruptive technology proactively think about the potential unintended consequences, even the ones glaring us in the face. If we are to design a technology that is meant to solve inefficiencies and be good for humankind, at the very minimum we need to be mindful at least to solve for the "known-knowns" negative externalities.

51% Attacks

Proof of work (commonly abbreviated to PoW) is a mechanism for preventing double-spends—a method for securing the cryptocurrency's ledger. Proof of work was the first consensus algorithm to surface, and, to date, remains the dominant one. Most major cryptocurrencies use this as their consensus algorithm. It was introduced by Satoshi Nakamoto in the 2008 Bitcoin white paper, but the technology itself was conceived long before then.

The PoW that protects the Bitcoin blockchain has proven to be very efficient over the years. However, there are a few potential attacks that can be performed against blockchain networks. The 51% attacks are among the most discussed. For more on this, see "What Is a 51% Attack?" (Binance Academy, 2019).

Such an attack may happen if one entity manages to control more than 50% of the network hashing power, which would eventually allow them to disrupt the network and systematically manipulate the system for personal gain by intentionally excluding or modifying the ordering of transactions.

Despite being theoretically possible, there was never a successful 51% attack on the Bitcoin blockchain. As the network grows larger, the security increases and it is quite unlikely that miners will invest large amounts of money and resources to attack Bitcoin because they are better rewarded for acting honestly.

Other than that, a successful 51% attack would only be able to modify the most recent transactions for a short period of time because blocks are linked through cryptographic proofs (changing older blocks would require intangible levels of computing power). Also, the Bitcoin blockchain is very resilient and would quickly adapt as a response to an attack.

Loss of Private Keys

Blockchain uses public-key (or asymmetric) cryptography to give users ownership over their cryptocurrency units (or any other blockchain data). Each blockchain address has a corresponding private key. While the address can be shared, the private key should be kept secret. Users need their private key to access their transactions or funds, meaning that they act as their own bank. If a user loses their private key, the money is effectively lost, and there is nothing they can do about it. If you die and no one else in the family knows the private keys, essentially those assets die with you!

A *New York Times* article explored a few real-life examples of people painfully stuck in this predicament (Popper, 2021). One such person is Stefan Thomas, a German-born programmer living in San Francisco who had two guesses left to figure out a password worth, as of April 2021, about $439 million. The password would let him unlock a small hard drive, known as an IronKey, which contains the private keys to a digital wallet that holds 7,002 Bitcoin.

An Even More Permanent Internet (Immutability)

Anonymity, immutability, and distributed control make blockchain a disruptive technology. They are also its greatest vulnerabilities.

Blockchain by design does not allow information to be erased unless all blockchain servers agree (which is very hard). This results in issues in removing private or illicit data. In cases when blockchain is used to store other information, such as criminal records, this information will become significantly more permanent, and individuals will have even less control over their data and their privacy.

As an example, in 2019, somebody added images of child pornography to the BSV ledger. Although a filter was quickly put in place, the images could not be actually removed from the ledger (Somers, 2019).

Storage Limitations

When you write in a book, eventually you run out of pages and need a new book. The situation is similar with blockchain ledgers, which can grow very large. At the time of this writing, the Bitcoin blockchain currently requires around 320 GB of storage. The current growth in blockchain size appears to be outstripping the growth of hard drives. The network risks losing nodes if the ledger becomes too large for individuals to download and store. In addition, the unintended consequence of electronic waste (which we will discuss in depth in upcoming chapters) is enormous.

WHAT'S BEING DONE TO ADDRESS THESE UCOTs?

Laying out the risks of Bitcoin big and small is important. From the systems level to the operational level, Bitcoin is still one of the most volatile investments you can make in 2021. It has a bit of an identity crisis and is not regulated by any central bank or nation. Despite all these challenges, it has generated major disruptive and ever-growing interest and buzz worldwide that's hard to ignore. The engineers, mathematicians, and solutionists in the Bitcoin community are working around the clock to address the challenges that face Bitcoin.

Solutions to Private Key Issues

Since there are no easy ways to store keys and no recovery options, there is a proposal to use *decentralized biometric identity verification* as a way to reclaim lost keys. The owner of the lost key may go to a secure facility and pass a combination of biometric tests, such as pulse, fingerprint, and retinal scanners. This idea is still in discussion with regulators around the world (Burt, 2018).

Solutions to 51% Attack Issues

This scenario is very unlikely, at the current cost of Bitcoin. The dollar amount any entity would need to pull off such a scheme is upwards of $15 billion USD. However, for blockchain technology in general, there have been ideas put forward about combating this problem. One such solution is *proof of stake* (Ghosh, 2020). After Ethereum was attacked, version 2.0 was introduced to use a proof of stake model to validate transactions. The way this system works is that a miner is randomly selected to validate and add blocks. This will not only make it harder (and more expensive) to gain a 51% holding but also deincentivizes criminals because the attack will then lead to a fall in the price of the holdings.

Solutions to Energy Inefficiency Issues

Without major fundamental changes in how the technology has been designed so far, this problem is bound to persist. One example of a solution for fundamental changes in the blockchain technology is the *red belly blockchain* (Red Belly Blockchain, 2021). This technique requires much less electricity and is much faster (at about 30,000 transactions per second versus 7 of the Bitcoin blockchain). The technology does not use the proof of work method but rather uses a unique algorithm and is also fork-free (meaning that it does not allow multiple branches and manages integrity by selecting the longest branch, like Bitcoin does). This may also address the scalability issues of Blockchain technology.

A second example is the use of alternative energy to mine. For instance, Cryptosolartech is Spain's largest Bitcoin miner. It uses the sun as the energy source (CryptoGlobe Staff Writer, 2018). They have built a 300-megawatt solar farm specifically for Bitcoin mining. By using sustainable methods in crypto mining, the environmental impact can be mitigated.

Solutions to Security and Criminal Activity Issues

Multiple companies, such as ComplyAdvantage and Elliptic, are taking on the challenge of screening transactions and working with law enforcement to catch cryptocurrency-aided crime, such as money laundering. They can prevent laundering by analyzing the cryptocurrency exchanges. A few private security companies use Blockchain's feature of immutability to their advantage. It allows banks or exchanges to screen transactions by tracing the origins of the Bitcoin. They can then discover that the origins may be a dark web marketplace, for example (Perez, 2019.)

In 2013, the FBI shut down the dark web marketplace Silk Road. This made the U.S. government the largest owner of Bitcoin, because they seized over $1 billion USD worth of Bitcoin as of 2020. The site was enabled by using cryptocurrency as the method of payment, in order to keep anonymity in the illegal transactions taking place on the site. The FBI found a bug on the site, which leaked a server IP address, and along with investigative work, they were able to crack the case (CBS News, 2020).

THE FUTURE OF BLOCKCHAIN

We have seen decentralization gaining a great deal of steam in recent years. Decentralized finance is replacing Wall Street. Social media is replacing the traditional mass media, remote work is replacing the 9–5 job, and Bitcoin is slowly ushering out giant centralized banking systems. Hyperledger, which is an open-source initiative by the Linux Foundation, is trying to unify the blockchain solutions under one big umbrella. This would improve the way that enterprises adopt blockchain technology, including frameworks, tools, APIs, and so on. The train is moving at high speed.

I do believe that Bitcoin will soon replace gold, because Bitcoin is better at being "gold" than gold itself. For instance, most commodity-money advocates choose gold as a medium of exchange because of its intrinsic properties. It is impossible to perfectly counterfeit and has a fixed stock—there is only so much gold on Earth, and inflation is limited to the speed of mining. Now check out how Bitcoin stocks up to gold in terms of these features:

Features	Bitcoin	Gold
Scarce	Fixed inelastic supply	Limited elastic supply
Transfer method	Email (very quick)	Moving heavy bricks (time consuming)
Storage	Low-cost space in the cloud	High-cost physical space
Decentralized	Yes	No
Durable	Yes (digital asset)	Yes (physical asset)
Fungible	Yes	Yes
Verifiable	Yes	Susceptible to fakes
Privacy	No Identity reveal	Receiver and sender identity are needed
Divisible	Yes. 1B =100m Satoshis	Not easily

Though there is room for Bitcoin and gold to coexist, the history of money tells us that winners usually take all.

Bitcoin as a currency may seem strange to some and hard to understand, but throughout history, humans have utilized interesting and sometimes strange currencies, from bartering to beads to paper money and even black tulip bulbs. At the height of the bubble, black tulips sold for approximately 10,000 guilders, equal to the value of a mansion on the Amsterdam Grand Canal.

Some people may argue that Bitcoin is a fad, that it's a bubble that will just disappear like tulips as currency. To the doubters I say—not so fast. I do not own Bitcoin as of this writing; I am just an observer, but I can clearly see that Bitcoin is here to stay.

So why compare Bitcoin to gold and not to the dollar? Well, less than 5% of the world's population transacts in U.S. dollars. I believe Bitcoin is going to be bigger than the dollar in value, hence the comparison to gold. You see, gold is an asset, and as such it has intrinsic value. Less than 5% of the world population lives in a nation where the U.S. dollar is the national currency. The role of gold as a currency is ubiquitous around the world and has been throughout history. The ancient philosopher Aristotle wrote that money must be durable, divisible, consistent, and convenient, and possess value in itself. Gold meets all of these characteristics.

There is also a psychological factor attached to the value of gold. The price of gold is often sensitive to the overall perceived value of *fiat* (government-issued currency that is not backed by a commodity) or paper currencies in general terms. During times of fear or geopolitical turmoil, the price of this historic metal tends to rise as faith in governments falls. During times of calm, the price of gold tends to fall. As perhaps the world's oldest and most storied currency, gold is an important barometer in terms of global economic and political well-being. I believe that metal gold will soon be replaced by digital gold!

REFERENCES

Baraniuk, Chris. (2019). "Bitcoin's energy consumption 'equals that of Switzerland.'" https://www.bbc.com/news/technology-48853230

BBC News. (2013). "Dark net marketplace Silk Road 'back online.'" https://www.bbc.com/news/technology-24842410

Binance Academy. (2019). "What Is a 51% Attack?" https://academy.binance.com/en/articles/what-is-a-51-percent-attack

Binance Academy. (2021). "What Is a Blockchain Consensus Algorithm?" https://academy.binance.com/en/articles/what-is-a-blockchain-consensus-algorithm

Burt, Chris. (2018). "Are multi-modal biometrics the solution to blockchain's private key-loss conundrum?" https://www.biometricupdate.com/201805/are-multi-modal-biometrics-the-solution-to-blockchains-private-key-loss-conundrum

CBS News. (2020). "Inside the FBI takedown of the mastermind behind website offering drugs, guns and murders for hire." https://www.cbsnews.com/news/ross-ulbricht-dread-pirate-roberts-silk-road-fbi/

CryptoGlobe Staff Writer. (2018). "Bitcoin Miner to Build 300MW Solar Farm for Sustainable Crypto Mining." https://www.cryptoglobe.com/latest/2018/10/bitcoin-miner-to-build-300mw-solar-farm-for-sustainable-crypto-mining/

Cuban, Mark. (2021). "Why gold did not have a bright future as a store of value asset." https://latoken.com/moments/2471/mark-cuban-explains-to-peter-schiff-why-gold-is-going-to-die-as-a-store-of-value/

Digiconomics. (2020). "Bitcoin Energy Consumption Index." https://digiconomist.net/bitcoin-energy-consumption

Gensler, Gary. (2021). "SEC Chair Candidate Gary Gensler Calls Bitcoin the "Catalyst of Change."" https://newsdol.com/ukraineeng/sec-chair-candidate-gary-gensler-calls-bitcoin-the-catalyst-of-change/

Ghosh, Monika. (2020). "Understanding 51% Attacks on Blockchains." https://www.jumpstartmag.com/understanding-51-attacks-on-blockchains/

Irrera, Anna. (2020). "Criminals getting smarter in use of digital currencies to launder money." https://www.reuters.com/article/crypto-currencies-criminals/criminals-getting-smarter-in-use-of-digital-currencies-to-launder-money-idUSKBN28J1IX

Latoken. (2021). "Insurance broker aon is dipping a toe in decentralized finance." https://latoken.com/moments/2498/insurance-broker-aon-is-dipping-a-toe-in-decentralized-finance-defi/

Perez, Yessi Bello. (2019). "Here's how law enforcement catches cryptocurrency criminals." https://thenextweb.com/hardfork/2019/12/26/bitcoin-cryptocurrency-criminals-law-enforcement/

Popper, Nathaniel. (2021). "Lost Passwords Lock Millionaires Out of Their Bitcoin Fortunes." https://www.nytimes.com/2021/01/12/technology/bitcoin-passwords-wallets-fortunes.html#:~:text=Stefan%20Thomas%2C%20a%20German%2Dborn,wallet%20that%20holds%20207%2C002%20Bitcoin.

Red Belly Blockchain. (2021). "No Leader Machine for Higher Bandwidth." https://www.redbellyblockchain.io/#:~:text=In%20RedBelly%20blockchain%20there%20is,computers%20to%20aggregate%20the%20results

Reuters. (2021). "S&P Dow Jones brings Bitcoin, Ethereum to Wall St with cryptocurrency indexes." https://www.reuters.com/technology/sp-dow-jones-indices-launches-crypto-indices-2021-05-04/?utm_campaign=trueAnthem%3A%20Trending%20Content&utm_medium=trueAnthem&utm_source=facebook&fbclid=IwAR0_KblAtkTPVUo5PA1MwgUrmMAz2OZ3bp-7pesWAJ2hOfg33oJwT_aVnH_k

Russo, Camila. (2020). *The Infinite Machine: How an Army of Crypto-hackers Is Building the Next Internet with Ethereum*. Harper Business.

SEC. (2021). "Tesla SEC filings." https://www.sec.gov/ix?doc=/Archives/edgar/data/1318605/000156459021004599/tsla-10k_20201231.htm

Somers, Meredith. (2019). "The risks and unintended consequences of blockchain." https://mitsloan.mit.edu/ideas-made-to-matter/risks-and-unintended-consequences-blockchain

Vincent, Danny. (2016). "We looked inside a secret Chinese Bitcoin mine." https://www.bbc.com/future/article/20160504-we-looked-inside-a-secret-chinese-bitcoin-mine

CHAPTER 6

Conditioning: From Human to User to an Addicted "Drug" User?

If you could control someone's attention, what would you do with it? Let's reverse that—if someone else had control of your attention, what would you be comfortable with them doing with it? Modern technology is changing humans, society, and our planet. The "attention economy" has commoditized our time and turned us into products to be bought and sold. Digital media can modify behavior at a scale never seen before. If it's free, you are the product. Even if you pay for it, and it has the ability to collect data about you, you are still partly the product. The attention economy and mass behavior modification are the topics of this chapter.

How can someone or some entity hold your attention so well, and you give it willingly without too many questions asked? Well, this can be achieved with what I call *conditioning*, which is the use of basic learning techniques, such as biofeedback, assertiveness training, positive or negative reinforcement, hypnosis, and aversion therapy, to change an individual or a group's behavior. For the purposes of this chapter, we will focus on one of these techniques—the use of positive or negative reinforcement to change people's behavior. Technology has used this method to reveal the true nature of humanity and brought out the best and the worst of us.

According to an article by Harvard University researcher Trevor Haynes, when you get a social media notification, your brain sends a chemical messenger called dopamine along a reward pathway, which makes you feel good (Haynes, 2018). Dopamine is associated with food, exercise, love, sex, gambling, drugs—and now, social media. When rewards are delivered randomly (as with a slot machine or a positive interaction on social media), and checking for the reward is easy, the dopamine-triggering behavior becomes a habit.

In 1997, a man named Michael Goldhaber helped popularize the term "attention economy" with an essay in *Wired* magazine (Warzel, 2021). He predicted that the Internet would upend the advertising industry and create a "star system" in which whoever you are, however you express yourself, you can now have a crack at the global audience. He said that one of the most finite resources in the world is human attention. To describe its scarcity, he latched on to what was then an obscure term, coined by a psychologist, Herbert A. Simon: "the attention economy." Attention has always been a currency, but as we've begun to live our lives increasingly online, it's now *the* currency. Any discussion of power is now, ultimately, a conversation about attention and how we extract it, wield it, waste it, abuse it, sell it, lose it, and profit from it

Social media and other online platforms are good examples of how technology uses these reinforcement techniques to tap into our strongest emotions and modify behavior at an unprecedented scale.

A Quick History of Media

The evolution of media has been fraught with concerns and problems since the beginning. Accusations of mind control, bias, and poor quality have been thrown at the media at every turn on a regular basis, especially when the media form is relatively new. Yet there are many advantages of the growth of communications technology. It has allowed humanity to find more information more easily. Each generation has a much better and more sophisticated mass media technology than the previous generation. When it comes to the use of this technology, people have used it for better or for worse.

So, what is *mass media*? It refers to a diverse array of media technologies that reach a large audience via mass communication. This can be print, radio, television, or online news. They can be local, national, or international. They can be broad or limited in their focus. The choices are tremendous.

It all started with print media (still images), followed by radio (sound) in the 1920s. Then television combined the best attributes of print and radio (a moving picture with sound). This changed media forever. The first official broadcast in the United States was President Franklin Roosevelt's speech at the opening of the 1939 World's Fair in New York. The appearance was broadcast to a handful of TV sets in the New York area. FDR had already mastered the medium of his time—radio. His "fireside chats" aired across the nation soothed Americans troubled by the hard times of the Great Depression (PBS, 1998).

Television brought new possibilities. Some of the best examples of the power of television occurred when presidents used television to inspire and comfort the population during a national emergency. These speeches aided in the "rally round the flag" phenomenon.

Next came the invention of cable in the 1980s and the expansion of the Internet in the 2000s. These opened more options for media consumers than ever before.

Print, radio, and TV all involve a regulatory framework on moderation, costs, pre- and post-production, and many other barriers that affect scalability and how fast information can get to consumers—and most important, accountability.

With the advent of digital mass media, such as social media and its freemium model, viewers can watch nearly anything, anywhere in the world, at any time with the click of a button. In addition, anyone can also post anything for all to read, true or not, with little to no accountability. This model of information democratization has a lot of both advantages and disadvantages.

ADVANTAGES OF MASS DIGITAL MEDIA

The ability of users to easily stay informed about the world and stay in touch with friends, family, and loved ones, both near and far, are the major merits of social media and other mass digital media. Being able to connect with like-minded people is great as well. The ability to start and expand a business with the click of a button, drive up sales, and stay in touch with customers is certainly amazing.

In addition, one of the most important advantages of social media is the speed and efficiency at which it allows communication between people. It has been used to increase awareness of social and political issues and organize demonstrations around the world. From Myanmar to Egypt, the United States to Nigeria, Russia to Uganda, social media organizing is a powerful tool and its force is global in reach.

For example, in 2019, the protests that took place in Hong Kong, also known as the Anti-Extradition Law Amendment Bill Movement, were triggered by the introduction of the Fugitive Offenders amendment bill by the Hong Kong government. Hundreds of thousands of demonstrators in Hong Kong gathered for a march that became the start of the semiautonomous Chinese region's biggest political crisis and the broadest expression of public anger with Beijing in decades (Ramzy and Ives, 2020).

Social media played a vital role in communication. Many of the protesters were young men and women, students, and they organized the protests using social media. The plans for where and how the protests would take place spread through social media accounts rapidly, resulting in some of the biggest protests that the Hong Kong government and people had witnessed in their history. This is a great example of how social media can be used for change and for public mobilization. Similar examples took place during the Arab Spring and other incidents across the world. Social media has given people, especially the very computer-savvy new generation, a new and effective instrument to come together on issues, they believe in.

Like most things, social media has real benefits of convenience and connectivity, and it also has its cautionary tales. Sadly, there is an ugly side to all that technology offers. Let's now explore the many unintended consequences of mass media.

THE UNINTENDED OR WILLFULLY IGNORED NEGATIVE CONSEQUENCES OF MASS MEDIA

As described, media serves many purposes, but there are five main functions of media content: to entertain, to inspire, to educate, to archive, and to persuade or convince.

Fast-forward to the 21st century. Social media has taken over the world and it's doing all these functions and much more.

"Users," formerly known as humans, state actors, and non-state actors, are employing these tools in ways that are not serving humanity and our planet's best interests. Following are a few examples of unintended and willfully ignored consequences of media technology.

Addiction (Social Media Disorder)

In order to understand social media addiction, we need to first understand the forces behind the disorder. *Positive reinforcement* is when a behavior is followed by a response that is rewarding, therefore increasing the occurrence of that behavior. *Negative reinforcement* is when a behavior is followed by the removal of something, such as when a toy is taken away from a child to stop the child from picking on a sibling, resulting in an increase in the desired behavior (in this case, no more teasing). *Punishment* is a consequence that decreases the frequency of a behavior.

Then there is *extinction*, which occurs when there is no consequence or response at all, eventually leading to a decline in that behavior. Consider a child whining and crying for attention, being ignored, crying a bit more, but with no attention given, the child decides to stop crying and moves on. That's extinction.

So why is social media so addictive? As mentioned at the onset, social networking sites are full of opportunities for positive and negative reinforcement. Today, there are more opportunities for positive social reinforcement now than at any other point in human history.

Facebook is the most powerful network of social reinforcement. Every like, comment, and share has the effect of reinforcing our behavior on Facebook, thus making us more likely to engage in it again and again. This has been a huge part of Facebook's success and a prime reason some people spend so much time checking their notifications. Before Facebook someone who had just gotten a new job had to inform each person individually or via mass email, but now, with a quick status update, the excitement can begin instantly with hundreds of friends and family.

On Twitter, whenever someone follows you, retweets, or favorites a tweet, replies to you, or mentions you, it acts as a positive form of reinforcement for that behavior. On LinkedIn, endorsements and recommendations are not as instantaneous or as constant as forms of positive reinforcement like Twitter and Facebook, but they nevertheless act as a reward that increases engagement levels. These are just a few examples out of millions out there on the Internet with reinforcement mechanisms built into their business model.

With all of this positive reinforcement of each other's behavior through social networks, it's no wonder that it's so easy to get addicted to them. Not only is there more opportunity for reinforcement, but there is less time between the event and reinforcement. Studies have found that the shorter the time interval between the action and the reinforcement, the more powerful the learning is (Walinga and Stangor, 2021).

We also see examples of punishment happening through social media. For example, someone can complain about a brand's poor customer service on Twitter, thus publicizing their opinion, leading to much more accountability and modification of that brand's behavior. Brands are increasingly aware of conversations happening about them on social media and are making efforts to avoid any negative publicity on these platforms.

Cancel Culture

Cancel culture (or call-out culture) is a modern form of ostracism in which someone or some business is thrust out of social or professional circles, whether it be online, on social media, or in person. Those who are subject to this ostracism are said to have been "cancelled." People, businesses, and fictional characters are all fair game.

As of this writing, there are two well-known targets of "cancel culture," which are examples of negative reinforcement in the media. One is work by Theodor Seuss Geisel, known to the world as Dr. Seuss, whose children's books are loved by many, since they are easy to read, and based on imaginative characters and rhymes. In an attempt to curtail some racist imagery, Dr. Seuss's family decided to recall some of his books (Engle, 2021).

Another focus of cancel culture is Pepé Le Pew, the animated French skunk that has appeared in Looney Tunes cartoons since 1945. His shtick revolves around being lovestruck with a female cat that looks similar to him and continually presenting unwanted advances toward her. In 2021, the cartoon was removed over concerns that the fictional character promoted "rape culture," in the latest string of outrage over children's characters.

Although cancel culture is a sign of our times in terms of reckoning with things that have been offensive and harmful to many for a long time, it goes without saying that for every good a technology is able to provide, there is a bad to counter it.

Cancel culture is not all bad, for it has helped expose and and hold accountable powerful people who felt invincible for a long time. However, it tends to turn the spotlight on simplistic and easy solutions. Rather than merely cancel Pepé Le Pew or Dr. Seuss, for example, we need to have real conversations, followed up by services for victims of date rape or victims of racism.

Society has very much benefited from being more sensitive to and in tune with the plight of with minority groups that have long been ignored, including people of color, women, the LGBT+ community, and others, yet the way this issue is often dealt with superficially on social media is not a true path to the equity our great country espouses.

Positive and negative reinforcements have played an integral role in the popularity of social media, which is the reason some networks fail while others thrive and keep us coming back for more. It is an invaluable social learning tool for brands, marketers, and individuals alike. The true impact that social media behavior modification has on shaping our behavior will likely only be revealed in years to come, but it sure is interesting!

Social Acceptance and Consumerism

Humans are particularly vulnerable to social acceptance, which feeds our self-esteem. We are social animals and we need to feel connected to others and part of a group. Jeff Siebert, a former Twitter executive, says, "If you get a notification saying that your friend just tagged you in a photo, of course you are going to click on it. It is not something you can just decide to ignore" (Siebert, 2020).

Facebook, for instance, can rank a new post or picture higher in the newsfeed so it sticks around for longer and more friends will like or comment on it. Even the more straightlaced LinkedIn publicly displays how many professional connections users have, targeting people's need for social approval and popularity. This feeds into consumerism where you need to get more of that validation. If many people like your shoes, you might want to get a new pair so you can get more likes. And if you see people liking someone else's material item, subconsciously you might want that similar item, so you too can get the same likes. This leads to an unhappy vicious cycle of consumerism. We are much less likely to be happy with what we have.

Facebook users fall into the trap of comparing someone else's outside with their insides. Furthermore, notifications put them on constant alert—this is the feeling of urgency to engage on social media. The average U.S. consumer checks their phone 52 times a day. This plays on the modern fear of missing out. Once interrupted, every interaction is designed to keep our attention. This might be a message notification pop-up or WhatsApp automatically telling the sender when you "saw" their message ("now that you know I've seen the message, I feel even more obligated to respond"). The use of ellipsis is similar—by showing that the other person is typing a message, we are less likely to turn away. Although we might think it will take a few seconds to deal with some social media notifications, studies show that it can take 25 minutes to return to our original task (Wong, 2015).

It's no surprise that these psychological tactics work. In his book *Ca$hvertising*, Drew Eric Whitman (2008) discusses absolute human instincts hardwired into all of us. These "life-force" motivations include superiority, social approval, enjoyment of life, and sexual companionship.

Cyberbullying

Online harassment can take different forms, and the legal definition of cyberbullying often varies depending on where the victim lives. What makes online gossip and vicious harassment so effective is that it can be posted anonymously. This allows these posts to be read by numerous other people anywhere else in the world and also makes it much easier for other people to join in and become part of the bullying. This also means that children and teenagers no longer face bullying only at school; it now follows them home on their phone or computer and is always there. This has the biggest impact on teens and young adults as they are maturing and forming their identities.

Cyberbullying comes in many forms. Here are a few examples:

- *Shaming*: These practices involve a video or a photo from a person's social media page getting comments that shame and ridicule the person, including everything from slut-shaming and fat-shaming to public shaming.

- *Cyberbaiting:* This occurs when perpetrators taunt their victims to the point of an outburst. Then they capture the victim's reaction on video and post it for others to see.

- *Happy slapping:* This form of cyberbullying originated in the UK. It involves using a camera phone to videotape a bullying incident. Typically, the bullying includes one or more kids slapping, hitting, kicking, or punching a victim. Then the videotape is downloaded and posted for a broader audience.

- *Todding:* This term was made popular by Internet trolls after Canadian teen Amanda Todd committed suicide. The 15-year-old posted a cry-for-help video on YouTube using note cards to detail the torment she endured from classmates and strangers in the wake of a revealing topless video chat photo being released to her Facebook friends and others by an extorting stranger. She got depressed and anxious and experimented with drugs and alcohol. She cut herself and had at least two previous attempts at suicide. Instead of mourning her death or feeling regret for their actions, many of the bullies in Todd's life began posting cruel messages on her Facebook page. People commented on her Facebook page that she should try harder to kill herself: "I hope she dies this time and isn't so stupid." Unfortunately, on October 10, 2012, she did (Patchin, 2012). This obviously created a great deal of pain and anguish for her family and friends.

Sometimes when young people have been bullied to the point of suicide, the bullies in their lives still do not relent, nor do they feel empathy for those suffering from the loss. Instead, they post on an account that has been memorialized and bring even more pain into the lives of the victim's family.

Polarization: The Us versus Them Mentality

With polarized information access, low-quality discourse driven by virality, toxicity, and stereotype-laden communication prevalent on social media platforms, users have a harder time engaging in quality discourse. As a result, people either stop engaging in meaningful conversations or resort to closed groups, which result in *echo chambers*. These are environments in which a person encounters only beliefs or opinions that coincide with their own, so that their existing views are reinforced and alternative ideas are not considered.

Humans are social beings. We have a deep need to belong, stemming from our evolutionary requirement of having to work together in groups to survive, reproduce, and flourish. As a result, the human mind has a tendency to categorize people into social groups. And often these social groups can create an "us versus them" mentality toward people who may be different from them in some way, whether because of race, gender, age, nationality, culture, religion, or socioeconomic status. Add exponential instantaneous technology to the mix, and the grouping and division scales exponentially. We have seen this play out in many recent examples of local, national, international, and global politics, such as Trumpism and Brexit. Groupings like these tend to fall to irrational favoritism, which ends up dividing society instead of bringing it together. With social media, when groupthink and identity politics are in place, a charismatic leader can excite and incite. The existence of us versus them leaves little room for openness, debate, and respectful oppositional conversations. Post-election anger and hysteria, over-the-top hyper-partisan criticism, false and misleading half-truths, malignant and very public insults are all possible in the "us versus them" polarized world.

Cultifiction and Radicalization

In the past, cults were hard to scale up. Any aspiring cult leader had to organically convince and convert followers one at a time. Cults usually started with a small group of people who had a direct physical connection to the leader. They would get indoctrinated (drink the Kool-Aid, if you will) one at a time, then if the group had enough people (usually a couple hundred) and the leader didn't have enough hours in the day to meet in person with everyone, the leader would create disciples to spread the message. Again, this is still a small group, a trusted inner circle of confidants. If a cult was successful, it would take many years to build and get to a few thousand followers. Leadership has to keep a close eye on all that's going on at all times in order to control followers and not have revolts within. It's hard to keep a close eye on tens of thousands of people. That's why the largest cults have been a few hundred people to a few thousand.

A good example of this is the charismatic cult leader Jim Jones, who was a preacher from the Pentecostal tradition. Although white, Jones attracted a large African American following because of his preaching style as well as dedication to integration and racial equality. Jones began the People's Temple in the 1950s in Indianapolis. After reading in *Esquire* magazine about places to survive a nuclear holocaust, he moved his congregation to Ukiah, California, in 1965. In the next five years, the People's Temple membership grew, with thriving churches in San Francisco and Los Angeles. Jones also began building a commune called Jonestown in Guyana, a socialist-led, largely English-speaking country in South America. In 1977, when Jones heard that *New West* magazine was to publish an expose on life in the People's Temple as "a mixture of Spartan regimentation, fear, and self-imposed humiliation," he and his congregation quickly fled to the commune.

Convinced by concerned former members and relatives of members, U.S. Congressman Leo Ryan flew down to visit Jonestown to learn more about it. Just before Ryan was about to leave Guyana, on November 18, 1978, Jones's men arrived at the airstrip and shot and killed the congressman as well as several others. That same day, Jones convinced his congregation to kill themselves by drinking a flavor aid drink laced with cyanide. More than 900 people died, including 276 children.

Although that's a huge number of people to die in one go, it's small compared what could have happened if social media existed in those days. (Chiu, 2020).

Fast-forward to the 21st century. The invention of social media and the instant dissemination and transfer of information can give a charismatic cult leader the ability to share their doctrine to fifty million or even a hundred million followers at the click of a button. Unlike in previous eras, followers do not need to meet the leader in person to believe. Targeted texts or a series of videos directed to a specific demographic can indoctrinate people; we've seen this in politics and other arenas, like military extremism. It is very scalable.

Social media and other aspects of the Internet are playing an increasing role in radicalization—it's an easily accessible incubator that, with just a few clicks, provides a wealth of influential material. Evidence suggests that the extremist terrorist organization Al Qaeda has embraced modern technology. This is despite its attempt to restore what its members consider a glorified past and avoid the dangers of modernization, globalization, and democratization that threaten to upset traditional ways. Nowhere is this more apparent than in Al Qaeda's use of the Internet and other new media technologies to build its support base and recruit new terrorists and terrorist sympathizers. In 2006, Al Qaeda quadrupled its production of videos and used an estimated 4500 jihadist websites to spread its messages within a one-year span (Guadagno et al., 2010).

Mental Health and Loneliness

This is a public health crisis. Loneliness is the feeling of being alone, regardless of the amount of social contact. Social isolation is a lack of real, meaningful social connections. Social isolation can lead to loneliness in some people, whereas others can feel lonely without being socially isolated.

Because loneliness is a state of mind, being physically alone is not required to experience loneliness. One can experience a lonely state of mind while having millions of "friends" or followers on social media or being with people at work, at home, or even in a marriage. Income, education, gender, and ethnicity don't necessarily protect you from loneliness.

With all the technology we have, we are increasingly connected but feel disconnected. Technology addiction and depression are on the rise. Addiction to technology is a relatively new phenomenon, but it is one of the fastest-growing addictions we have ever seen.

In fact, there is a new business in town: Tech rehab centers designed to rehabilitate addiction victims the same way facilities treat all the other types of additions, such as alcohol, drugs, or sex. They are really big in Asian countries and are coming to a neighborhood near you.

The UK now has a Minister for Loneliness. The first appointee, Tracey Crouch, said, "Nobody should feel alone or be left with no one to turn to. Loneliness is a serious issue that affects people of all ages and backgrounds, and it is right that we tackle it head on. Our strategy sets out a powerful vision for addressing this generational challenge." More than nine million people in the UK often or always feel lonely, according to a 2017 report published by the Jo Cox Commission on Loneliness. "There were so many university students in the UK who just lock themselves in their rooms for days because they feel rejected or that they don't fit in" (Yeginsu, 2018).

Suicide

There is increasing evidence that the Internet and social media can influence suicide-related behavior. The first documented use of the Internet to form a suicide pact was reported in Japan in 2000. A suicide pact is an agreed plan between two or more individuals to commit suicide. The plan may be to die together, or separately and closely timed. It has now become a more common form of suicide in Japan. The Internet has also provided a way for people to obtain how-to descriptions of suicide as well as lethal means to kill themselves. Message boards or forums have been used to spread information on how to die by suicide.

In a bid to tackle mental health issues in Japan, the government has also recently appointed Tetsushi Sakamoto as the minister in charge of dealing with problems of isolation and loneliness. The initiative was made after Japan saw a spike in suicide rates for the first time in 11 years. According to the National Police Agency, 20,919 people in Japan died by suicide in 2020, an increase of 750 deaths compared to 2019 (Skopeliti, 2021).

Another disturbing phenomenon is the livestreaming of social media suicides. A 12-year-old girl in Georgia hanged herself from a tree while broadcasting on the video streaming app Live.me. A 33-year-old aspiring actor in California, who had been arrested and posted bond after accusations of domestic violence, shot himself in the head as his world watched on Facebook Live. A 14-year-old girl was on Facebook, broadcasting from a bathroom at her foster home in southeastern Florida. Then she was hanging from a scarf tied to a shower's glass door frame. Mental health experts say there is no question that social media is becoming a new platform for public suicide. The concern is that people who are planning to take their own lives can broadcast their own deaths in real time, which is not only devastating for those who die but also for those watching it happen online (Bever, 2017). The effect of broadcasting one's death goes beyond the victim, and may include inspiring others to do the same. It's distressing to the viewing audience and inflicts additional trauma beyond the death itself on the loved ones of the deceased.

How to Mitigate the UCOTs of Mass Media

As noted, there are many unintended consequences of mass media. However, many people, groups, and lawmakers are working hard to find ways to mitigate them. This section discusses a few examples of what's being done now and what can be done.

Action Against False Information

Labeling misleading content can be a great tool to fight this epidemic. A new and still debated action that social media platforms have taken is labeling fake news. Companies like Facebook and Twitter have signed a "Code of Practice on Disinformation" in 2018, which is a pledge to tackle potentially false information. There have been heated debates among the general public and in the board rooms on who is the arbiter of truth. Should tech companies be regulating speech? Twitter, for example, implemented a system of monitoring content and labeling those identified as false with labels that alert viewers of potentially misleading information (Roth and Pickles, 2020). The jury is out as to whether this is legal or effective.

Additionally, many use technology to fight falsehoods. Platforms such as snopes.com and others like it are used for fact-checking. Snopes has been described as a "well-regarded reference for sorting out myths and rumors" on the Internet. It has also been seen as a source for validating and debunking urban legends and similar stories in popular culture.

Action Against Addiction

In this section, we'll look at personal, group, and intuitional actions we can take to mitigate the effects of social media addiction.

Personal Action

Many smartphones now have built-in features that can limit your use of apps. Many Android phones have "Digital Wellbeing" functionality that lets you track your use of apps and set time limits on them. On iOS, the Screen Time feature in Settings performs a similar function. On your computer, free apps like Cold Turkey can help block websites. Turning off notifications or putting your phone on Do Not Disturb are also effective ways to control your social media use (Cold Turkey, 2021). Set up rules and restrictions in your home or in your relationships, such as no devices at the dinner table or no devices after a certain time of day, or institute a "device-free" day once a week. This is particularly important if you have children.

Group Action

According to the Kaiser Family Foundation, young people spend an average of 7.5 hours a day consuming media—and this doesn't include computer use for schoolwork. There are scholarships available for young folks to help them understand the negative effects of screen time and how to mitigate them, and to educate their peers about the issue. With technology always at the ready, it can be a challenge to unplug. But taking a break from technology is healthy for the mind and for the body (Digital Responsibility, 2021).

Institutional Action

As mentioned, tech addiction centers are opening in many parts of the world. They are very popular in Japan. Since addiction to technology is a relatively new phenomenon, it is one of the fastest-growing ones. Many people are addicted to the sensation that only device input can provide.

For the digital addict, it is the perceived need to interact with their digital devices, whether it be gaming, texting, chatting on their social networks, or surfing pornography, news, or other sites. Personal relationships suffer as they withdraw from normal and healthy engagement with friends and family. Professional relationships suffer as work often plays second fiddle to digital devices, or fatigue from a lack of sleep hinders the work life. That's why tech addiction rehab centers are popping up in a city near you. There is one called "A Place of Hope" in Edmunds, Washington. During the patient's stay, issues addressed include dependency, behavioral addiction, mental health, and social relationships (Jantz, 2021).

Action Against Polarization

Ways to *break the algorithm* and find alternative technology platforms are becoming popular. Search engines like Brave, Qwant, and you.com are being developed. Encrypted social platforms like Signal also offer alternatives to large platforms like WhatsApp and Facebook, which through its algorithm feeds users the same content and rarely shows them opposing views, which has resulted in polarization.

Qwant, for instance, is a search engine that does not store user search history or collect personal data from users, and does not personalize search results by feeding past search results into algorithms. Signal offers an alternative to Facebook-owned WhatsApp. When there was an announcement for an upcoming update to WhatsApp, with a privacy policy that allowed Facebook and its subsidiaries to access user's WhatsApp data, many users moved to Signal for its focus on privacy. It does not harvest data to build its algorithm, as it is sourced through grants and donations rather than advertisements.

Algorithmic Recommendations

Based on what you consumed in the past, YouTube and Facebook present a lot of recommended videos or posts, which are fed to you based on the algorithm. These recommendation features could be the main culprit when looking at connection between polarization and social media. Realizing this and actively avoiding recommendations is a positive step. Using a Chrome extension to block these recommendations can also be helpful (e.g., the Chrome extension Unhook can do this).

Social Solutions

Polarization is an unintended (or sometimes purposeful) consequence of social media, but it is still a social issue. Thus, many social solutions have been put forward. For example, one of the ideas to reduce political polarization is the civic model of Citizen's Assembly, where selected citizens (similar to selection for jury duty) come together to deliberate different solutions to issues. This model has been put in place in Britain, where selected participants came together for two weekends to discuss issues and options on Brexit (Citizens' Assembly on Brexit, 2017).

Action Against Cyberbullying and Suicide

As noted, social media suicide-related incidences have increased significantly. Thus, there have been calls to increase the age minimum to use social media platforms from the current age of 13 for the majority of platforms. In addition, advocates have also suggested requiring proof of age when users open their account to help enforce the age minimum (Hedegaard, Curtin, and Warner, 2020). This strategy has been used to control underage alcohol and tobacco consumption for many years. We should apply it to technology so we can protect our youngsters.

BEHAVIOR MODIFICATION TECHNIQUES

The solutions discussed in the last section might feel a bit like a Band-Aid—addressing the symptoms but not necessarily the root of the problem. When it comes to mass media, we need to find and address the root cause instead. For one, we need a reset!

Mass and social media require a perspective shift in many people's lives. Online connections, likes, posts, and so on should never become more important than actual ("IRL") relationships we have with other people. That's the hard truth, made even harder by the COVID-19 pandemic, which literally meant we were putting our lives in danger if we wanted to have real connections with other humans. Let's look at ways all of us can adjust and reset the importance that media has in our lives.

Digital Detox

The best thing that you can do is learn to live without it. This doesn't mean abandoning social media entirely; it just means spending some time away from it. This is called a digital detox. A friend of mine wrote a book that is a good resource for unplugging (Shlain, 2019). Titled *24/6*, it explores her decade-long family tradition of going completely off the waves for a day every week. The book is rooted in the ancient Jewish tradition of Shabbat, and the author suggests we all take a technology Shabbat once a week, a restorative 24 hours that reminds us why we are lucky to have technology in the first place.

Place Less Importance on Your Social Media Appearance

Easier said than done, I know. However, one of the big signs of social media addiction is that you spend a lot of time overthinking and overplanning your posts, or you feel the need to continually check for new posts from friends or people you follow. This causes anxiety and stress. If you place less importance on how and what you post, as well as whether you catch all the posts coming in, you will be able to free up your mind from this stress.

I have seen people apply certain techniques and strategies. For example, my partner deletes some of the apps she deems "too distracting" off her phone during the week and checks them on the weekend, then deletes them at the start of the week. There are other routines for screen time that can help as well. You can put time limits on screen use, for instance, using one of the many apps available to help with this. Some of the apps will literally lock you out to help you avoid the temptations.

Analogue Alternatives

Make time for real-life, real-time connections. Make it a point to incorporate and enjoy non-screen-based activities, such as arts and crafts, reading, or exercising. Make a plan to get outside for walks, weather permitting. Play a board game with others. Have a "no technology" day in your house.

No Phone in the Bedroom

Create physical distance between you and your devices. Keep them away to avoid the temptations. "Half of phone users scroll through social media instead of sleeping and do the same immediately after they wake up" (Nicholls, 2021).

Turn Off Notifications

We're constantly drawn to our phones with every sound, buzz, or flash from the notifications. One of the easiest ways to reduce your time spent on social media is to turn off these push notifications, and mute any apps that trigger an insatiable urge to check for updates.

In summary, conditioning in mass media is here and it's here to stay. Many technology companies depend on it. Thus, there is an incentive to keep it going. But how can we make it better? It all starts with the concept of "user experience," a term popularized by Don Norman (1988) in his book *The Design of Everyday Things*. The idea was to look past the visuals and functions, and toward the feelings and thoughts that a "user" has when interacting with the product. Improving the user experience was meant to make utilizing a product more joyful, more convenient. However, just like anything with technology, there is a downside.

User experience (UX) design has led us to use a certain vocabulary; instead of seeing human beings with goals, wants, and desires, we see users. We refer to them with words like *subscribers, subs, visitors, spenders, whales,* or even just *traffic* or *installs*. We assign a role to them. UX design has led to dehumanizing people, and has thus made us numb to the negative consequences of the products we create and put out into the world. We started as humans, became users, and in some cases became users who are addicts. So how do we get back to humans again? Well, we need to go back to seeing each other—as humans who have needs but also have agency and honor.

References

Bever, Lindsey. (2017). "The disturbing trend of live-streamed suicides." https://www.chicagotribune.com/lifestyles/health/ct-the-disturbing-trend-of-live-streamed-suicides-20170208-story.html

Chiu, David. (2020). "Jonestown: 13 Things You Should Know About Cult Massacre." https://www.rollingstone.com/feature/jonestown-13-things-you-should-know-about-cult-massacre-121974/

Citizens' Assembly on Brexit. (2017). "Citizens detailed, reflective and informed discussions about what the UK's post-Brexit." https://www.ucl.ac.uk/constitution-unit/research/deliberative-democracy/citizens-assembly-brexit

Cold Turkey. (2021). "A dose of discipline, built in." https://getcoldturkey.com/

Digital Responsibility. (2021). "Technology Addiction Awareness Scholarship." http://www.digitalresponsibility.org/technology-addiction-awareness-scholarship

Engle, Jeremy. (2021). "Lesson of the Day: 'Dr. Seuss Books Are Pulled, and a "Cancel Culture" Controversy Erupts.'" https://www.nytimes.com/2021/03/05/learning/lesson-of-the-day-dr-seuss-books-are-pulled-and-a-cancel-culture-controversy-erupts.html

Guadagno, Rosanna E., Adam Lankford, Nicole L. Muscanell, Bradley M. Okdie, and Debra M. McCallum. (2010). "Social Influence in the Online Recruitment of Terrorists and Terrorist Sympathizers: Implications for Social Psychology Research." https://www.cairn.info/revue-internationale-de-psychologie-sociale-2010-1-page-25.htm

Haynes, Trevor. (2018). "Dopamine, Smartphones & You: A Battle for Your Time." https://sitn.hms.harvard.edu/flash/2018/dopamine-smartphones-battle-time/

Hedegaard, Holly, Sally C. Curtin, and Margaret Warner. (2020). "Increase in Suicide Mortality in the United States, 1999–2018." https://www.cdc.gov/nchs/data/databriefs/db362.h.pdf

Jantz, Gregg. (2021). "Internet & Digital Addiction Doesn't Define You." https://www.aplaceofhope.com/internet-digital-addiction-treatment/

Nelson, Ted. (2012). "Computers for Cynics: The Myth of Technology." youtube.com/watch?v=KdnGPQaICjk

Nicholls, Kat. (2021). "Young people turning to social media to avoid emotions." https://happiful.com/young-people-turning-to-social-media-to-avoid-emotions/

Norman, Don. (1988). *The Design of Everyday Things*. Basic Books.

Patchin, Justin W. (2012). "Amanda Todd, Cyberbullying, and Suicide." https://cyberbullying.org/amanda-todd-cyberbullying-and-suicide

PBS. (1998). "Franklin D. Roosevelt became the first president of the United States to appear on television." https://www.pbs.org/30secondcandidate/timeline/years/1939.html

Ramzy, Austin, and Mike Ives. (2020). "Hong Kong Protests, One Year Later." https://www.nytimes.com/2020/06/09/world/asia/hong-kong-protests-one-year-later.html

Roth, Yoel, and Nick Pickles. (2020). "Updating our approach to misleading information." https://blog.twitter.com/en_us/topics/product/2020/updating-our-approach-to-misleading-information.html

Shlain, Tiffany. (2019). *24/6: The Power of Unplugging One Day a Week*. Gallery Books.

Siebert, Jeff. (2020). *The Social Dilemma*. https://www.thesocialdilemma.com/

Skopeliti, Clea. (2021). "Japan appoints 'Minister for Loneliness' after rise in suicides." https://www.independent.co.uk/news/world/asia/japan-minister-loneliness-suicides-tetsushi-sakamoto-b1807236.html

Walinga, Jennifer, and Charles Stangor. (2021). "Changing Behaviour Through Reinforcement and Punishment: Operant Conditioning." In *Introduction to Psychology*. https://opentextbc.ca/introductiontopsychology/chapter/7-2-changing-behavior-through-reinforcement-and-punishment-operant-conditioning/

Warzel, Charlie. (2021). "The internet rewired our brains. He predicted it would." https://www.nytimes.com/2021/02/04/opinion/michael-goldhaber-internet.html

Whitman, Drew Eric. (2008). *Ca$hvertising: How to Use More Than 100 Secrets of Ad-Agency Psychology to Make BIG MONEY Selling Anything to Anyone*. Career Press.

Wong, Kristin. (2015). "How Long It Takes to Get Back on Track After a Distraction." https://lifehacker.com/how-long-it-takes-to-get-back-on-track-after-a-distract-1720708353

Yeginsu, Ceylan. (2018). "U.K. Appoints a Minister for Loneliness." https://www.nytimes.com/2018/01/17/world/europe/uk-britain-loneliness.html

CHAPTER 7

Genomics: What Happens When Humans Play God?

*G*enome editing, also known as *gene editing*, is the manipulation of the genetic material of a living organism by deleting, replacing, or inserting a DNA sequence, typically with the aim of improving a crop or farmed animal. It has more recently been used in humans. CRISPR-Cas9 is the most recent revolutionary technology that's making gene editing possible, with incredible results.

Plants, animals, and microorganisms like bacteria that have been genetically engineered are termed *genetically modified organisms* (GMOs). If the genetic material introduced to the host is from an organism that normally would not be able to breed with the host species, the new organism is called *transgenic*.

There are two ways that gene editing can be carried out. Genes and chromosomes mutate in one of two ways. One way is *somatic mutation*, which occurs in a single body cell and cannot be inherited (only tissues derived from the mutated cell are affected). The second way is *germline mutations*, which occur in gametes (reproductive cells) and can be passed to offspring (every cell in the entire organism will be affected).

HOW DOES GENE EDITING WORK?

Genetic engineers choose the gene they want to insert into the target organism. Next, they isolate the gene and purify the DNA. The purified DNA is either cut into segments to remove traits or *amplified* (reproduced) as it is. This DNA is then inserted into a bacterium along with other genetic material, such as promoters and terminators, to initiate and stop the genes' reproduction. Researchers also insert genetic markers to help determine which cells have been successfully transformed. The bacterium containing the new DNA is then inserted into the target, or host, and then reproduced. Techniques to modify DNA in the genome have existed for several decades, but the conversation about the science and ethics of genome editing has grown louder due to faster, cheaper, and more efficient technologies (National Human Genome Research Institute, 2021).

A Quick Look at the History of Gene Editing

Selective breeding, or artificial selection (dog breeding, animal husbandry, etc.), has been used by humans for thousands of years. More recently, mutation breeding uses exposure to radiation or chemicals to produce a high frequency of random mutations for selective breeding purposes.

The term "genetic engineering" was first coined by Jack Williamson in his sci-fi novel *Dragon's Island*, published in 1951. It wasn't until 1972, though, that the first *recombinant* (combined from two or more sources) DNA molecule was made by Paul Berg. The first GMO was a bacterium generated in 1973, and in 1974, the first genetically modified animal was created when foreign DNA was introduced into a mouse. Genetically engineered human insulin was produced in 1978 and commercialized in 1982. Genetically modified food has been on the market since 1994—the Flavr Savr tomato. This tomato was developed through the use of anti-sense RNA to regulate the expression of the enzyme polygalacturonase (PG) in ripening tomato fruit. This enzyme is one of the most abundant proteins in ripe tomato fruit and has long been thought to be responsible for softening in ripe tomatoes. The engineering of this tomato was intended to improve its shelf life (Bruening and Lyons, 2000).

A biotech company called Advanced Genetic Sciences applied for U.S. government authorization in 1983 to perform field tests with GM bacteria sprayed on crops to protect them from frost. Protestors delayed the tests for four years with legal challenges, but in 1987 the first GMO to be released into the environment was sprayed on two fields in California. Both fields were trashed by activists the night before spraying

(Borel, 2014). In 2009, 11 transgenic crops were grown commercially in 25 countries, including the United States, Brazil, Argentina, India, and China, and the FDA approved a drug genetically engineered and produced in goat's milk.

In 2012, a technique was developed to easily and specifically alter the genome of any organism, known as the CRISPR-Cas9 System (Synthego, 2021). In October 2020, the Nobel Prize in Chemistry was awarded to Emmanuelle Charpentier and Jennifer Doudna for their CRISPR genome editing. It was a stunning choice, both as a DNA-altering tool and because it was the first time two women won such a prize in chemistry. CRISPR has completely revolutionized biological research since its arrival (Cohen, 2020).

Scientists have since published more than 300,000 studies using the tool to manipulate the genomes of many types of organisms. It's cheap, fast, and easy enough for almost anyone to use. Today, scientists can order custom-made CRISPR components with the click of a button.

Positive Use Cases of Gene Editing

Gene editing technology can be used to create "gene drives" that ensure a genetic modification will be inherited by all the offspring, spreading throughout an animal population over several generations. There are many advantages to this "godlike" technology.

For example, exotic pet breeding and faster racehorses are now possible. This technology also enables designer babies whose genetic makeup has been selected in order to eradicate particular defects, or to ensure that a particular gene is present. Just like an Amazon shopping cart, theoretically one could preselect hair color, eye color, height, sex, intersex, half human/half horse—anything is possible.

For example, in 2021, monkey embryos containing human cells were made in a laboratory in China. The scientists injected human stem cells—which have the ability to develop into many different body tissues—into macaque embryos. Other so-called mixed-species embryos, or chimeras, have been produced in the past, with human cells implanted into sheep and pig embryos. The scientists were led by Professor Juan Carlos Izpisua

Belmonte of the Salk Institute in the United States, who, in 2017, helped make the first human-pig hybrid (Briggs, 2021).

Furthermore, removing allergens from foods and genetically creating decaf coffee beans is now possible. Controlling or eradicating invasive species or pests such as like malaria-causing mosquitoes is possible. Employing a strategy known as *population modification*, which involves using a CRISPR-Cas9 gene drive system to introduce genes preventing parasite transmission into mosquito chromosomes, University of California researchers have made a major advance in the use of genetic technologies to control the transmission of malaria parasites (University of California – Irvine, 2020).

There are many more use cases, such as de-extinction of species, bringing back birds like passenger pigeons and animals like the mammoth (Marcus, 2018). Gene editing can be used in conservation and natural area management, to vaccinate a threatened fauna from disease or to confer resistance to pathogens among wild animal populations.

Gene editing can also be used to create a DNA tape recorder of sorts (Yandell, 2014); you can modify a gene so that it acts as a recorder of events in the lifetime of a cell, such as exposure to antibiotics, nutrients, bacteria, viruses, and light.

Gene editing can be used in microbial art, thereby producing black and white photographs, and novelties, such as blue roses, lavender carnations, and glowing fish.

One of the more well-known and controversial uses for gene editing is creating genetically modified crops or livestock to produce genetically modified foods or to increase production. On the plant side, there are already two gene-edited products in the United States. Canola oil from herbicide-resistant plants was first available in 2019. And the soybean is edited to be high in oleic acid, a healthier fat found in olive oil and avocados. CRISPR has put powerful genetic-modification capabilities into the hands of small agricultural firms, rather than big agribusinesses, because it is easy and inexpensive to use. The gene-editing tool allows scientists to alter an organism's genome with unprecedented precision (Hall, 2016).

Gene editing can increase tolerance to stressors such as insects, drought, and herbicides, or increase the nutritional value of food

(Parmar, 2017). It's also an important research tool, because it enables the creation of transgenic organisms—one of the most important tools for the analysis of gene function.

One of the most fascinating use cases of gene editing is its capabilities in medicine. In this industry, genetic engineering is used for mass production of insulin, mass production of human growth hormones, mass production of a specific protein or enzyme, treating infertility, production of antibodies, increasing the success of organ transplantation, and the production of food supplements and foods like cheese. And that's just the beginning!

Cancer treatments are also possible. In 2015, gene therapy was successfully used to treat a rare skin disease in humans. Researchers successfully treated a boy with epidermolysis bullosa using skin grafts grown from his own skin cells, genetically altered to repair the mutation that caused his disease. A seven-year-old who had lost most of his skin to this rare genetic disease made a dramatic recovery after receiving an experimental gene therapy (Servick, 2017).

At the time of this writing, one amazing application of gene editing technology is the development of vaccines used to fight COVID-19. Pharmaceutical companies Moderna and Pfizer/BioNTech created a novel type of vaccine made from messenger RNA (mRNA) that can offer high levels of protection by preventing COVID-19 and death among people who are vaccinated.

So how does mRNA vaccine work exactly? Vaccines traditionally contain either weakened viruses or purified signature proteins of the virus. The mRNA vaccine is different, because rather than having the viral protein injected, a person receives genetic material—the mRNA—that encodes the viral protein. When these genetic instructions are injected into the upper arm, the muscle cells translate them to make the viral protein directly in the body. The vaccines train the immune system to recognize the disease-causing part of a virus (Centers for Disease Control, 2021).

This approach mimics what the COVID-19 virus does in nature—but the vaccine mRNA codes only for the critical fragment of the viral protein. This gives the immune system a preview of what the real virus looks like without causing disease. This preview gives the immune system time to design powerful antibodies that can neutralize the real virus if the individual is ever infected. After the protein piece is made, the cell breaks down the instructions and gets rid of them, just like deleting the PDF of an Ikea user manual. Pretty remarkable.

While this synthetic mRNA is genetic material, it cannot be transmitted to the next generation. After an mRNA injection, this molecule guides the protein production inside the muscle cells.

As you can see, the possibilities are endless. However, with great technology comes great responsibility. How do we ensure that anyone using this technology has the best intentions for humanity and our planet? It's sad but true that, just as there are endless positive use cases, there are negative harmful use cases as well. Next, we will explore the possible negative unintended consequences (UCOTs) of gene editing.

THE UNINTENDED OR WILLFULLY IGNORED NEGATIVE CONSEQUENCES OF GENE EDITING

There are many ethical, social, ecological, and economic concerns over gene editing and its use cases. Let's dive in.

Justice and Equity Concerns

As with many new technologies, there is concern that genome editing will only be accessible to the wealthy and will increase existing disparities in access to healthcare and other interventions. Some worry that taken to its extreme, gene editing could create classes of individuals defined by the quality of their engineered genome. That it could lead to a resurgence of the eugenics movement. Furthermore, folks in control of the technology could control the food supply with the use of intellectual property rights.

Perhaps this could even lead to the "patenting" of life itself. A gene patent is the exclusive rights to a specific sequence of DNA (a gene) given by a government to the individual, organization, or corporation who claims to have first identified the gene. Gene patents have often resulted in companies having sole ownership of genetic testing for patented genes.

Safety Concerns

Safety concerns include the possibility of off-target effects (edits in the wrong place) and *mosaicism* (when some cells carry the edit but others do not), or even unexpected or harmful genetic changes and mutations. For example, an attempt to control or eradicate invasive species or pests such as the malaria-causing mosquito could lead to an accidental eradication of bees. Without bees, we have no pollination, which means no food. And lack of food would lead to the extinction of humanity!

It is possible there could be bad actors who would engineer bees or humans directly with the intent of eradicating the species.

Rogue Army

Gene editing technology could theoretically be used to enhance, modify, or alter a human being's appearance, adaptability, intelligence, character, or behavior. It's not hard to imagine a dictator creating a rogue army that has been genetically modified not to have feelings.

One of the worst humans ever to walk the Earth was Adolf Hitler. He had no regard for human life and committed some of the worst acts of human rights abuse and murders in history and in the worst way possible. One of his maniacal plans was to create a "pure" Aryan race. What if, in the future, someone like Hitler were to emerge who believes a certain race or people should be eradicated, and decides to genetically modify them so that the targeted group dies off?

Bioweaponry

The 20th century was dominated by advances in physics that led to the development of the most destructive weapons humanity has ever created. Advances in biotechnology over the last few decades promise to make the same true for the 21st century. The biological revolution is set to produce tools that could be turned into weapons of war. Gene editing is the latest in a series of biological advances that will fundamentally change how humans live and die.

One of the potential dangers of gene editing is the accidental or purposeful creation and release of harmful organisms. The real danger here will come from organisms that already exist. Viruses should be our major concern. Anyone who has lived through a pandemic like the Spanish flu in 1918 or coronavirus in 2020 can tell you how such a small organism can bring the whole world and life to a standstill.

It's not hard to imagine an individual or a state actor motivated to create something similar to disrupt the world. Smallpox, for example, is very potent, and we are not protected against it. The smallpox sequence is published online, so anyone can recover it by synthesis and create significant harm.

In short, advances in genetic engineering have offered bad actors an opportunity to create low-cost, low-profile, potentially catastrophic weapons of mass destruction (Cropper, 2020).

Concerns Over Using Embryos

Genome-editing research sometimes involves using embryos. Many people have moral and religious objections to the use of human embryos for research. Federal funds cannot be used for any research that creates or destroys embryos. Furthermore, government agencies in the United States such as the National Institutes of Health (NIH) go as far as not funding any use of gene editing in human embryos. The concept of altering the human germline in embryos for clinical purposes has been debated over many years, from many different perspectives, and has been viewed almost universally as a line that should not be crossed. Advances in technology have given us an elegant new way of carrying out genome editing, but the strong arguments against engaging in this activity remain (National Institutes of Health, 2015).

GMOs

Economic growth, population dynamics, land availability, and volatile weather are all variables in an increasingly complex and interdependent global agriculture industry. The world's population is expected to grow to almost 10 billion by 2050, leading to an increase in agricultural demand by roughly 50% compared to 2013 levels. As consumption continues on an upward trajectory in the coming decades, scientists have turned to bioengineering to fill the need for global food supplies (Borel, 2017). There has been plenty of research on how GMOs negatively affect human health. This could result from differences in nutritional content, allergic response, or undesired side effects such as toxicity, organ damage, or gene transfer.

WHAT HAS BEEN DONE TO MITIGATE THE UCOTs OF GENE EDITING

As you can see, there are many unintended consequences of such a powerful technology. Experts and policy makers around the world are working hard to find ways to mitigate some of these negative effects. This section covers some of the measures people have taken.

U.S. Domestic Regulatory Oversight and Policies

In 1979, the National Commission for the Protection of Human Subjects in Biomedical and Behavioral Research released the "Belmont Report." The report provided landmark guidelines in medicine and biotechnology that "focused on avoiding infliction of harm, accepting a duty of beneficence, and maintaining a commitment to justice" (National Institutes of Health, 2017).

The committee created principles aimed at protecting and promoting the health and well-being of individuals; approaching novel technologies with careful attention to constantly evolving information; respecting individual rights; guarding against unwanted societal effects; and equitably distributing information, burdens, and benefits. Differences in social and legal culture inevitably will lead to different domestic policies governing specific applications of genome editing. Nonetheless, some principles can be shared across national borders. Thus, while the overarching principles presented in the report were aimed primarily at the U.S. government, they and the responsibilities that underlie them are universal in nature. These principles include:

- *Promoting well-being*: The principle of promoting well-being supports providing benefit for and preventing harm to those affected, often referred to in the bioethics literature as the principles of beneficence and non-maleficence.

- *Transparency*: The principle of transparency requires openness and sharing of information in ways that are accessible and understandable to stakeholders.

- *Due care*: The principle of due care for patients enrolled in research studies or receiving clinical care requires proceeding carefully and deliberately, and only when supported by sufficient and robust evidence.

- *Responsible science*: The principle of responsible science underpins adherence to the highest standards of research, from bench to bedside, in accordance with international and professional norms.

- *Respect for persons*: The principle of respect for persons requires recognition of the personal dignity of all individuals, acknowledgment of the centrality of personal choice, and respect for individual decisions. All people have equal moral value, regardless of their genetic qualities.

- *Fairness*: The principle of fairness requires that like cases be treated alike, and that risks and benefits be equitably distributed (distributive justice).

- *Transnational cooperation*: The principle of transnational cooperation supports a commitment to collaborative approaches to research and governance while respecting different cultural contexts.

In U.S. regulation, these principles underlie the insistence on voluntary, informed consent from competent persons; special protections for those lacking competence; a reasonable balance between the risks of harm and potential benefits; attention to minimizing risks whenever possible; and equitable selection of research participants.

In 2019, the House of Representatives passed a bill reinstating a ban on genetically modified human technology (CRISPR) in the United States (U.S. Congress, 2019). The bill on appropriations was focused on federal health and food oversight through the Food and Drug Administration (FDA), and included language that prohibits the FDA from acting on genetically modified technology on humans (Regalado, 2019). This ban on genetically modified in vitro fertilization technology has been in place since 2015.

As of this writing, laboratory work related to gene editing is overseen by local institutional biosafety committees and often federally through the Clinical Laboratory Improvement Amendments regulated through the Centers for Disease Control and Prevention, the Center for Medicaid Services, and the FDA. Clinical trials related to this research are overseen and reviewed by the National Institutes of Health Recombinant DNA Advisory Committee, as well as the FDA and institutional review boards. Any potential medical products will be reviewed by the FDA's Center for Biologics Evaluation and Research. The National Bioethics Commissions serve as advisories to public policy and bioethics recommendations.

International Regulations and Policies

In France, restrictions on gene editing under the Oviedo Convention allow modifications to the human genome only for somatic gene editing and no modification for heritable traits, for "preventive, diagnostic, or therapeutic purposes."

France also embraced a plan for genomic medicine focused on addressing cancer and diseases that can be aided by gene technology (Vogel, 2018).

Germany passed the Embryo Protection Act of 1990, which prohibits the use of embryos for scientific research, but there remains a debate over whether nonviable embryos can be used.

South Korea's Bioethics and Biosafety Act restricts genetic experimentation with or modification of human embryos. The Notification Act prohibits the sale of products that alter genes.

Canada created a law that says "all germline" editing is prohibited under the Assisted Human Reproduction Act.

Various stakeholders in European countries have voiced concerns about how to accommodate genome-editing techniques such as CRISPR-Cas9 within the existing regulatory framework for genetically modified organisms. The European Union has established a legal and regulatory framework for safeguarding the development of genetically modified organisms and protecting humans, animals, and the environment. However, comprehensive international regulations on human gene editing do not exist due to varying evaluations of safety and implications of embracing this technology (Vogel, 2018).

Restricting Funding for Germline Gene Editing

Many somatic gene-editing technologies are funded by large investors. The potential danger of companies investing in germline gene editing is that the desire for profits could drive the research and production in a destructive ethical direction.

Human genome editing poses some hefty ethical questions. For families who have watched their children suffer from devastating genetic diseases, the technology offers the hope of editing cruel mutations out of the gene pool. For those living in poverty, it is yet another way for the privileged to vault ahead. One open question is where to draw the line between disease treatment and enhancement, and how to enforce it, considering differing attitudes toward conditions such as deafness (Bergman, 2019).

Action Against GMOs

To address the domination of genetically modified crops, pesticides, and other products of bioengineering in the modern agricultural system, more regenerative agriculture practices ought to be adopted internationally. Reducing monoculture farming through diversity of crop rotation and decreasing inputs such as pesticides and herbicides is one great approach. This was in response to the rapid increase in the production of biotechnology products, and a realization of the need for some sort of guidelines to ensure that public health and the environment are adequately protected from the potential risks of this technology (Environmental Protection Agency, 2021).

At the same time, bioengineering and gene editing can be used to help formulate solutions in sustainable farming. Some argue that bioengineering methods in crops to improve efficiency and safety can be sources of positive solutions: reducing environmental waste, improving soil health, and helping to "reclaim" misused farmland (Peters, 2003). Gene-editing techniques are being used to increase livestock resistance to disease and crop resilience. Adequate oversight and regulation of bioengineering in agriculture on a global scale is lacking. (Beaver and Talapatra, 2018).

Again, long-standing concerns in the scientific community early on in genetic engineering led to the development of a regulatory framework, started in 1975. Later, the Cartagena Protocol on Biosafety, an international treaty that governs the transfer, handling, and use of GMOs, was adopted in 2000. Currently, 157 countries are members of the protocol, and many countries use it as a reference point for their own regulations concerning GMOs.

Still, the legal and regulatory status of GMOs varies widely by country. Here, the United States established a committee at the Office of Science and Technology that assigned regulatory assessment and approval of GM food to the U.S. Department of Agriculture (USDA), the Food and Drug Administration (FDA), and the Environmental Protection Agency (EPA). EPA regulation of bioengineered products is largely focused on plant products that incorporate pesticide substances and toxic materials. The USDA focuses on agriculture and, for biotechnology purposes, this mostly relates to plant health and safety. The FDA is largely tasked with keeping genetically engineered foods safe.

Grass Roots Organizing and Working to Build Solutions

The Human Gene Editing Initiative of the National Academies of Sciences, Engineering, and Medicine hosts international summits to convene nations and experts to consider the safety, ethics, and applications of human gene editing. It has hosted three conferences so far. Its main mission is to provide researchers, clinicians, policy makers, and societies around the world with a comprehensive understanding of human genome editing to help inform decision-making about this research and its application (National Academies of Sciences, Engineering, and Medicine, 2015).

THE RESET ON GENE EDITING

The mitigation efforts described here, although well meaning, still fall short of having the ability to manage or handle the fallout of any potential damage gene editing and synthetic biology are capable of causing. We need to do more.

As mentioned, genetic editing is being used in medicinal research to find therapies and cures for such things as cancer, obesity, heart disease, diabetes, arthritis, substance abuse, anxiety, aging, and Parkinson's disease, among others. This points to the fact that the potential good that can result from genetic engineering is invaluable.

However, processes like germline modification, which would result in any genetic modifications being inheritable, can't simply be ignored. As seen in a few examples, the germline is the population of a multicellular organism's cells that pass on their genetic material to their offspring. Germline modification is currently banned in 40 countries, but that does not stop people from doing it.

So far, the concerns over engineered plants and animals have proven unfounded, but the potential for great benefits and great risk to the human race calls for a cautious approach to genetic engineering.

If there is any technological development that personally scares me the most, it's gene editing. Playing "god" can create a life. That same power can destroy all living things. It would be great if all humans were well meaning and used this powerful technology all for good and *only* for good. However, we should not underestimate human stupidity and human evil. We need better safeguards.

REFERENCES

Beaver, Nathan A., and Sunit Talapatra. (2018). "Agricultural Bioengineering: The Shifting Landscape." https://www.foley.com/en/insights/publications/2018/07/agricultural-bioengineering-the-shifting-landscape

Bergman, Mary Todd. (2019). "Perspectives on gene editing." https://news.harvard.edu/gazette/story/2019/01/perspectives-on-gene-editing/

Borel, Brooke. (2014). "The First GMO Field Tests." https://modernfarmer.com/2014/05/even-first-gmo-field-tests-controversial-will-ever-end-fight/

Borel, Brooke. (2017). "The U.S. Regulations for Biotechnology Are Woefully Out of Date." http://www.slate.com/articles/technology/future_tense/2017/04/u_s_biotechnology_regulations_are_woefully_out_of_date.html

Briggs, Helen. (2021). "Human cells grown in monkey embryos spark ethical debate." https://www.bbc.com/news/science-environment-56767517

Bruening, G., and Lyons, J.M. (2000). "The case of the FLAVR SAVR tomato." http://calag.ucanr.edu/Archive/?article=ca.v054n04p6#:~:text=The%20FLAVR%20SAVR%20tomato%20was,crop%20product%20to%20be%20commercialized.&text=By%201987%2C%20Calgene%20research-ers%20identified,inserted%20PG%20antisense%20DNA%20constructions

Centers for Disease Control. (2021). "Understanding mRNA COVID-19 Vaccines." https://www.cdc.gov/coronavirus/2019-ncov/vaccines/different-vaccines/mrna.html

Cohen, Jon. (2020). "CRISPR, the revolutionary genetic 'scissors,' honored by Chemistry Nobel." https://www.sciencemag.org/news/2020/10/crispr-revolu-tionary-genetic-scissors-honored-chemistry-nobel

Cropper, Nicholas. (2020). "CRISPR Is Making Bioweapons More Accessible Posted." https://www.americansecurityproject.org/crispr-is-making-bioweapons-more_accessible/

Environmental Protection Agency. (2021). "Introduction to Biotechnology Regu-lation for Pesticides." https://www.epa.gov/regulation-biotechnology-under-tsca-and-fifra/introduction-biotechnology-regulation-pesticides

Hall, Stephen S. (2016). "Transform Food Crops—or Die on the Vine." https://www.scientificamerican.com/article/new-gene-editing-techniques-could-transform-food-crops-or-die-on-the-vine/

Marcus, Amy Dockser. (2018). "Meet the Scientists Bringing Extinct Species Back from the Dead." https://www.wsj.com/articles/meet-the-scientists-bringing-extinct-species-back-from-the-dead-1539093600

National Academies of Sciences, Engineering, and Medicine. (2015). "Human Genome Editing Initiative." https://www.nationalacademies.org/our-work/human-gene-editing-initiative

National Human Genome Research Institute. (2021). "How Does Genome Editing Work?" https://www.genome.gov/about-genomics/policy-issues/Genome-Editing/How-genome-editing-works

National Institutes of Health. (2015). "Statement on NIH funding of research using gene-editing technologies in human embryos." https://www.nih.gov/about-nih/who-we-are/nihdirector/statements/statement-nih-funding-research-using-gene-editing-technologies-human-embryos

National Institutes of Health (2017). "Oversight of Human Genome Editing and Overarching Principles for Governance." https://www.ncbi.nlm.nih.gov/books/NBK447266/

Parmar, N. (2017). "Genetic engineering strategies for biotic and abiotic stress." https://www.ncbi.nlm.nih.gov

Peters, L. David. (2003). "Sustainable farming needs bioengineering." https://yale-dailynews.com/blog/2003/10/27/sustainable-farming-needs-bioengineering/

Regalado, Antonio. (2019) "Congress is about to renew its ban on creating CRISPR babies in the US." https://www.technologyreview.com/2019/01/10/137871/congress-is-going-to-renew-its-ban-on-creating-crispr-babies-in-the-us/

Servick, Kelly. (2017). "A boy with a rare disease gets new skin, thanks to gene-corrected stem cells." https://www.sciencemag.org/news/2017/11/boy-rare-disease-gets-new-skin-thanks-gene-corrected-stem-cells

Synthego. (2021). "History of Genetic Engineering and the Rise of Genome Editing Tools." https://www.synthego.com/learn/genome-engineering-history

University of California – Irvine, (2020). "Researchers pioneer more effective way to block malaria transmission in mosquitoes." https://www.sciencedaily.com/releases/2020/11/201103140613.htm

U.S. Congress. (2019). "H.R.265—Agriculture, Rural Development, Food and Drug Administration, and Related Agencies Appropriations Act, 2019." https://www.congress.gov/bill/116th-congress/house-bill/265

Vogel, Kathleen M. (2018). "Crispr goes global: A snapshot of rules, policies, and attitudes." https://thebulletin.org/2018/06/crispr-goes-global-a-snapshot-of-rules-policies-and-attitudes/

Yandell, Kate. (2014). "DNA Tape Recorder." https://www.the-scientist.com/daily-news/dna-tape-recorder-36429

CHAPTER 8

5G: Is This a New "Cold War" You've Never Heard Of?

You may have never heard of 5G. You might have heard of it in bizarre conspiracy theories, such as 5G giving people headaches, causing erectile dysfunction, sickening cows, causing chickens to lay fewer eggs, or even causing the coronavirus. Every time you've heard such theories, before you even wrap your mind around them, you might wonder, "What the heck is this monster"?

This chapter explores the new wireless network technology known as 5G. Whether you've never heard of it, or have heard of it but don't really understand it, or have incomplete, out-of-context information that seems like a mess of conspiracy theories, this chapter offers some answers.

The 5G technology is the fifth-generation wireless network technology. It is faster and can handle more connected devices than the existing 4G LTE network. These improvements have enabled a wave of new kinds of technologies. 5G instantly connects and supports millions of devices at ultrafast speeds, and is 10 to 100 times faster than 4G. This is a big deal! Let's dive into the why.

A QUICK LOOK AT THE HISTORY OF 5G

In the last 50 years, mobile phones, more than any other technology, have quietly changed our lives forever. Do you remember how much you loved your 2G Nokia 3310?

Here is how it has changed over the years. In 1979, 1G "the first generation" of telecom networks that enabled *talk and mobile*, came to market. Twelve years later, in 1991, 2G digital networks surfaced. With this new technology, you were able to talk, send messages, and travel (with roaming services).

Half a dozen years went by. In 1997, there was an upgrade to 2.5G and 2.75G. This new technology brought some improvement to data services. General Packet Radio Service (GPRS) was a packet-oriented mobile data standard on the cellular communication network's global system for mobile communications. This enabled video calling, email accessing, multimedia messaging, and the like. GPRS was established by the European Telecommunications Standards Institute. GPRS was soon replaced by EDGE, which was slightly faster than GPRS, with a download speed over two times faster at 384Kbps.

In 1998, 3G, "the third generation" of the telecoms, was introduced and it brought a better mobile Internet experience (with limited success). This was soon replaced by 3.5G, in 2001. This allowed a truly mobile Internet experience, unleashing the mobile apps ecosystem.

Ten years later, in 2008, 4G, "the fourth generation" of the telecom's networks, hit the market. This brought all-IP services. Voice and data were possible. 4G was a fast broadband Internet experience, with unified networks architectures and protocols. As you guessed it, 4G was soon replaced by 4G LTE (Long-Term Evolution) in 2009. This new capability enabled doubled data speeds. 4G LTE was "faster" than 4G. But what did that actually mean when it came to using our phones? It meant downloads 10 times faster. It meant web pages loading in an instant. It meant smoother video and music streaming. In short, 4G LTE gave us the ability to utilize and experience the Internet on our phones in a quicker, richer way.

By enabling video viewing and data sharing at a pace not realized before, LTE turned our smartphones into powerful connected devices that we can carry anywhere. And it's opened up new possibilities for our personal and professional lives. Whether you were skimming reviews on Yelp! to find a great new restaurant, using GPS to find your way around, or streaming videos on YouTube, 4G LTE lets you do it all—seamlessly.

All was going great until connected devices hit the market. *Connected devices* are physical objects—such as smart home devices, appliances, thermostats, or cars—that can connect to each other and to other systems through the Internet, via various wired and wireless networks and protocols, such as Wi-Fi, NFC, 3G, and 4G networks. The bigger and more sophisticated the network of devices that need to connect and "speak" to each other, the bigger the need for faster and more efficient speeds.

In 2019, 5G technology was introduced to address this need. This "fifth generation" of the telecom networks expanded broadband wireless services beyond mobile Internet to the Internet of Things (IoT), connected devices, and critical communications segments. This technological advancement may be the most consequential thus far, because it's promising to revolutionize all aspects of our lives—from what you wear to everything in your house, from how you travel to how you enjoy experiences. Everything is promising to be infused with smart technology and interconnected via a 5G network.

5G wireless technology is meant to deliver higher multi-Gbps peak data speeds, ultra-low latency, more reliability, massive network capacity, increased availability, and a more uniform experience to more users. So what does this actually mean when it comes to using devices and being connected to the world around you? Let's consider that question next.

POSITIVE USE CASES FOR 5G

As of this writing, 5G is being deployed everywhere, opening up exciting new opportunities as well as concerns, as we will see later. I have identified a few of the most important positive use cases of 5G and their impacts across industries and society.

Entertainment and Media

We will get near-instantaneous 4K transmissions over mobile, cloud gaming, VR/AR, and other platforms. 4K, also known as UHD (Ultra-High Definition), provides high-quality images.

5G's incredibly fast speeds use millimeter wave spectrum wireless technology. This will be huge in the movie and video gaming industries, among others. The advantages of 5G's fast speeds provide a higher capacity for production. Traditionally, directors viewed their raw unedited footage the day after they shot it on film. It took time to process the film and sync the sound. That changed with the introduction of digital equipment. But 5G can further improve that process. The super-fast speeds could allow filmmakers to transfer massive amounts of video to their editors extremely quickly, and not be bound by wired connections.

Furthermore, lower latency means that applications like augmented and virtual reality will run more smoothly. It means that when you're wearing those VR glasses and turn your head, the virtual world responds in what feels like real time.

5G promises mass connectivity that will provide the ability to connect millions of devices in an area. To put this in perspective, Wi-Fi can only connect hundreds of devices.

The entertainment industry may have a blockbuster opportunity with 5G. Whether providing faster speeds for data transfer on set or creating innovative film or venue experiences, the combination of 5G, EDGE computing, artificial intelligence, and mixed reality may just usher in yet another golden age of Hollywood (Katibeh, 2019).

Smart Cities and Unlocking the Industrial Internet

Smart cities put data and digital technology to work to make better decisions and improve the quality of life of their citizens.

For example, in the event of an emergency in a connected city, police are notified about accidents immediately, traffic lights adjust to divert traffic and control volume, and change in real-time to allow emergency vehicles access to the accident without stopping. Imagine if everything was connected—lampposts, manhole covers, street signs, water pipes, sensors on pedestrians via their phones and smart watches, smart clothing, every gas pipe, every sewage outlet, and so on. The implications of a truly connected city are hard to articulate, but easy to imagine. That's what's going to be possible with 5G.

A truly connected home is not so ridiculous anymore either—smart fridges and smart vacuums are now everywhere. Now food can automatically be reordered and remotely delivered, and when you spill that bag of chips, the vacuum will automatically come and take care of the mess. It's all happening quickly.

In addition, 5G will help the three layers of a smart city work together. First is the technology base, which includes a critical mass of smartphones and sensors connected by high-speed communication networks. The second layer consists of specific applications. Translating raw data into alerts, insight, and action requires the right tools, and this is where technology providers and app developers come in. The third layer is usage by cities, companies, and the general public. Applications succeed only if they are widely adopted and manage to change behavior. They encourage people to use transit during off-hours, to change routes, to use less energy and water and to do so at different times of day, and to reduce strains on the healthcare system through preventive self-care.

5G will facilitate numbers that could translate into lives saved, fewer crime incidents, shorter commutes, a reduced health burden, and carbon emissions averted (Grijpink, Ménard, Sigurdsson, and Vucevic, 2018).

Autonomous Vehicles: Unlocking Mobility

A self-driving car—also known as an autonomous vehicle, driverless car, or robo-car—is a vehicle that is capable of sensing its environment and moving safely with little or no human input.

As of this writing, the technology is "nearly there," but just needs more training data.

Commercial applications are happening in controlled environments, not because of the car, but because of everything around the car (pedestrians, human drivers, animals, etc.). Self-driving cars will get here very shortly, and how they are deployed will change how we get around forever. From Tesla to Google to Uber to all the major automakers, the race is on for who gets to the finish line first.

At the moment, scaled autonomous driving is not fully possible until everything in the city is connected. Visual signals are not enough; there must also be real-time data. Truly autonomous driving requires 5G deployment. That's why it's still difficult to connect even 6 million cars in Los Angeles to a 4G network, not to mention every pedestrian.

Another hindrance of scaled autonomous driving is that motor vehicle operating laws, impaired driving laws, insurance laws, and most other laws addressing the operation of vehicles in most parts of the world are premised on a significant assumption—that a human is behind the wheel, operating the vehicle. State lawmakers around the world need to consider the ramifications of driverless cars, including how existing laws and systems may need to be modified in order to facilitate the implementation of this new technology.

With 5G connectivity, it's on the way. Laws are on the way. It's not a matter of if, but when.

Healthcare: Unlocking Access

The future of surgery could be remote. Doctors can now perform heart surgeries using a 5G mobile Internet connection. The appeal of long-distance surgery is that the leading specialist can help with or even intervene in operations far away from where they live. But having a reliable and fast enough connection is key.

In April 2019, surgeons in Gaozhou, China, remotely performed heart surgery on a woman while a team of experts monitored and provided instructions from Guangzhou, 400 kilometers away. The one-millisecond latency and data throughput (the rate at which data is processed) was what made this possible. 400MBs images were received in one second, versus the three-minute rate at which one is able to receive images on a non-5G network. These 5G capabilities will allow for scaled healthcare across populations and across landmass (Ye, 2019).

Military Benefits

In 2019, the Defense Innovation Board (an independent government advisory to the U.S. Department of Defense) released a paper on the implications of 5G, with the explicit assessment that the United States is behind and at significant risk. The primary focus was on control of standards and first-mover advantage.

Military industrial complex advancement with 5G translates to increased awareness development and deployment of next-generation weaponry such as nuclear and hypersonic.

Localized 5G also means connectivity in war environments like jungles where satellite communications are impossible. Of course, controlling primary communications networks also allows for intelligence gathering (which is a benign term for government-sanctioned espionage or surveillance).

Primary access in the United States today is 4G and 3G, but it's likely to fall behind on 5G in the future. The country that owns 5G will own many of its innovations, and these first-mover advantages will set standards for the rest of the world. As of this writing, the country in the lead of this race is not the United States. So, what country is leading? You will know before the end of this chapter. But first. . .

5G is the new "cold war" that you've never heard of. Let's dive a bit into how and why the United States fell behind and the long-term implications of this predicament.

How the United States Lost Its Telecom Dominance

To understand this issue, we need to look back at the history of telecom. In 1837, Samuel Morse invented the telegraph, and in 1876 Alexander Graham Bell invented the telephone. From the founding days up until recently, the United States was the global leader in telecommunications. That held for 150 years. How and why did that change?

It began with a critical mobile standards decision, which was *not* to have a standard:

- In 1987, Europe chose GSM, a cross-continent mobile development focused on a single standard. The Global System for Mobile (GSM) communications is a standard developed by the European Telecommunications Standards Institute to describe the protocols for second-generation digital cellular networks used by mobile devices such as mobile phones and tablets. It was first deployed in Finland.

- The United States allowed choice—GSM or CDMA. Code-division multiple access (CDMA) is a channel access method used by various radio communication technologies and is an example of multiple access, where several transmitters can send information simultaneously over a single communication channel. This allows several users to share a band of frequencies. Verizon, one of the largest telecom companies, chose CDMA, partially because Qualcomm—an American company—invented the hardware.

- Deregulation (the Telecommunications Act of 1996) led to further fragmentation of the telecom industry in the United States. According to the Federal Communications Commission (FCC), the goal of the law was to "let anyone enter any communications business—to let any communications business compete in any market against any other." The legislation's primary goal was deregulation of the converging broadcasting and telecommunications markets.

- This led to the rise of competing telecoms and standards.

- This led to spin-off of Bell Labs from AT&T, named Lucent. A $3B IPO, it was originally seen as a huge success.

Multiple standards meant slow development and market difficulties:

- In 2006, Lucent was sold to Alcatel.

- In 2010, Nokia bought Motorola.

- In 2016, Nokia bought Alcatel.

This leaves the United States without a major mobile hardware manufacturer. CISCO was still providing wired infrastructure, but mostly in the commercial markets.

Without a major company, the U.S. market was forced to work with Samsung, Nokia, and Ericsson, thus allowing these telecompanies to define development. On top of all of those hurdles, the United States chose millimeter wave spectrum (mmWave), which is the band between 30 GHz and 300 GHz. Wedged between microwave and infrared waves, this spectrum can be used for high-speed wireless communications. This was another GSM versus CDMA mistake, but one with far greater ramifications:

- It had major interoperability problems.

- There was less reach and penetration.

- It was much more costly to acquire, upgrade, and maintain physical assets such as property, plants, buildings, technology, and equipment.

To deliver 5G to 72% of the U.S. population requires 13 million base stations and $400 billion USD in funding. However, at the time of this writing, Verizon, AT&T, Sprint, and T-Mobile have a combined debt of $360 billion, thus massively limiting their capital expenditure investments.

The Implications of a Country's 5G Dominance

There's a financial gain for a country to dominate 5G. As we've seen with 4G, whichever country leads in the development and deployment of the latest technology sees more economic growth from that technology. And that translates into not just technological and economic power but into geopolitical power as well.

Let's look at China as an example. Here are the numbers:

- Three major telecoms are now piloting 5G in more than 12 cities. That's a combined population of 167 million and that many commercial licenses granted.

- China is far ahead in global patents: 30% compared to 13% for the United States. As of early February 2021, the numbers are dynamic and keep changing by the day.

- 5G is part of China's 2025 plan. Think of this as a country's vision board followed by an implementation strategy. China's plan set specific targets by 2025. China aimed to achieve 70% self-sufficiency in high-tech industries, and by 2049—the hundredth anniversary of the People's Republic of China—it seeks a dominant position in global markets.

- By 2025, China will have 460 million 5G connections, accounting for 28% of total Internet connections in the country.

- China will spend between $130 and $220B USD in 5G infrastructure between 2020 and 2025.

- China is home to Huawei and ZTE, two of the largest companies dominating the market with the best and cheapest 5G hardware.

Allies of the United States are not bending to U.S. diplomatic demands of cutting Chinese manufacturers out of their networks, partly because of these factors:

- The Chinese options are already embedded, cheaper, and better.

- There is no reasonable alternative!

- Nokia and Ericsson cost two to three times as much.

- The UK, Germany, Italy, and France all continue to allow Huawei in their networks.

- Southeast Asia is also heavily reliant on Chinese infrastructure and technology. The belt roads mean export throughout Central Asia, the Middle East, and Africa. For those who may not know, the Belt and Road Initiative is a global infrastructure development strategy adopted by the Chinese government in 2013 to invest in developing roads and other infrastructure in nearly 70 countries. This is another strategy by the Chinese government to get a large portion of the world population to rely on their infrastructure.

Last but not least: hundreds of billions of dollars, regulations, standards, military, and intelligence are at stake—and that's a lot.

Thus, though unrealistic, there is a need for some form of a universal body governing the development and deployment of 5G, so that it's not fully dominated by one state power. Otherwise, it's going to be a major source of conflict among the superpower countries.

Tensions began to rise between the United States and China's company Huawei in 2018. Huawei is a major global telecommunications supplier and phone manufacturer, but it remains a pariah in countries like the United States. The company has come under huge scrutiny in recent years, where lawmakers and intelligence officials have claimed that the telecommunications giant could be exploited by the Chinese government for espionage, presenting a potentially grave national security risks.

Huawei's phones are also virtually invisible in the United States, despite their huge popularity around the world. Rumors have it that all the scrutiny is due to Huawei's superiority in 5G technology, which is making the United States nervous as they watch their global leadership in technology wither away. Applying pressure, inconvenience, and frustration to Huawei is designed to dwarf its growth and global takeover.

The United States cites as the core issue it has with Huawei technology the company's coziness with the Chinese government. The U.S fears that Huawei's equipment could be used to spy on other countries and companies. It's the reason why, in 2012, the United States banned companies from using Huawei's networking equipment and why the company was added to the U.S. Department of Commerce's Bureau of Industry and Security Entity List in May 2019. This followed an executive order from then-President Trump that effectively banned Huawei from U.S. communications networks. A year later, Trump extended the order until 2021 (Keane, 2021). The United States is not alone in this pressure campaign; countries like the UK and Sweden have banned the use of its equipment in their 5G networks.

Clearly, as you can see, there is a lot going on at an individual level, at the company level, and at nation-state level. However, the doozy of them all is the underlying negative externalities of 5G technology on humanity and our planet.

THE UNINTENDED OR WILLFULLY IGNORED NEGATIVE CONSEQUENCES OF 5G

There's a lot of confusion about the negative impact of 5G on human health and the environment. The reality is that since this is a new technology, the full effect is yet to be known. However, the full deployment of 5G is bound to have a disruptive impact on ecosystems. 5G will offer unprecedented speed and bandwidth, but just like any other technology we have talked about in this book, there will be many unintended consequences. Let's look at a few examples.

5G Technologies Leading to Consumption Increases

The wasteful nature of manufacturing and maintenance of individual devices and the devices used to deliver 5G connections could become a major contributor to climate change. The promise of 5G technology to expand the number of devices might be the most troubling aspect of the new technology. Cell phones, computers, and other everyday devices are manufactured and later dumped. This will put dramatic stress on the environment.

The Fear of a Subdivided Internet

As nation-states (and their native companies) continue the battle in creating unique incompatible 5G hardware and software, there is a likelihood of having two competing Internets, stopping global cooperation and shared progress.

On the consumer side, there's the annoyance of having to carry both a CDMA and a GSM phone. If you are a traveler like me, this is really an inconvenience.

Increased Energy Usage of the 5G Network

The whole aim of the new 5G network is to allow for more devices to be used by consumers at faster rates than ever before. Because of this, there will certainly be a global increase in energy usage, which is one of the main contributors to climate change. An increase in energy usage would cause climate change to increase drastically as well.

The Impact of 5G on Ecosystems

There is some evidence that the new devices and technologies associated with 5G will be harmful to delicate ecosystems. The main component of the 5G network that will affect the Earth's ecosystems are the millimeter waves.

More than 240 scientists who have published peer-reviewed research on the biologic and health effects of nonionizing electromagnetic fields (EMF) signed the International EMF Scientist Appeal, which calls for stronger exposure limits. The appeal makes the following assertions: "Numerous recent scientific publications have shown that EMF affects living organisms. . . effects include increased cancer risk, cellular stress, increase in harmful free radicals, genetic damages, structural and functional changes of the reproductive system, learning and memory deficits, neurological disorders, and negative impacts on general well-being in humans. Damage goes well beyond the human race, as there is growing evidence of harmful effects to both plant and animal life" (Moskowitz, 2019).

The impact that the cell towers have on birds and bees is important to understand, and we have not done much study on it. There will be an impact on all ecosystems of the Earth because they are interconnected. If one component of an ecosystem is disrupted, the whole system will be affected. Cell tower disturbances among birds would only increase, because with 5G a larger number of small radio-tower-like devices would be necessary to ensure high-quality connection for users. Having a larger number of high concentrations of these millimeter waves in the form of small cells would cause a wider exposure to bees and birds, and possibly other species that are also important to our environment.

The 5G technology employs millimeter waves in addition to microwaves that have been in use for older cellular technologies, 2G through 4G. Given the limited reach, 5G will require cell antennas every 100 to 200 meters, exposing many people to millimeter wave radiation. 5G also employs new technologies (e.g., active antennas capable of beam forming; phased arrays; and massive multiple inputs and outputs, known as MIMO), which pose unique challenges for measuring exposures with its diversity and complexity of wireless onboard systems and the large electrical size of the test (Walkenhorst, Pelland, Leifert, and Berbeci, 2020).

Scientific American says, "Millimeter waves are mostly absorbed within a few millimeters of human skin and in the surface layers of the cornea. Short-term exposure can have adverse physiological effects in the peripheral nervous system, the immune system and the cardiovascular system. Research has suggested that long-term exposure may pose health risks to the skin (e.g. melanoma), the eyes (e.g. ocular melanoma), and the testes (e.g. sterility)" (Moskowitz, 2019). Since 5G is a new technology, there is no research on health effects, so we are all "flying blind."

Network Security Concerns

Distributed Denial of Service (DDoS) attacks are when so many requests are artificially generated and sent to a website that it prevents the website from functioning correctly. 5G enables faster connections among many devices, which potentially leads to more attacks. Devices connected to 5G can generate traffic at a higher rate and make more significant DDoS attacks, not only in frequency but also in how far and fast those attacks could spread (Bacon, 2019).

A *network backdoor* refers to any method by which authorized and unauthorized users are able to get around normal security measures and gain high-level user access (aka root access) on a computer system, network, or software application. The European Commission and European Agency for Cybersecurity published a report highlighting that there is a grave concern when a single company is the builder of the *network backdoors*. The report outlined concern that implementing the 5G network with foreign technology can be susceptible to backdoors. It is also a national intelligence threat: the report states that a Huawei 5G network, for example, would be a counterintelligence nightmare. These are the same concerns at the center of the U.S. government and the Huawei technology (Duckett, 2019).

Interference

The radio frequencies used by the 5G technology come close to the frequency used in weather forecasting. A study at Rutgers University found that 5G frequencies could lead to less accurate weather forecasting because of this. Unintended frequencies from a 5G transmitter could leak into an adjacent frequency used by weather sensors. The study uses modeling to find that leakage power when above a certain point (–15 to –20 decibel watts) does affect the accuracy of forecasting precipitation. The World Meteorological Organization and similar organizations have voiced warnings about such interferences and advocated for more restriction or solutions (Rutgers University, 2020).

How to Mitigate the UCOTs of 5G

Mobile speeds are soon to reach ten times today's performance. There is minimal to no attention being paid to the many possible negative effects. As I have pointed out so far, the benefits are great, but the dangers are real. Let's look at a few efforts toward mitigating the UCOTs of 5G.

Action Against Security Concerns

Many nations—including the United States, Australia, and the UK—have taken action to restrict the use of Chinese equipment for security. The UK Parliament's Defense Committee has also been looking into the connection between Huawei and the Chinese state, and has concluded there is clear evidence of collusion, thus their recommendation of removal of Huawei equipment from the 5G network. In my opinion, this is a Band-Aid solution, because it does not solve the underlying cause, which is that both Europe and the Americas are behind on the development of the technology. Banning one company does not solve this issue.

Action Against Environmental Concerns

Efficient cooling: The 5G networks need to be cooled (similar to most laptops, which have a fan). New technologies have been implemented to address this, and 5G implementation is, as a whole, more energy efficient. Nokia, for example, has been the first to use liquid cooling in their 5G technology (particularly the base station), which they claim reduces energy consumption by 30% and CO_2 emission by 80% (Nokia, 2021).

5G network infrastructure sharing: In countries where there are competing mobile operators, infrastructure sharing could reduce the environmental impact of building redundant infrastructure. Although it is still a rarity, China's competing mobile operators China Telecom and China Unicom have reached an agreement to build out and share base stations. Cost savings is the largest motivator, but there are also environmental benefits in the implementation phase (McKinsey Global Institute, 2018).

Action on Health Concerns

5G waves still use radio wavelengths, but at a higher energy, meaning that each cycle of the wave is closer together. These millimeter waves are like other portions of the non-ionizing electromagnetic spectrum, such as visible light and traditional broadcast frequencies. Non-ionizing radiation is any type of radiation that does not carry enough energy per quantum to completely remove an electron from an atom or molecule.

Research about the health effects of long-term exposure to radio wave frequencies, such as that done by the IEEE's International Committee on Electromagnetic Safety, concludes that there are no adverse health effects. Additionally, FCC and their counterpart organizations in other countries set limits on the energy emitted in these waves to limit any type of adverse health effects (Hern, 2020).

THE RESET ON 5G

It is important that big mobile companies around the world consider the impact that 5G will have on humanity and our planet before pushing to have it widely implemented. The companies pushing for the expansion of 5G may stand to make short-term economic gains, but at the expense of our global health. (If you doubt the power of capitalism, refer to Chapter 1.)

While the new network will undoubtedly benefit consumers greatly, looking at 5G's long-term human and environmental impacts is also very important. We need to clearly understand, articulate, and mitigate those risks.

The technology needed to power the new 5G network will inevitably change how mobile devices are used, as well as what capabilities they have. This technological advancement will also change the way technology and the environment interacts. While it is unrealistic to call for an end to 5G, companies, governments, and consumers should be proactive and understand the impact that this new technology will have on humanity and our planet.

Health experts and 5G developers should carry out environmental and human impact assessments that fully estimate the impact that the new technology will have before rushing to implement it widely. This process will help identify, mitigate, and prevent harm, which is imperative to ensuring that humanity and the planet are sustainable and sound in the future.

As a society, if we are able to invest hundreds of billions of dollars deploying 5G—a cellular technology that requires the installation of 800,000 or more new cell antenna sites in the United States close to where we live, work, and play—we should be able to invest the same amount to fund the research needed to understand biologically based exposure limits that protect the health and safety of humanity and of our planet.

REFERENCES

Bacon, Madelyn. (2019). "DDoS attacks among top 5G security concerns." https://searchsecurity.techtarget.com/feature/DDoS-attacks-among-top-5G-security-concerns

Duckett, Chris. (2019). "Europe warns 5G will increase attack paths for state actors." https://www.zdnet.com/article/europe-warns-5g-will-increase-attack-paths-for-state-actors/

Grijpink, Ferry, Alexandre Ménard, Halldor Sigurdsson, and Nemanja Vucevic. (2018). "Network sharing and 5G: A turning point for lone riders." https://www.mckinsey.com/industries/technology-media-and-telecommunications/our-insights/network-sharing-and-5g-a-turning-point-for-lone-riders

Hern, Alex. (2020). "5G confirmed safe by radiation watchdog." https://www.theguardian.com/technology/2020/mar/12/5g-safe-radiation-watchdog-health

Katibeh, Mo. (2019). "Lights, Camera, 5G: Transforming the Entertainment Industry with 5G." https://www.forbes.com/sites/forbestechcouncil/2019/11/27/lights-camera-5g-transforming-the-entertainment-industry-with-5g/?sh=2c370c07467e

Keane, Sean. (2021). "Huawei ban timeline: Chinese company will charge royalties for its 5G tech." https://www.cnet.com/news/huawei-ban-full-timeline-us-sanctions-china-5g-royalties/

McKinsey Global Institute. (2018). "Smart cities: Digital solutions for a more livable future." https://www.mckinsey.com/business-functions/operations/our-insights/smart-cities-digital-solutions-for-a-more-livable-future#

Moskowitz, Joel M. (2019). "We Have No Reason to Believe 5G Is Safe." https://blogs.scientificamerican.com/observations/we-have-no-reason-to-believe-5g-is-safe/

Nokia. (2021). "Nokia and Elisa see sustainability leap in world-first 5G liquid cooling deployment." https://www.nokia.com/about-us/news/releases/2020/06/03/nokia-and-elisa-see-sustainability-leap-in-world-first-5g-liquid-cooling-deployment/

Rutgers University. (2020). "5G wireless may lead to inaccurate weather forecasts." https://www.sciencedaily.com/releases/2020/09/200924082706.htm

Walkenhorst, B. T., P. Pelland, T. Leifert, and M. Berbeci. (2020). "A Survey of MIMO OTA Test Methodologies for Automotive Applications," 2020 IEEE International Symposium on Antennas and Propagation and North American Radio Science Meeting, Montreal, QC, Canada, 2020, pp. 1793-1794, doi: 10.1109/IEEECONF35879.2020.9330254.

Ye, Yvaine. (2019). "Doctors in China are using 5G internet to do surgery from far away." https://www.newscientist.com/article/2198922-doctors-in-china-are-using-5g-internet-to-do-surgery-from-far-away/

CHAPTER 9

Truth In the Era of Willful Ignorance: Is Trust Over?

In his 2007 book, *The Cult of the Amateur*, Silicon Valley entrepreneur Andrew Keen warned that the Internet not only had democratized information beyond people's wildest imaginings but also was replacing genuine knowledge with "the wisdom of the crowd," thus dangerously blurring the lines between fact and opinion, informed argument and blustering speculation (Kakutani, 2018).

From post-modernism to filter bubbles, "truth decay" has been spreading for decades. How can we stop alternative facts from bringing society down with them? Well, we need to get back to basics, as well as to understand the incentive structures that got us here.

Truth is the property of being in accord with fact or reality. In everyday language, truth is typically ascribed to things that aim to represent reality or otherwise correspond to it, such as propositions and declarative sentences. Truth is usually held to be the opposite of falsehood.

Truth is the metaphysics and the philosophy of language, the property of sentences, assertions, beliefs, thoughts, or propositions that are said, in accordance with reality.

The opposite of truth is falsehood or lie or mistruth or misinformation. Misinformation can also often mean disinformation, fake news, a rumor, urban legend, conspiracy theories, spam, and trolls.

In recent years, the world has been facing an unprecedented assault on truth. Add exponential technology to the mix, and you have an infodemic. Houston, we have a truth problem!

Fake news. Misinformation on social media platforms like Facebook and Twitter. Conspiracy theories concerning democracies, vaccines, and climate change. Alternative facts from politicians and people of high influence. The truth is being attacked.

There is a basic assumption that people evaluate information coming at them and arrive at reasoned conclusions or judgments. But this system depends on an agreement about the state of the world. People should be able to agree about what is true. As Daniel Moynihan once famously said, "Everyone is entitled to his own opinion, but not his own facts." (Roberts, 2018). But now we can't seem to agree on the facts. The problem isn't your fault or my fault, really. We are being peddled false information by many people. The worst part is that some people come to believe the falsehoods and then spread the misinformation. Everyone is susceptible to misleading information, which can lead people to create false personal memories and to believe false things about the state of the world.

Words matter. Words can heal, words can hurt, and words can even kill. The foundation of our society and its success is grounded in our ability to tell the truth and stay in reality.

THEORIES ON TRUTH

Truth has existed since the beginning of time. It has been one of the central and largest subjects in philosophy for thousands of years. However, it's the recording of the events, the analysis and the theories that surround truth, that are of continuous interest. Many theories about the nature of truth have emerged over time. Here are the most important ones:

- *The correspondence theory of truth* states that the truth or falsity of a statement is determined only by how it relates to the world and whether it accurately describes that world. For example, "A woman is riding a bicycle" is true if, and only if, there is in the world a woman and a bicycle and the woman is related to the bicycle by virtue of riding it.

- *The semantic theory of truth* was developed by Alfred Tarski in the 1930s. This theory is a philosophy of language that holds that truth is a property of sentences. "The sky is blue" is true if and only if the sky is blue. However, there are times when semantics come into play. For example, "destination" and "last stop" can technically mean the same thing, but students of semantics can analyze their subtle shades of meaning.

- *The deflationary theory of truth* is one of a family of theories that all have in common the claim that assertions of predicate truth of a statement do not attribute a property called "truth" to such a statement. For example, to say that "snow is white" is true, or that it is true that snow is white, is equivalent to saying simply that snow is white, and this, according to the deflationary theory, is all that can be said significantly about the truth of "snow is white."

- *The coherence theory of truth* regards truth as coherence within some specified set of sentences, propositions, or beliefs. For example, it is true that "water boils at 100°C." However, you have to ask under what conditions it is true. It may be true of water at sea level but not at high altitudes. When coherence theorists say that every statement is only partly true, they usually seem to mean that every statement is only part of the truth, since nothing but the whole system of statements can give the whole of the truth.

- *The pragmatic theory of truth* has the effect of shifting attention away from what makes a statement true and toward what people mean or do in describing a statement as true. For example, if humans commonly perceive the ocean as beautiful, then the ocean is beautiful.

Again, these are just a few of the many theories of truth. Whichever theory you examine or advance to settle the principal issue, there are a number of additional issues to be addressed: Can claims about the future be true now? Or in this nuanced world, can we build technologies and algorithm for finding truth—some recipe or procedure for deciding, for any claim in the system of, say, arithmetic, whether the claim is true?

Furthermore, the opposite of truth are lies and falsehoods. These too have been around for as long as truth has existed. With all these theories on how to deduce an event as true, there are as many ways that humans have figured out how to bend or break these theories to their advantage. In the advent of exponential technology and mass media, we are living in the *era of willful ignorance*. People reject truth, fact, and reason and increasingly become comfortable with lies and falsehoods. Let's dive into the question of why this happens.

Why Do People Tell Falsehoods?

There are many incentives for people to tell untruths:

- To obtain a reward not otherwise readily obtainable. For example, someone might falsely claim work experience during a job interview to increase chances of being hired. Or a politician might lie about their accomplishments so they can be reelected.

- To gain a reward like money and other material things or immaterial things like power or fame.

- To avoid being punished. Telling lies and getting caught can have negative consequences.

- To protect another person from being punished. This occurs between coworkers, friends, family, and even between strangers!

- To protect oneself from the threat of physical harm. This is different from being punished; the threat of harm in this case is not for a misdeed. For example, a hostage victim might lie to avoid being tortured.

- To win the admiration of others. Telling lies to increase your popularity can range from "little white lies" to embellishing a story to create an entirely new (fabricated) persona.

- To get out of an awkward social situation, such as lying to get out of a rather awkward date, or ending a telephone conversation by saying there is someone at the door.

- To avoid embarrassment. An example is the child who claims the wet bed resulted from water spilling, not from wetting her pants.

- To maintain privacy without notifying others of that intention. For example, a celebrity might use a pseudonym to evade people knowing their real names, or a couple might claim to have eloped because the cost of a wedding was beyond their means when, in reality, they were avoiding the obligation to invite their families.

- To exercise power over others by controlling the information the target receives. This has famously been employed by Hitler, Trump, and other authoritarian/Orwellian leaders. This is arguably the most dangerous motive for telling lies.

As you can see, there are many reasons and motivations for why people lie. The negative consequences of any lie vary depending on the power and the motive of the person telling the lie.

Whether it's election integrity issues, vaccination conspiracies, or rumors, the spread of disinformation online continues to undermine not only democracies, but also the very foundations of global civil society.

WHY POLITICAL LIES ARE ESPECIALLY DAMAGING

In the last 10 years, there has been a lot of local and international political assault on truth by leaders in democracies and dictatorships alike, at a level and scale never seen before. Most of the falsehoods have been aided by exponential technologies that seem to reward snark and outrage more than logic and civility. This phenomenon has created a generation that has abandoned reality and only accepts something to be true if it confirms their existing beliefs and biases (called *confirmation bias*)—self-fulfilling prophecies. So how did we get here?

Politicians and other people with self-interests tend to sow discord on the word "truth" by bending it or outright breaking it and telling falsehoods. Many of the lies are trivial, often bizarrely so, like a politician repeatedly claiming to have received an award that doesn't even exist, or being on the cover of a magazine that the publisher confirms never existed. However, some falsehoods and misinformation and other mass content manipulation tactics have serious real-world consequences.

The presidential elections in the United States and Brexit in the UK are two famous cases dealing with harmful falsehoods and with massive real-world implications. Even worse, the real big danger is the millions of citizens who take these leaders at their word and spread it as if it were true.

According to the *Washington Post*, former U.S. president Donald J. Trump was one of the most powerful people in the world whose words and truth telling (or lack thereof) were carefully tracked, documented, and counted. The paper pointed out in an article published on January 24, 2021, that he overstated the "carnage" he was inheriting, then later exaggerated his "massive" crowd and claimed, despite clear evidence to the contrary, that it had not rained during his address. Over time, Trump unleashed his falsehoods with increasing frequency and ferocity, scores of them in a single campaign speech or tweetstorm.

The final tally of Trump's presidency was 30,573 false or misleading claims, with nearly half coming in his final year (Kessler, 2021).

This was a very specific strategy Trump mastered with the intent of eroding the truth. And it's not just the discernible falsehoods. He also attacked the media, experts, and anyone who presented facts. He strategically attacked truth itself. His administration discredited the media by naming them "fake news," flooding the news cycle with disinformation and distractions on Twitter, until his account was suspended on January 8, 2021 (Conger and Isaac, 2021). His administration restricted White House access for reporters he disagreed with and created a dynamic whereby if the media wasn't to be trusted, then President Trump would be, by definition, the sole arbiter of truth. The political polarization and echo chambers undermined trusted institutions and truth itself.

Trump was not alone in this strategy. The assault on truth is not confined only to America. Around the world, waves of populism and fundamentalism are elevating appeals to fear and anger over reasoned debate, eroding democratic institutions and replacing expertise with the "wisdom" of the crowd. This tactic continues to be used around the world in what feels like a playbook in which democratically elected populist leaders are pulling their countries toward authoritarian regimes. Consider these examples:

- In India, Prime Minister Narendra Modi exploited religion to reforge the world's largest democracy in the mold of a Hindu nationalist ideology. "He used Hindutva ideology to restyle the country as one with only the trappings of democracy" (Ibrahim, 2020).

- In Brazil, President Jair Bolsonaro used brutal and oppressive policies to weaponize fear (Jarrett, 2019).

- In Hungary, a media consortium controlled by Prime Minister Viktor Orban's associates and political allies controls the news and is recasting the historical narrative of the country (Kingsley, 2018).

The list goes on and on. Italy, Poland, Colombia, the Philippines, and Egypt are all places where leaders seem to be systematically undercutting the democracies that elected them by simply breaking the truth.

THE UNINTENDED OR WILLFULLY IGNORED NEGATIVE CONSEQUENCES OF EXPONENTIAL TECHNOLOGY ON TRUTH

The spread of selective truths, untruths, falsehoods, and misinformation has created a new world disorder. Our willingness to knowingly or unknowingly share content without thinking critically about it has been exploited by the powers that be and has trapped us in a vortex. Technology has played a huge role in facilitating this dangerous precedent. We've been getting misinformation from so many corners—uncles, friends, and from a president or prime minister and other elected officials. People we trust are supposed to be respectable and trustworthy. Sometimes it's not people at all; we also get information from computer bots. It's becoming increasingly difficult to tell the difference. Never in history have we had such a fast technology that facilitates the spread of so much misinformation, which hits us like an avalanche from so many corners all at one time.

The severity of the negative impact of any falsehood depends on the number of the people it affects as well as the power of the person or entity that instigates and spreads that lie. There are many types of falsehoods and untruths. Let's look at a few examples and the effects and dangers of misinformation.

Persona Copycat Falsehoods

Persona copycats, also known as *deepfakes*, are a form of deceptive image about a person's reality. They are fake videos or audio recordings that look and sound just like the real person. Some of the usage is benignly used for humor, but in other forms it can be dangerous. Deepfakes have garnered widespread attention for their uses in celebrity pornographic videos, revenge porn, fake news, hoaxes, and financial fraud. Yes, we need to understand deepfakes because they are a major player in eroding truth.

Soon, it's going to be increasingly difficult to know whether what you are looking at is real or is a doctored version. This has many real-world consequences.

Until recently, when children were asked what they want to be when they grow up, common answers were teacher, engineer, doctor, nurse, fire-fighter, or pilot. Today, that answer is likely to be "social media influencer."

An *influencer* is simply someone who has influence over others' buying decisions. In other words, it's someone who has authority over and/or is trusted by a certain group of people. In the social media world, an influencer is someone who has lots of followers, from hundreds of thousands to millions of people.

In the past, becoming an influencer was very hard. You had to be a charismatic politician like former president Barack Obama, who legitimately put in the work of grassroots organizing, which along with his policy decisions, led to people admiring and following him. Or you had to be someone whose "influence" is primarily grounded in talent, such as a famous musician like singer Arianna Grande selling out arenas for concerts, or an athlete like soccer star Cristiano Ronaldo filling stadiums with people who come to see him play.

In today's world, talent does not seem to be a requirement. One can "doctor" influence. And skip being a doctor altogether. Fake personas and lifestyles are becoming an epidemic in eroding the truth. These profiles create an illusion of living large, luxurious lives in order to acquire the admiration of others. This strategy works sometimes, and you get real people to fall for the ruse. But when that fails you can always fake the extent of your influence by paying for computer bots to create the illusion that you have millions of followers in a bizarre influencer world where followers, likes, and comments function as a cultural currency.

Another example is the *decentralized persona copycat*. The latest example of a persona copycat is the new blockchain social platform called BitClout, which generates social tokens that represent actual people. In most sovereign states, it is well established that a person or company cannot knowingly use another's name, voice, signature, photograph, or likeness in any manner for purpose of selling or soliciting purchases. However, prominent users of Crypto Twitter have suddenly discovered they have another profile on BitClout, where others are buying and selling tokens representing their identities, often without their consent.

BitClout's creator says it's a new way to monetize a following. The platform appears to use profiles pulled from Twitter, regardless of whether the Twitter user has actually signed up to BitClout. Defending the platform, BitClout's lead creator, who goes by "Diamondhands," told CoinDesk in a phone call, "The core insight behind BitClout is that if you can mix speculation and content together, you can not only get a 10x product that creates innovative ways for creators to monetize, but you also get a new business model that's not ad-driven anymore" (Dale, 2021).

Falsehoods Based on Real-World Events

Some falsehoods can be total lies, fabrications that never happened. But in recent years we've seen many falsehoods and conspiracies that have roots in things that actually happened. One example is how big tobacco lied about cancer.

Tobacco companies "falsely marketed and promoted low-tar and light cigarettes as less harmful" (Truth Initiative, 2021) than regular cigarettes to keep people smoking and sustain revenues. Furthermore, tobacco companies concealed evidence and publicly denied that nicotine is addictive. They went as far as to acknowledge internally that second-hand smoke is hazardous to nonsmokers, yet still gave false and misleading public statements denying the fact. Research has proven that there is no safe cigarette, and all cigarettes cause cancer, lung disease, heart attacks, and premature death. People died, lots of them (Truth Initiative, 2021)! Granted, most of this happened before social media really took off, but it's certainly one of the many examples that laid the groundwork for what has now transpired in the Internet age.

Toxic Falsehoods Dangerous to Oneself

One good example of toxic falsehoods is *science denialism*. Since we are living through a pandemic as of this writing, let's take the example of falsehoods surrounding the COVID-19 virus. Public health officials, fact checkers, and doctors tried to quash hundreds of rumors in myriad ways.

But misinformation around the pandemic has endured as much as the virus itself. A scary number of people think that masks do not protect you from the virus. Other people think the virus is no worse than the flu. Others think the whole thing is a hoax and the vaccines are merely a ploy by Bill Gates and the government to get chips into all of us. Let's break down virus-related issues a bit to see how we got here:

- *Masks do not protect from the virus.* Mixed messaging early on caused some confusion. The U.S. government and health officials initially told Americans they did not need masks, at a time when there was a shortage of N95 masks for health workers and there was concern that others would buy up the limited supply. Experts later reversed course, urging the public to wear cloth masks and face coverings outside. The early messaging gave people "a little more room to take up these narratives" against wearing masks, explained Stephanie Edgerly, a communications professor at Northwestern University (Seitz and Dupuy, 2020).

- *COVID-19 is similar to the flu.* Not true, for the virus has proved to be far deadlier. Early similarities between the symptoms of COVID-19 and influenza led many to speculate that there was not much difference between the two illnesses. Social media posts and videos viewed thousands of times online also claim that COVID-19 is no deadlier than the flu. Trump tweeted a faulty comparison between the flu and COVID-19 in March and October of 2020, as states implemented stay-at-home orders. COVID19 has been blamed for nearly 600,000 American deaths and has killed roughly 3.5 million worldwide as of this writing. COVID-19 symptoms can be far more serious and persist for many months. Health experts have also uncovered a range of bizarre coronavirus symptoms, from brain fog to swollen toes (healthline. com, 2021).

- *The virus is man-made or is a result of a "lab leak."* Social media users and fringe websites weaved together a conspiracy theory that the virus was leaked—either accidentally or intentionally— from a lab in Wuhan, China, before the World Health Organization declared COVID-19 a pandemic in March 2020. The falsehood was espoused by elected officials, including former

U.S. President Trump, which gave it more room to gain ground. Although the origins of the virus are not yet fully substantiated, they are likely to be far less scandalous. It likely originated in nature. Bats are thought to be the original or intermediary hosts for several viruses that have triggered recent epidemics, including COVID-19. U.S. intelligence agencies also concluded the virus is not man-made. Yet the conspiracy theory continues to travel online. This misconception had a resurgence when a Chinese virologist repeated the claim on Fox News that the Chinese government intentionally manufactured and released the COVID-19 virus that led to mass shutdowns and deaths across the world (Dorman, 2020).

- *The virus is a ploy to force global vaccinations.* Anti-vaccine supporters have been pushing this conspiracy theory since the invention of the vaccines, when some falsely claimed online that the virus had been patented by pharmaceutical companies as a scheme to cash in on the illness. Some have targeted billionaire and vaccine advocate Bill Gates, claiming he was part of a global plan around COVID-19 to microchip billions of people through mass vaccinations. Gates has not threatened to microchip anyone. Instead, he suggested creating a database of people who have been inoculated against the virus (Goodman and Carmichael, 2020).

Falsehoods Detached from or Escaping Reality

There are many falsehoods that are detached from or *escape reality*, also known as conspiracy theories. The theories attempt to explain events as the result of the actions of small but powerful groups. Examples include Area 51, Pizzagate, and QAnon.

The Area 51 Conspiracy

Officially named the Nevada Test and Training Range at Groom Lake, this is a high-security open training range for the U.S. Air Force in southern Nevada, although the site is still very secretive. The public found out that Area 51 officially existed after Dr. Jeffrey T. Richelson, a senior fellow at the George Washington University National Security Archive, submitted a Freedom of Information Act Request in 2005 for information on the CIA's Lockheed U-2 plane reconnaissance program. Declassified information later revealed that the location is for the secret construction and testing of spy planes used to gather intelligence.

Area 51 became the subject of so many conspiracy theories because of the many rumors that alien secrets are held there. They claim a UFO crashed in Roswell, New Mexico, in 1947, which the Roswell Army Airfield later said was a weather balloon. The Air Force began investigating claims of UFO sightings in 1947, which later became known as Project Blue Book in 1952. By the time Project Blue Book ended in 1969, the Air Force had investigated over 12,000 claims. Meanwhile, people in the southern Nevada region continued to report UFO sightings, which in hindsight were probably sightings of the top-secret spy planes being constructed. Even so, imaginations have run wild ever since.

Area 51 has been shrouded in mystery for decades, so it only makes sense that the rumored alien secrets held within the remote desert site would get a reboot in the social media age. The Internet has been invaded by Area 51 memes inspired by a joke Facebook event to take over the secretive military site and find the supposed aliens kept inside. The event, called "Storm Area 51, They Can't Stop All of Us," was planned for September 20, 2020 and as many as 1.5 million people signed on (Aguilera, 2019).

The Pizzagate Conspiracy

Another falsehood detached from reality is "Pizzagate," a debunked conspiracy theory that went viral during the 2016 U.S. presidential election cycle. It has been extensively discredited by a wide range of organizations, including the Washington, DC, police (LaCapria, 2016).

In March 2016, the personal email account of John Podesta, Hillary Clinton's campaign manager, was hacked in a spear-phishing attack. WikiLeaks published his emails in November 2016. Proponents of the Pizzagate conspiracy theory falsely claimed the emails contained coded messages that connected several high-ranking Democratic Party officials and U.S. restaurants with an alleged human trafficking and child sex ring.

One of the establishments allegedly involved was the Comet Ping Pong pizzeria in Washington, DC. Members of the alt-right, conservative journalists, and others who had urged Clinton's prosecution over the emails, spread the conspiracy theory on social media outlets such as 4chan, 8chan, and Twitter.

In response, a man from North Carolina traveled to Comet Ping Pong to investigate the conspiracy and fired a rifle inside the restaurant to break the lock on a door to a storage room during his search. The restaurant owner and staff also received death threats from conspiracy theorists (Kang, 2016).

Pizzagate resurged in 2020, an election year, mainly due to QAnon. While it was initially spread by only the far-right, it has since been dispersed by children and teenagers on TikTok "who don't otherwise fit a right-wing conspiracy theorist mold" (Richter, 2020). The conspiracy theory has developed and become less partisan and political in nature, with less emphasis on Clinton and more on the alleged worldwide elite of child sex traffickers.

Pizzagate is generally considered a predecessor to the QAnon conspiracy theory.

The QAnon Conspiracy

QAnon, also known as "Q," is a disproven and discredited American far-right conspiracy theory alleging that a secret cabal of Satan-worshipping, cannibalistic pedophiles is running a global child sex-trafficking ring and plotted against former U.S. President Donald Trump while he was in office. QAnon commonly asserts that Trump has been planning a day of reckoning known as the "Storm," when thousands of members of the cabal will be arrested.

We saw this manifest itself in the January 6th attacks on the U.S. Capitol. QAnon supporters believed marching on the Capitol could trigger the Storm, and Trump's foes would be punished in mass executions (Porter, 2021). Even when their theories do not come to pass on the anticipated date, they move the goal post, and adjust the theory itself. After the January 6th failure, QAnon's most devoted fans believed bizarrely that Trump would be sworn in as the 19th president on March 4, 2021. Of course, that did not happen. The sad part is that they still believe it's all part of the plan.

In addition, QAnon supporters have accused many liberal Hollywood actors, Democratic politicians, and high-ranking government officials of being members of the cabal. They have also claimed that Trump feigned conspiracy with Russians to enlist Robert Mueller to join him in exposing the sex trafficking ring and preventing a coup d'état by Barack Obama, Hillary Clinton, and George Soros (Laviola, 2018).

Selective Facts, Confirmation Bias, and Echo Chambers

Echo chambers increase social and political polarization and extremism. The term is a metaphor based on an acoustic echo chamber, in which sounds reverberate in a hollow enclosure. Another emerging term for this echoing and homogenizing effect within social media communities on the Internet is *cultural tribalism*.

Fake information has made it harder for people to see the truth. This has led to people resorting to creating bubbles with folks they know, the ones who agree with them and they are comfortable being around. Sometimes they have to reimagine the definition of certain words or statements to make it conform to what they already believe.

A Pew Research Center study (Graham, 2019) found that those on the right and the left of the political spectrum have different ideas about the definition of "fake news." The study suggests that fake-news panic, rather than driving people to abandon ideological outlets and the fringe, may actually be accelerating the process of polarization. It's driving consumers to drop some outlets, to simply consume less information overall, and even to cut out social relationships.

Depending on your political leanings, it can be hard to find a news source that's not biased in some form. Algorithms are trained by an individual's consumption habits. The type of news you click on more often is essentially saying "give me more of that." If you don't click on a source, you are basically voting it, so algorithms will not show those types to you. It's becoming increasingly difficult to find content sources that strive to provide accurate, neutral coverage of major events, simply because even the curated network channels have to create content the viewers want to hear.

The flow of both information and misinformation on media platforms is a function of both human and technical factors. Human biases play an important role: Since we're more likely to react to content that taps into our existing grievances and beliefs, inflammatory tweets will generate quick engagement. It's only after that engagement happens that the technical side kicks in: If a tweet is retweeted, favorited, or replied to by enough of its first viewers, the newsfeed algorithm will show it to more users, at which point it will tap into the biases of those users too—prompting even more engagement, and so on. At its worst, this cycle can turn social media and other platforms into a kind of confirmation bias machine, one perfectly tailored for the spread of misinformation.

Misinformation Turned Deadly

The spread of misinformation can also be lethal. A percentage of the nearly 600,000 Americans and the roughly 3,000,000 people worldwide who died from the COVID-19 virus lost their lives as a result of misinformation. There's no way to know the exact numbers, common sense tells us that some of these deaths could have been avoided if the advice of health experts and science was properly followed. COVID-19 misinformation led to the death of many prominent people, including two heads of state in East Africa: Burundi's Pierre Nkurunziza in 2020 and Tanzania's John Magufuli in 2021. Both leaders drew criticism for their denial of and approach to the pandemic and eventually paid the ultimate price—their lives (Onyuloi, 2021).

President Trump suggested that people take the anti-malaria drug hydroxychloroquine to combat the effects of COVID-19. Even though Mr. Trump's own Food and Drug Administration cautioned against using the drug outside a hospital, due to potential heart problems, that did not stop some people from taking it, many of whom died. An Arizona man lost his life and his wife was in critical condition after they ingested chloroquine phosphate, an aquarium cleaning product similar to drugs named by President Trump as potential treatments for the coronavirus infection. The couple, in their 60s, experienced immediate distress after swallowing the drug, an additive used at aquariums to clean fish tanks, according to Banner Health Hospital in Phoenix (Beasley, 2020).

Falsehoods also led to the deadly insurrection at the Capitol building. The 2021 storming of the U.S. Capitol was a violent attack against the U.S. Congress. The riot was carried out by a mob of Donald Trump supporters in a failed attempt to overturn his defeat by Joe Biden in the November 2020 presidential election (McLaughlin, 2021). Five people died: four rioters and one police officer. Experts believe that the January 6 Capitol siege could have been much deadlier if lawmakers hadn't been whisked away to secure rooms.

How to Mitigate the UCOTs of Falsehoods

There are several ways to deal with falsehoods and disinformation that can be undertaken by various organizations. These solutions combat fake news and disinformation without endangering freedom of expression and investigative journalism.

The Role of the Government

Avoid censoring content and make online platforms liable for misinformation. Avoid crackdowns on the news media's ability to cover the news. Encourage independent, professional journalism. The general public needs reporters who help them make sense of complicated developments and deal with the ever-changing nature of social, economic, and political events. Policy makers should put regulations in place to manage information flow as well as real consequences and punishments for those who knowingly spread misinformation.

As concerns about fake news, hoaxes, and misinformation continue to heighten around the world, some governments are taking action, ranging from anti-fake news laws in Malaysia to media literacy initiatives in Denmark; the platform Poynter is keeping track of them in more than 80 countries. Actions include laws, bills, a task force, media literacy amendments, committees, and media regulation (Funke and Flamini, 2021).

The Role of Tech Companies

Invest in technology to find fake news and identify it for users through algorithms and crowdsourcing. There are innovations in fake news and hoax detection that are useful to media platforms. Don't profit off fake news manufacturers, and make it hard to monetize hoaxes. Strengthen online accountability through stronger real-persona policies and enforcement against fake accounts and bots.

Fighting technology with technology is also an option. Websites have been put in place to help people to discern fact from fiction. For example, sites like Snopes and FactCheck.org have a mission to fact-check the media, especially memes, political speeches, and stories going viral on the Internet. In Ukraine, an organization known as StopFake relies upon "peer-to-peer counter propaganda" to dispel false stories.

The Role of Educational Systems

Educate young people about this growing epidemic. Create programs to educate folks trapped in the conspiracy theories and misinformation vortex. Work with people who left the cult and create "truth advocates" from people the victim may trust better.

The Role of the News Industry

Focus on high-quality journalism that builds trust and attracts greater audiences. Call out fake news and disinformation without legitimizing it. Rely on in-house professionals and well-respected fact-checkers.

The Role of Individuals

Have a diversity of people, news sources, and perspectives you follow. Learn how to judge news sites, and when in doubt use fact-checking sites before sharing so you don't disseminate inaccurate information.

THE RESET ON TECHNOLOGY AND TRUTH

As noted, fake news, untruths, and misinformation have become a major problem of the modern, connected world.

Who is being affected by falsehoods depends on the issue and the context. The impact of a falsehood depends on the power of the originator and their motivation for sharing it. That's why the effect of any lie varies widely. But it's pretty safe to say all of humanity is now affected. Mistruths about climate change, antivaccination in the middle of a pandemic, or lies about marginalized groups—just these three broad topics alone affect the entirety of the human population. If society becomes so fake that the truth is what bothers people, well, it goes without saying that we need a giant reset.

Many social and cultural factors have shaped the war on truth. The culture of convenience, distrust in authority, cultural inertia, and economic and political incentives/drivers all play a role in eroding the truth.

The misinformation epidemic on a global scale is not an easy one to solve. The assisters and resistors in solving this challenge include organized conspiracy rings, state actors/governments, non-state actors such as corporations, and lone individuals and the general public. The important questions we need to ask ourselves as a society are:

- For people who already "drank the Kool-Aid," how might we make it sexy for them to update/refine/open their minds when presented with facts?

- How might we help people confirm or reject the information they read?

- How might we inspire trust, reconciliation, and action?

- How might we change the incentives structures on truth such as power, influence, money, and politics?

The problem is too big, multifaceted, complex, and global to have simple answers. However, we must do something about this epidemic.

Because of the lack of Internet gatekeepers due to the decentralized nature and structure of the Internet, writers can easily publish content without being required to subject it to peer review, prove their qualifications, or provide backup documentation. Whereas a book found in a library generally has been reviewed and edited by a second person, Internet sources cannot be assumed to be vetted by anyone other than their authors. They may be produced and posted as soon as the writing is finished. In addition, the presence of trolls and bots used to spread willful misinformation needs to be addressed on the social media platforms.

When you consider the areas where truth is under attack, remember that you have a voice and a calling to stand for truth and to be a light in a dark world. Protecting the truth is critical for democracies around the world, and for making personal decisions (such as vaccinating your children). When the truth is under attack, each of us must engage in careful critical evaluation of news. But our news sources, both traditional and social media platforms, also have some ethical obligations to defend the truth (Hyman, 2018).

What gives me hope is that truth is truth. It's grounded in facts and reality. On the other hand, falsehoods don't exist unless they are created and amended to be kept up-to-date. When it's all said and done, I believe truth will prevail.

REFERENCES

Aguilera, Jasmine. (2019). "Area 51 Is the Internet's Latest Fascination. Here's Everything to Know About the Mysterious Site." https://time.com/5627694/area-51-history/

Beasley, Deena. (2020). "Arizona Man Dies After Taking Chloroquine for Coronavirus." https://www.usnews.com/news/us/articles/2020-03-23/arizona-man-dies-after-taking-chloroquine-for-coronavirus

Conger, Kate, and Mike Isaac. (2021). "Twitter Permanently Bans Trump, Capping Online Revolt." https://www.nytimes.com/2021/01/08/technology/twitter-trump-suspended.html

Dale, Brady. (2021). "What Is BitClout? The Social Media Experiment Sparking Controversy on Twitter." https://www.coindesk.com/what-is-bitclout-the-social-media-experiment-stoking-controversy-on-twitter

Dorman, Sam. (2020). "Chinese virologist: China's government 'intentionally' released COVID-19." https://www.foxnews.com/media/chinese-virologist-government-intentionally-coronavirus

Funke, Daniel, and Daniela Flamini. (2021). "A guide to anti-misinformation actions around the world." https://www.poynter.org/ifcn/anti-misinformation-actions/

Goodman, Jack, and Flora Carmichael. (2020). "Coronavirus: Bill Gates 'microchip' conspiracy theory and other vaccine claims fact-checked." https://www.bbc.com/news/52847648

Graham, David A. (2019). "Some real news about fake news." https://www.theatlantic.com/ideas/archive/2019/06/fake-news-republicans-democrats/591211/

Healthline. (2021). "What to Know About COVID-19 and Brain Fog." https://www.healthline.com/health/covid-brain-fog

Hyman, Ira. (2018). "The Truth Is Under Attack" https://www.psychologytoday.com/us/blog/mental-mishaps/201808/the-truth-is-under-attack.

Ibrahim, Azeem. (2020). "Modi's Slide Toward Autocracy." https://foreignpolicy.com/2020/07/13/modi-india-hindutva-hindu-nationalism-autocracy/

Jarrett, Tracy. (2019). "Democracy undone: How Trump sells his war on truth." https://thegroundtruthproject.org/democracy-undone-how-trump-sells-his-war-on-truth-authoritarianism-authoritarian-authoritarians-playbook/

Kakutani, Michiko. (2018). "The death of truth: How we gave up on facts and ended up with Trump." https://www.theguardian.com/books/2018/jul/14/the-death-of-truth-how-we-gave-up-on-facts-and-ended-up-with-trump

Kang, Cecilia. (2016). "Fake News Onslaught Targets Pizzeria as Nest of Child-Trafficking." https://www.nytimes.com/2016/11/21/technology/fact-check-this-pizzeria-is-not-a-child-trafficking-site.html

Kang, Cecilia, and Sheera Frenkel. (2020). "'PizzaGate's Conspiracy Theory Thrives Anew in the TikTok Era." https://www.nytimes.com/2020/06/27/technology/pizzagate-justin-bieber-qanon-tiktok.html

Katz, Leslie. (2021). "In HBO's Fake Famous, social media influencers buy their way to glory." https://www.cnet.com/news/in-hbo-documentary-fake-famous-social-media-influencers-buy-their-way-to-fame/?TheTime=2021-02-02T20%3A29%3A41&ftag=COS-05-10aaa0a&UniqueID=61291E06--6595-11EB-90C3-1F3216F31EAE&ServiceType=facebook_page&PostType=link&fbclid=IwAR0WB2EZVuRsz4LjHsfpVuty5uvDx4iRgqhONRsodsuOG77F0BSLlLk6sm0

Kessler, Glenn. (2021). "Trump made 30,573 false or misleading claims as president. Nearly half came in his final year." https://www.washingtonpost.com/politics/how-fact-checker-tracked-trump-claims/2021/01/23/ad04b69a-5c1d-11eb-a976-bad6431e03e2_story.html

Kingsley, Patrick. (2018). "Orban and His Allies Cement Control of Hungary's News Media." https://www.nytimes.com/2018/11/29/world/europe/hungary-orban-media.html

LaCapria, Kim. (2016). "Is Comet Ping Pong Pizzeria Home to a Child Abuse Ring Led by Hillary Clinton?" https://www.snopes.com/fact-check/pizzagate-conspiracy/

Laviola, Erin. (2018). "QAnon Conspiracy: 5 Fast Facts You Need to Know." https://heavy.com/news/2018/08/qanon-conspiracy-trump/

McLaughlin, Kelly. (2021). "5 people died in the Capitol insurrection. Experts say it could have been so much worse." https://www.businessinsider.com/capitol-insurrection-could-have-been-deadlier-experts-say-2021-1

Porter, Tom. (2021). "QAnon supporters believed marching on the Capitol could trigger 'The Storm,' an event where they hope Trump's foes will be punished in mass executions. https://www.businessinsider.com/qanon-trump-capitol-attack-belief-precursor-the-storm-2021-1

Onyuloi, Tonny. (2021). "COVID-19 God's Punishment? African Christians Debate as Their Presidents Die." https://www.christianitytoday.com/news/2021/march/tanzania-magufuli-dies-covid-president-burundi-god-punishme.html

Richter, Right. (2020). "Pizzagate is taking over TikTok." https://newsletry.com/Home/The%20Daily%20Beast/dcb7d527-eeca-4e3c-e88e-08d816300c2d

Roberts, Sam. (2018). "Daniel Patrick Moynihan, the American Politics." https://www.nytimes.com/2018/10/11/opinion/sunday/daniel-patrick-moynihan.html

Seitz, Amanda, and Beatrice Dupuy. (2020). "Here are 5 debunked COVID-19 myths that just won't die." https://www.denverpost.com/2020/12/18/covid-19-myths-debunked/

Truth Initiative. (2021). "The 5 ways tobacco companies lied about the dangers of smoking cigarettes." https://tinyurl.com/34sjcapf

West, Darrell M. (2017). "How to combat fake news and disinformation." https://www.brookings.edu/research/how-to-combat-fake-news-and-disinformation/

CHAPTER **10**

Warfare: Is "Cyber" the New Gunpowder?

Traditionally, war is known as an intense armed conflict between states, governments, societies, or paramilitary groups such as mercenaries, insurgents, and militias. It is generally characterized by extreme violence, aggression, destruction, and mortality, using regular or irregular military forces.

Warfare is also known as an engagement in a violent conflict or a struggle between competing entities. Activities are undertaken by Unit A to weaken or destroy Unit B. There are four levels of warfare: political, strategic, operational, and tactical. At any given moment, any war is attempting to accomplish one or more of the four levels.

Warfare and conflicts spin all aspects of human existence in society on a physical, mental, spiritual, economic, social levels. These conflicts come in many forms. For example, in instances where the poor and the rich conflict, that's a form of class warfare. One country bombing another when they get into a dispute or two countries bombing each other in the territory of a third country is an action of waging military war.

Then there is *proxy war,* which is an armed conflict between two states or non-state actors acting on the instigation or on behalf of other parties that are not directly involved, such as the hostilities in the Korean War, the Vietnam War, and Soviet Afghanistan. Another example is the United States and the Soviet Union fighting the Cold War by demonstrating their power and technology.

Another form of warfare is when people in power pit one ethnic group or a class of people against another. This type of warfare has led to some of the worst genocides humanity has seen. Violent conflict is normally caused mainly by social and political systems that lead to inequality and grievances and do not offer options for the peaceful expression of differences.

As you can see, there are many forms of war. However, warfare is generally understood to be the controlled and systematic waging of armed conflict between sovereign nations or states, using military might and strategy, until one opponent is defeated on the field or surrenders in the face of inevitable destruction and greater loss of human life.

Yet this is just one type of war. The other types move battlegrounds to involve the social, political, and economic systems of the enemy with the goal of weakening or domination. With the advent of cyber technologies, our new exponential modern technology, warfare is taking on a whole new meaning where you can wage a full blown "remote war" without physically setting foot in the enemy state territory. The tactics of remote war that can be appropriately adjusted apply militarily, socially, politically, and economically on the enemy state.

Economic warfare is a strategy based on the use of measures to weaken the economy of another state. A patent warfare is a "battle" between corporations or individuals to secure patents for litigation, whether offensively or defensively. There are ongoing patent wars between the world's largest technologies and software corporations. The intellectual property (IP) wars are rampant in the 21st century, where the creations of the mind, such as inventions; literary and artistic works; designs; and symbols, names, and images used in commerce are constantly stolen. This can lead to trade wars, where an economic conflict results from extreme protectionism in which states raise or create tariffs or other trade barriers against each other in response to trade barriers created by the other party, as we have seen in the battle between powerful countries like the United States and China.

As of this writing, there is an ongoing economic conflict between China and the United States. In 2018, then-President Donald Trump began setting tariffs and other trade barriers on China with the goal of forcing it to make changes to what the United States claims are "unfair trade practices" and intellectual property theft.

The United States imposed tariffs on more than $360 billion of Chinese goods, and China has retaliated with tariffs on more than

$110 billion of U.S. products. Washington delivered three rounds of tariffs in 2018, and a fourth one in September 2019. The most recent round targeted Chinese imports, from meat to musical instruments, with a 15% duty. Beijing hit back with tariffs ranging from 5% to 25% on U.S. goods (BBC, 2020). This is a typical example of a trade war.

A QUICK HISTORY OF MODERN WARFARE

As mentioned, conflicts and war have existed since the beginning of humanity. However, the "gunpowder revolution" marked the start of early modern warfare. The use of the machine guns, aircrafts, tanks, and radio in World War I signified a new era. These developments led to the introduction of *total war*, a war that is unrestricted in terms of the weapons used, the territory or combatants involved, or the objectives pursued, especially one in which the laws of war are disregarded.

Then there was *industrial warfare*. This is a period in the history of warfare ranging roughly from the early 19th century and the start of the industrial revolution to the beginning of the atomic age, which saw the rise of nation-states, capable of creating and equipping large armies, navies, and air forces, through the process of industrialization. The era featured mass-conscripted armies, rapid transportation (first on railroads, then by sea and air), telegraph and wireless communications, and the concept of total war. In terms of technology, this era saw the rise of rifled breech-loading infantry weapons capable of high rates of fire, high-velocity breech-loading artillery, chemical weapons, armored equipment, metal warships, submarines, and aircraft. This *mechanized warfare* brought about the modern mobile attack and defense tactics that depend on machines, more particularly on vehicles powered by gasoline and diesel engines. Central to the waging of mechanized warfare are the tank and armored vehicles, with support and supply from motorized columns and aircraft.

Then came the *nuclear warfare*, sometimes referred to as atomic warfare or thermonuclear warfare. This is a military conflict or political strategy that deploys nuclear weaponry. This was a terrifying time, with the possibility of a global catastrophe by design, miscalculation, or by pure madness. Then the nuclear-weapon states—China, France, Russia, the United Kingdom, and the United States—were officially recognized as possessing nuclear weapons by the Non-Proliferation Treaty (NPT). The objective of this landmark international treaty was to prevent the spread of nuclear weapons and weapons technology, to promote cooperation in the peaceful uses of nuclear energy, and to further the goal of achieving nuclear disarmament and general and complete disarmament.

As countries became more powerful but were still targeted by enemies, there was a rise in *counterinsurgency* movement/strategy, which is defined by the U.S. Department of State as "comprehensive civilian and military efforts taken to simultaneously defeat and contain insurgency and address its root causes" (U.S. Department of State, 2020).

The counterinsurgency movement more recently gave rise to *asymmetric warfare*, a conflict between nations or groups that have significantly disparate military capabilities and strategies. This is typically a war between a standing, professional army and an insurgency or resistance-movement militias, who often have status of unlawful combatants. This is a very complex strategy that gave rise to terrorism as a strategy. Every bomb dropped killed militants but also the families and friends of these groups. Since they do not have the same military power as the forces attacking them, they had to come up with a plan. The goal was to inflict carnage and pain on the countries they deem enemy states. The 9/11 terrorist attacks and the war in Afghanistan are among the best-known recent examples of asymmetric warfare.

As if we do not have enough strategies to approach war, the "cyber revolution" has marked the start of new warfare. The exponential technology development and deployment of the 21st-century has now introduced *NextGen warfare*, which is complex and long term and involves cyber technologies.

So, what is *cyber warfare*? Well, it's the use of technology to attack a nation's computers or information networks, causing harm comparable to actual warfare—financial or economic damage, death, or destruction. Destructive digital "weapons" have evolved and today they can be deployed simply by sending an email. When you click on this email, it sends a virus to affect your entire network of systems.

- In cyber warfare, digital terrorism (also known as cyberterrorism) is now a tactic. *Cyberterrorism* is the use of the Internet to conduct violent acts that result in, or threaten, loss of life or significant bodily harm, in order to achieve political or ideological gains through threat or intimidation. Sometimes it involves a direct attack on the enemy's culture, including the possibility of genocidal acts against civilians.

- Cyber warfare is also asymmetric, with players that are non-national or transnational and highly decentralized.

- Cyber warfare is highly sophisticated psychological warfare that uses propaganda, especially media manipulation, Internet trolls, bots, and lawfare, which is the misuse of legal systems and principles against an enemy by damaging or delegitimizing them, wasting their time and money (e.g., SLAPP suits), or winning a public relations victory.

This NextGen warfare sometimes lacks hierarchy. Though it can be big and include state and non-state actors, sometimes it's small, with a spread-out network of communication, financial support, and decentralized forces. Remote democratized and miniaturized weaponry (such as drones, bioweapons, sonic attacks, and more) are now at play.

In May 2021, law enforcement agencies were investigating two possible directed "energy attacks" on government employees on U.S. soil. One of these suspected attacks occurred on the south side of the White House in November 2020, and is believed to have sickened a White House aide (Morrow, 2021). That incident followed a similar one in 2019 in a Virginia suburb which reportedly injured an aide walking her dog (Pegues, 2021).

In the past, the National Security Agency has described an energy attack as a "high-powered microwave system weapon" that can "bathe a target in microwaves" and "kill the target over time and without leaving evidence" (Mackinnon, 2020). Energy attacks were suspected in Cuba and China in the past few years as U.S. personnel reported symptoms of ear popping, pounding headaches, and nausea. The symptoms have been referred to as "Havana Syndrome." There have been energy-directed attacks on U.S. personnel on multiple continents.

Each advancement in technological power brings a new set of challenges that are global in scale. With NextGen warfare, all areas of the enemy population are fair targets—political, economic, social, and military, all designed to disrupt or degrade the civil infrastructure.

How Do Bad Actors Gain Access to Systems?

Since cyber warfare often targets every aspect of the enemy population, not just the military, we need to look at how cyberattacks happen in general. The types of cyber threats are threefold:

- *Cybercrime:* Single actors or groups target systems for financial gain. This includes stealing money directly from financial accounts, stealing credit card information, causing data breaches, demanding ransom, and much more

- *Cyberattacks:* Often involving politically motivated information gathering, these types of attacks are divided into two categories: technical and psychological. The former encompasses network attacks relating to defense, counterattack, and exploitation. The latter involves information warfare with the attempt to change people's behavior or beliefs in favor of the attacking party or sow chaos among the enemy state population. Other times, they just cause disruptions, such as disabling systems, or use a breached computer as a launch point for other attacks.

- *Cyberterrorism:* Intended to undermine electronic systems to cause panic or fear.

The next sections discuss some common cyber warfare methods.

Malware

Malware means malicious software. One of the most common cyber threats, malware is software that a cybercriminal or hacker has created to disrupt or damage a legitimate user's computer. Often spread via an unsolicited email attachment or legitimate-looking download, malware may be used by cybercriminals to make money or in politically motivated cyberattacks. There are a number of different types of malware, including the following:

- *Virus*: A self-replicating program that attaches itself to clean files and spreads throughout a computer system, infecting files with malicious code.

- *Trojans*: A type of malware that is disguised as legitimate software. Cybercriminals trick users into uploading Trojans onto their computer, where they cause damage or collect data.

- *Spyware*: A program that secretly records what a user does, so that cybercriminals can use this information. For example, spyware could capture credit card details.

- *Ransomware*: Malware that locks down a user's files and data, with the threat of erasing it unless a ransom is paid.

- *Adware*: Advertising software that can be used to spread malware.

- *Botnets*: Networks of malware used by cybercriminals to infect computers to perform tasks online without the user's permission.

SQL Injection

An *SQL (structured language query) injection* is a type of cyberattack used to take control of and steal data from a database. Cybercriminals exploit vulnerabilities in data-driven applications to insert malicious code into a database via an SQL statement. This gives them access to the sensitive information contained in the database.

Phishing

Phishing is when cybercriminals target victims with emails that appear to be from a legitimate company asking for sensitive information. Phishing attacks are often used to dupe people into handing over credit card data and other personal information.

Spear phishing and *social engineering* are techniques deployed in order to get cybercriminals closer to the targeted systems. Threats from the inside pose a significant risk for states or organizations hoping to safeguard their systems against intruders

Man-in-the-Middle Attack

A man-in-the-middle attack is a type of cyberthreat where a cybercriminal intercepts communication between two individuals in order to steal data. For example, on an unsecure Wi-Fi network, an attacker could intercept data being passed from the victim's device and the network.

Denial-of-Service Attack

A denial-of-service attack is where cybercriminals prevent a computer system from fulfilling legitimate requests by overwhelming the networks and servers with traffic. This renders the system unusable, preventing an organization from carrying out vital functions.

Dridex Malware

In December 2019, the U.S. Department of Justice charged the leader of an organized cybercriminal group for their part in a global Dridex malware attack (U.S. Department of Justice, 2019). This malicious campaign affected the public, government, infrastructure, and business worldwide.

Dridex was a financial Trojan with a range of capabilities. Affecting victims since 2014, it infected computers though phishing emails or existing malware. Capable of stealing passwords, banking details, and personal data that can be used in fraudulent transactions, it has caused massive financial losses amounting to hundreds of millions of dollars.

In response to the Dridex attacks, the UK's National Cyber Security Centre advises the public to "ensure devices are patched, anti-virus is turned on and up to date, and files are backed up" (National Cyber Security Centre, 2019).

Romance Scams

In February 2020, the FBI warned U.S. citizens to be aware of confidence fraud that cybercriminals commit using dating sites, chat rooms, and apps. Perpetrators take advantage of people seeking new partners, duping victims into giving away personal data (FBI, 2020).

Emotet Malware

In late 2019, the Australian Cyber Security Centre warned national organizations about a widespread global cyberthreat from the malware called Emotet. Emotet is a sophisticated Trojan that can steal data and load other malware. Emotet thrives on unsophisticated passwords: a reminder of the importance of creating a secure password to guard against cyberthreats (Australian Cyber Security Centre, 2019).

THE INTENDED AND UNINTENDED CONSEQUENCES OF CYBER WARFARE

Advances in technology bring many benefits, but they also create new tensions across a host of areas. The use of automation in cyberspace has increased returns to capital and lowers the costs of goods, but at the same time it has raised concerns about cyber technologies becoming a battleground for war. This section discusses a few examples of the unintended (and purposeful) consequences of cyber warfare.

Wasted Resources

Cyberattacks have resulted in massive damages. The Council of Economic Advisers reported that in the year 2016 alone malicious cyber activity cost between $57 billion and $109 billion dollars (Epstein and Hagan, 2018). The report listed actors like Russia, China, Iran, and North Korea. Protection against these attacks also requires significant investment from governments around the world. The United States, for example, has a projected cybersecurity funding of $18.78 billion, according to Statista (Johnson, 2021).Governments not only have to allocate resources away from other, more directly meaningful programs, but larger businesses also have to invest in cyber protection. And these numbers are only projected to rise. It is predicted that cybersecurity spending will exceed $1 trillion from 2017 to 2021 (Morgan, 2021).

Infrastructure Systems Attacks

Stuxnet was a malicious computer worm first uncovered in 2010 and thought to have been in development since at least 2005 (Fruhlinger, 2017).

Stuxnet targeted supervisory control and data acquisition systems and was believed to be responsible for causing substantial damage to the nuclear program of Iran. Stuxnet is one of the best examples of cyber warfare in action.

Other significant events can be attributed to state-level attacks. One recent example comes from Russia, a country that has been accused of many state-level cyberattacks. Russia is accused of mounting multiple cyberattacks against Ukraine, including the BlackEnergy attack that cut the power to 700,000 homes in the country in 2015, and the NotPetya malware, which masqueraded as ransomware but was in reality designed purely to destroy the systems it infected (McCallion, 2021).

In 2020, we witnessed an unprecedented cyberattack on the U.S. electric grid system (Riley, 2020). Hackers used firewall vulnerabilities to cause periodic "blind spots" for grid operators in the western United States. It's the first known cyberattack to cause that kind of disruption.

The U.S. power grid has long been considered a logical target for a major cyberattack. Besides the intrinsic importance of the power grid to a functioning U.S. society, all 16 sectors of the U.S. economy deemed to make up the nation's critical infrastructure rely on electricity. Disabling or otherwise interfering with the power grid in a significant way could thus seriously harm the United States.

In early 2020, hackers secretly broke into Texas-based SolarWinds' systems and added malicious code to the company's software system (Jibilian and Canales, 2021a). The system, called Orion, is widely used by companies to manage IT resources. SolarWinds has 33,000 customers that use Orion, according to SEC documents. Most software providers regularly send out updates to their systems, whether it's fixing a bug or adding new features. SolarWinds is no exception. Beginning as early as March 2020, SolarWinds unwittingly sent out software updates to its customers that included the hacked code. The code created a backdoor to customers' information technology systems, which hackers then used to install even more malware that helped them spy on companies and organizations.

SolarWinds told the SEC that up to 18,000 of its customers installed updates that left them vulnerable to hackers. Since SolarWinds has many high-profile clients, including Fortune 500 companies and multiple agencies in the U.S. government, the breach was massive. Federal investigators and cybersecurity experts say that Russia's Foreign Intelligence Service, known as the SVR, is probably responsible for the attack (Jibilian and Canales, 2021b).

The water systems attack in 2021 shocked everyone when a cyberattacker significantly increased levels of lye into the Oldsmar water treatment system remotely (Peiser, 2021). An employee realized the attack was happening when their mouse began moving across the screen. The attack was quickly reversed. While the lye likely wouldn't have been enough to kill any of the 15,000 customers the water system serves, the damage a more sophisticated attacker might have done with the same access could have been much worse. Though this was a failed attempt, attackers are getting ideas on how to do the greatest harm to the largest number of people with minimum effort.

Cybersecurity experts have long warned that insecure remote work software is a major source of weakness for hacking (Levenson, 2021).

Election Tampering

The interference and cyberattacks on governments by other governments are often targeted to gain intelligence or break down government infrastructure, but another method is hacking to reveal information that can sway elections. For example, during the 2016 U.S. election, Russian military intelligence used phishing attacks to hack into the Clinton campaign (Abrams, 2019).

This attack was designed to interfere in the election with the goals of harming the campaign of Hillary Clinton, boosting the candidacy of Donald Trump, and increasing political and social discord in the United States. According to U.S. intelligence agencies, the operation—code named Project Lakht—was ordered directly by Russian president Vladimir Putin (Ross, Schwartz, and Meek, 2016).

The Internet Research Agency (IRA), based in Saint Petersburg, Russia, is described as a *troll farm*, an institutionalized group of Internet trolls. These people or companies make deliberately offensive or provocative online posts in order to cause conflict or manipulate public opinion. They created thousands of social media accounts that purported to be Americans supporting radical political groups and planned or promoted events in support of Trump and against Clinton. They reached millions of social media users between 2013 and 2017 (Lee, 2018). Fabricated articles and disinformation were spread from Russian government-controlled media and promoted on social media.

Additionally, computer hackers affiliated with the Russian military intelligence service (GRU) infiltrated information systems of the Democratic National Committee (DNC), the Democratic Congressional Campaign Committee (DCCC), and Clinton campaign officials, notably chairman John Podesta, and publicly released stolen files and emails through DCLeaks, Guccifer 2.0, and WikiLeaks during the election campaign (Whittaker, 2019).

Several individuals connected to Russia contacted various Trump campaign associates, offering business opportunities to the Trump Organization and proffering damaging information on Clinton (U.S. Department of Justice, 2019). Russian government officials have denied involvement in any of the hacks or leaks.

Russian interference activities triggered strong statements from U.S. intelligence agencies, a direct warning by then-President Barack Obama to Russian President Vladimir Putin, renewed economic sanctions against Russia, and closures of Russian diplomatic facilities and expulsion of their staff. The Senate and House Intelligence Committees conducted their own investigations into the matter (Tucker, 2020). Trump denied the interference had occurred, contending that it was a "hoax" perpetrated by the Democratic Party to explain Clinton's loss.

The Federal Bureau of Investigation (FBI) opened the Crossfire Hurricane investigation of Russian interference in July 2016, including a special focus on links between Trump associates and Russian officials and suspected coordination between the Trump campaign and the Russian government.

Russian attempts to interfere in the election were first disclosed publicly by members of the United States Congress in September 2016, confirmed by U.S. intelligence agencies in October 2016, and further detailed by the Director of National Intelligence office in January 2017 (Vesoulis and Simon, 2018).

This is hardly the only example of hacker interference in a country's elections. We have seen it in the UK with Brexit, as well as other forms of meddling in Africa and South America.

Tracing and Identifying the Sources

Unlike standard weapons of destruction, cyber warfare is harder to trace because elements like malware can be embedded into a system secretly. Often, state-sponsored attacks go unclaimed, leaving room for speculation. Then there are the occasions when hacking groups admit their crimes, but the problem is that they're never "officially" linked to a particular state.

We know that Russia and China are developing cyber weapons to use in any future cyber conflict, and the United States, France, and Israel are just as active as nation-states leading the way in this endeavor (Gilbert + Tobin, 2020). But that doesn't mean we can say any of these countries are using them, although we know they have the capability and have done so in the past. Stuxnet, for example, was a joint venture between Israel and the United States to destroy Iran's nuclear program capability.

In addition, instead of an entity, a state actor, or a non-state actor doing all of their dirty work, they have now resorted to hybrid cyber warfare. For example, in any given election, "Group A" may engage in efforts to alter sentiment through channels like social media while simultaneously targeting the websites of its main competitors, "Group B," in cyber vandalism—an attack without any obvious rational criminal, political, or ideological motive, usually defacement of a vulnerable website to display the hacker's prowess.

Often, it won't be Group A itself that engages in these activities, but instead it will outsource to companies that specialize in the spreading of disinformation and hackers for hire. This makes it more difficult to trace. This tactic is also seen in state-sponsored cyberattacks, where countries claim an attack originated from "patriotic hackers" acting on their own terms without any persuasion or reward from the state. Indeed, when it comes to nation states, we can see another aspect of hybrid cyber warfare when cyberattacks are carried out alongside "kinetic attacks," with traditional warfare machines like bombs. This is similar to when, in the past, saboteurs would target critical infrastructure ahead of an invasion, only now the attacks can happen remotely.

Furthermore, the one cyber weapon that is perhaps even more dangerous and disruptive is the *false flag*. This is when "Entity A" attacks "Entity B" pretending to be "Entity C." For example, we know that the attack by the so-called Cyber Caliphate claiming to be affiliated with ISIS on a U.S. military database was a false flag operation by the Russian state-sponsored hacking group APT 28. Why does this matter? Because the United States retaliated with kinetic attacks on cyber communication channels and drone strikes against human targets in Syria in retaliation against ISIS, while the perpetrator—Russia—went free, without blame or consequences.

Cyber Coupled with Democratization and Miniaturization of Drones

In recent years, three major trends have been driving developments in the field of unmanned aerial systems (drones): automation, swarming, and miniaturization. The benefits to the military are clear.

Applications such as *infrared and hyperspectral imaging* are of high interest. The most familiar uses of infrared technology by the military are airborne forward-looking infrared scanners, guidance heads for missiles, and night-vision goggles. People, vehicle engines, and aircraft glow in the infrared because they generate and retain heat. Thermal imaging cameras contain a special lens that focuses the heat, or infrared energy given off by an object onto a detector that's sensitive to heat. Consider these real-life cases:

- *Swarm*: In 2017, the U.S. military tested 103 miniature swarming drones called Perdix from a fighter jet in California. The drones, which have a wingspan of 12 inches (30 cm), operate autonomously and share a distributed brain. A military analyst said the devices are able to dodge air defense systems, which is very good for surveillance. "Perdix are not pre-programmed synchronized individuals, they are a collective organism, sharing one distributed brain for decision-making and adapting to each other like swarms in nature," said William Roper, director of the Strategic Capabilities Office (Baraniuk, 2017).

- *Mini*: In another example, the U.S. Army's standalone miniature drones have already been deployed to Afghanistan with air support literally in the palm of their hands. Soldiers were so enthused about the 1.16-ounce Black Hornet mini-drone that the Army ended up buying up to 9,000 systems, each with two drones. The Army is working to improve the technology so that, instead of one soldier remote-controlling one robot, they can have one soldier overseeing a largely autonomous swarm the same way they do with the other unmanned drones. The palmtop Black Hornet is already in the hands (literally) of a brigade of the elite 82nd Airborne. For the first time, a squad leader has the ability to scout ahead by air before exposing human soldiers on the ground (Freedberg, 2019).

This is just the United States; you better believe state actors, non-state actors, and individuals (allies and foes) are all testing these miniature systems in one way or another.

It's possible to load up a bioweapon on a swarm of drones and send it into large crowds in a stadium or across borders via cyberspace with the click of a button. The use cases and possibilities are endless. Humanity needs to devise means and ways to mitigate the unintended consequences. This is not fear-mongering or hyperbole—these are real concerns.

ACTIONS AGAINST CYBER WARFARE

Individuals, state actors, and non-state actors need to stay vigilant as the Internet keeps moving at lightning speed.

The issue of dealing with cyber warfare between governments and cyberattacks in general has been a source of debate and there has yet to be world consensus. But just as there are treaties to counter against the threat of "real" weapons, there has been discussion on actions against the threat of these new digital weapons. The next sections discuss a few actions on an individual as well as at the systems level to deal with this ever-evolving threat.

UN and Global Cooperation

The Convention on Cybercrime (also known as the Budapest Convention) was introduced in 2001 (Daskal and Kennedy-Mayo, 2020). It deals with violations of network security and aims to foster international cooperation as well as other cyber-related issues like copyright infringements. However, as of 2020, a resolution updating the Budapest Convention made what constitutes "Information and Communications Technologies" crime vaguer. It was introduced by Russia and opposed by Western nations such as the United States. There needs to be a strong body responsible for enforcing laws and punishing rule breakers (Hakmeh and Peters, 2020).

White Hat Hacker

White hat hackers, also called *ethical hackers*, hack into systems with the intention of revealing and fixing security flaws. Governments have recruited the help of these white hat hackers to improve the security of their systems. The U.S. Department of Homeland Security, for example, makes an appearance at cybersecurity convention DEF CON, which is one of the world's largest and most notable hacker conventions, held annually in Las Vegas, with over 30,000 attendees. They do so to enlist hackers to protect the U.S. government from cyberthreats (Peterson, 2015).

Laws and Government Actions

Naturally, the governments of the world are investing in cyber capabilities. For example, one U.S. government action is the Comprehensive National Cybersecurity Initiative. This included actions like implementing intrusion detection systems on federal systems as well as investments in expanding cyber education (White House Archives, 2009). These legislations are continually built upon; for example, former president Trump signed the Cybersecurity and Infrastructure Security Agency Act of 2018 (Cimpanu, 2018). Nations around the world are continually investing and improving cyber preparedness.

President Obama had identified cybersecurity as one of the most serious economic and national security challenges we face as a nation, that the government and the country were not adequately prepared to counter. Shortly after taking office, he ordered a thorough review of federal efforts to defend the U.S. information and communications infrastructure and the development of a comprehensive approach to securing America's digital infrastructure (White House Archives, 2009)

In May 2009, President Obama accepted the recommendations of the resulting Cyberspace Policy Review (U.S. Government Accountability Office, 2010). Among many things, the review included managing the federal enterprise network as a single network enterprise with trusted Internet connections, deploying an intrusion detection system of sensors across the federal enterprise, developing and implementing the government-wide cyber counterintelligence (CI) plan, coordinating and redirecting research and development (R&D) efforts, and selecting an Executive Branch Cybersecurity Coordinator who had regular access to the president (White House Archives, 2021).

Security Product Solutions

Companies have taken on the challenges of securing software and need to continue to do so. Products monitor for signs of any attacks, help secure data, and more. For example, Cisco sells solutions to these problems, often to governmental agencies.

So, how do you stay safe from a cyberattack? The answer is that you can't. It's a kinetic situation that requires kinetic vigilance. Here are some things you can do:

- Train your employees in cybersecurity principles.
- Install, use, and regularly update antivirus and antispyware software on every computer used in your business.
- Use a firewall for your Internet connection.
- Use two-factor or multi-factor authentication systems.
- Use encryption whenever that option is available.
- Download and install software updates to your operating systems and applications as they become available.

The global cyber threat continues to evolve at a rapid pace, with a rising number of breaches each year. To combat the proliferation of malicious code and aid in early detection, experts recommend continuous, real-time monitoring of all your electronic resources.

REFERENCES

Abrams, Abigail. (2019). "Here's What We Know So Far About Russia's 2016 Meddling." https://time.com/5565991/russia-influence-2016-election/

Australian Cyber Security Centre. (2019). "Australian Cyber Security Centre (ACSC) has warned in a new threat." https://www.cyber.gov.au/acsc/view-all-content/news

Baraniuk, Chris. (2017). "US military tests swarm of mini-drones launched from jets." https://www.bbc.com/news/technology-38569027#:~:text=The%20US%20military%20has%20launched,and%20share%20a%20distributed%20brain

BBC. (2020). "A quick guide to the US-China trade war." https://www.bbc.com/news/business-45899310

Cimpanu, Catalin. (2018). "Trump signs bill that creates the Cybersecurity and Infrastructure Security Agency." https://www.zdnet.com/article/trump-signs-bill-that-creates-the-cybersecurity-and-infrastructure-security-agency/

Daskal, Jennifer, and Debrae Kennedy-Mayo. (2020). "Budapest Convention: What Is It and How Is It Being Updated?" https://www.crossborderdataforum.org/budapest-convention-what-is-it-and-how-is-it-being-updated/#:~:text=Officially%20known%20as%20the%20Council,to%20focus%20explicitly%20on%20cybercrime

Epstein, Jennifer, and Shelly Hagan. (2018). "The Cost of Cyber Attacks to U.S. Economy." https://www.insurancejournal.com/news/national/2018/02/20/481121.htm#:~:text=Malicious%20cyber%20activity%20cost%20the,on%20U.S.%20government%20and%20industry.

FBI. (2020). "FBI warned U.S. citizens to be aware of confidence fraud." https://www.fbi.gov/contact-us/field-offices/saltlakecity/news/press-releases/fbi-warns-of-fraud-trend-online-romance-scams

Freedberg, Sydney J., Jr. (2019). "Army Buys 9,000 Mini-Drones, Rethinks Ground Robots." https://breakingdefense.com/2019/06/army-buys-9000-mini-drones-for-squads-rethinks-ground-robots-for-2020/

Fruhlinger, Josh. (2017). "What is Stuxnet, who created it and how does it work?" https://www.csoonline.com/article/3218104/what-is-stuxnet-who-created-it-and-how-does-it-work.html

Gilbert + Tobin, (2020). "Cyber warfare – is attack the best form of defence?" https://www.lexology.com/library/detail.aspx?g=be126908-c800-4ca4-a247-0737bb351bfb

Hakmeh, Joyce, and Allison Peters. (2020). "A New UN Cybercrime Treaty? The Way Forward for Supporters of an Open, Free, and Secure Internet." https://www.cfr.org/blog/new-un-cybercrime-treaty-way-forward-supporters-open-free-and-secure-internet

Jibilian, Isabella, and Katie Canales. (2021a). "Here's a simple explanation of how the massive SolarWinds hack happened and why it's such a big deal." https://www.businessinsider.com/solarwinds-hack-explained-government-agencies-cyber-security-2020-12

Jibilian, Isabella, and Katie Canales. (2021b). "What is SolarWinds?" https://www.businessinsider.com/solarwinds-hack-explained-government-agencies-cyber-security-2020-12#:~:text=In%20early%202020%2C%20hackers%20secretly,Orion%2C%20according%20to%20SEC%20documents.&text=SolarWinds%20is%20no%20exception

Johnson, Joseph. (2021). "U.S. government and cyber crime – Statistics & Facts." https://www.statista.com/topics/3387/us-government-and-cyber-crime/

Lee, Dave. (2018). "The tactics of a Russian troll farm." https://www.bbc.com/news/technology-43093390

Levenson, Eric. (2021). "Florida water hack highlights risks of remote access work without proper security." https://www.cnn.com/2021/02/13/us/florida-hack-remote-access/index.html

Mackinnon, Amy. (2020). "What's Behind the Mysterious Illness of U.S. Diplomats and Spies?" https://foreignpolicy.com/2020/10/21/whats-behind-mysterious-illness-us-diplomats-spies-cuba-china-russia-microwave-attack/

McCallion, Jane. (2021). "What is cyber warfare?" https://www.itpro.co.uk/security/28170/what-is-cyber-warfare

Morgan, Steve. (2021). "Global Cybersecurity Spending Predicted to Exceed $1 Trillion from 2017-2021." https://cybersecurityventures.com/cybersecurity-market-report/

Morrow, Brendan. (2021). "U.S. reportedly investigating a potential energy attack near the White House." https://www.yahoo.com/entertainment/u--reportedly-investigating-potential-energy-132607737.html

National Cyber Security Centre. (2019). "UK and US investigations into harmful international cyber campaigns." https://www.ncsc.gov.uk/news/uk-and-us-investigation-into-harmful-international-cyber-campaigns

Pegues, Jeff. (2021). "Suspected energy attack near White House." https://www.newsbreak.com/news/2223309084689/u-s-investigates-suspected-energy-attack-near-white-house

Peiser, Jaclyn. (2021). "A hacker tried to poison the water supply in Oldsmar, Florida." https://www.washingtonpost.com/nation/2021/02/09/oldsmar-water-supply-hack-florida/

Peterson, Andrea. (2015). "How the government tries to recruit hackers on their own turf." https://www.washingtonpost.com/news/the-switch/wp/2015/10/24/how-the-government-tries-to-recruit-hackers-on-their-own-turf/

Riley, Tonya. (2020). "Cybersecurity." https://www.washingtonpost.com/politics/2020/12/08/cybersecurity-202-securing-electric-grid-should-be-priority-biden-first-100-days-expert-says/

Ross, Brian, Rhonda Schwartz, and James Gordon Meek. (2016). "Officials: Master Spy Vladimir Putin Now Directly Linked to US Hacking." https://abcnews.go.com/International/officials-master-spy-vladimir-putin-now-directly-linked/story?id=44210901

Tucker, Eric. (2020). "Senate panel finds Russia interfered in the 2016 U.S. election." https://www.pbs.org/newshour/politics/senate-panel-finds-russia-interfered-in-the-2016-us-election

U.S. Department of Justice. (2019a). "Report on the Investigation into Russian Interference in the 2016 Presidential Election." https://www.justice.gov/archives/sco/file/1373816/download

U.S. Department of Justice. (2019b). "Russian National Charged with Decade-Long Series of Hacking and Bank Fraud Offenses Resulting in Tens of Millions in Losses." https://www.justice.gov/opa/pr/russian-national-charged-decade-long-series-hacking-and-bank-fraud-offenses-resulting-tens

U.S. Department of State. (2020). "Counter-insurgency." https://www.state.gov/

U.S. Government Accountability Office. (2010). "Cyberspace Policy: Executive Branch Is Making Progress Implementing 2009 Policy Review Recommendations." https://www.gao.gov/products/gao-11-24

Vesoulis, Abby, and Abigail Simon. (2018). "Here's Who Found That Russia Meddled in the 2016 Election." https://time.com/5340060/donald-trump-vladimir-putin-summit-russia-meddling/

White House Archives. (2009, 2021). "The Comprehensive National Cybersecurity Initiative." https://obamawhitehouse.archives.gov/issues/foreign-policy/cybersecurity/national-initiative

Whittaker, Zack. (2019). "Mueller report sheds new light on how the Russians hacked the DNC and the Clinton campaign." https://techcrunch.com/2019/04/18/mueller-clinton-arizona-hack/

CHAPTER 11

Work:
Why Do People Work?

ork is something everyone loves and sometimes hates. But what is
it? And why do most people you know work?

Work includes the duties that someone regularly performs in order
to earn wages or a salary. Work is an occupation, a job, something that
someone does or has done in order to achieve a result or serve a purpose.

A worker is someone who does work. Sometimes people are self-
employed, other times they are employed by an employer or a company.
The IRS says that a worker (an employee) gets paid wages, pays taxes
on those wages, receives benefits, and has a schedule dictated to them
by an employer. A worker can also be considered to be a member of the
working class.

WHY DO PEOPLE WORK?

In addition to the most elemental reason—to support themselves and their
dependents—there are many explicit and unspoken reasons why people
work. Here are a few:

- *Identity*: We derive our sense of identity from comparison with
  others, those we are like, those we differ from. So changing
  our job can change how we are seen and who we identify with.
  Through our work we find an identity, and we can find status and
  intellectual stimulation.

- *Sense of belonging*: This is the feeling of security and support when
  there is a sense of respect, acceptance, inclusion, and identity for

a member of a certain group or place. In order for people to feel like they belong, the environment (in this case the workplace) needs to be set up to be a diverse and inclusive place.

- *Safety and security*: When you work you earn wages. Money can buy you comfort. Instead of worrying about short-term problems, fretting about bills and debts, and stressing about essential things you cannot afford, you relax, live well, and do your best work. As a matter of fact, money can buy some level of happiness up to a point—studies indicate emotional well-being rises with income up to about $75,000 (Liles, 2020). According to the study from Princeton University the more a person's annual income falls below that benchmark, the unhappier he or she feels. But no matter how much more than $75,000 people make, they don't report any greater degree of happiness (Luscombe, 2010). Researchers have also found that money can buy you experiences that make people happier because they enhance social relationships and are a bigger part of one's identity.

- *Contribution to society*: When you work, you contribute to the good of society and move the world and everything in it positively forward (in theory, at least). Some work relieves people's suffering, fights for social justice, and improves lives and communities. The world desperately needs your contribution. It makes us better as people and better stewards of our planet.

- *Creativity*: This is the act of transforming new, innovative ideas into reality. Work gives people an arena for creativity, asking questions and finding new solutions to problems. It provides an area to create something novel for oneself or for the world.

- *Social benefits*: We are social beings. People work to be social. From drinking and partying together, to fun interesting personal conversations and discussions, to making friends with coworkers or people you meet through your job, work is also a social outlet.

- *Learning*: College, advanced degrees, training, or diplomas—those kinds of learning are obviously important for building a career. However, with the acceleration of technological innovations in all spheres of work, and the significant shortening of the life cycle of any particular skill in the market, creating and maintaining market leadership hinges on talent development's ability to help employees acquire and grow the right skills. We're curious animals by nature. Learning something new is invigorating. Going through the same routine, day after day, just isn't. There's a virtuous cycle in play here, too: the more you learn, the more engaged you are in your career, boosting individual skills. When you work, you are learning new things, gaining more skills and experiences.

- *Purpose, meaning, and value*: Someone works on a task, a task matters to a job, a job matters to an organization, the organization serves humanity, the planet, the world, or even the universe. The outcome is the feeling as though the task or the job you did is of service to something larger than yourself. Having this kind of impact in the world brings moments of joy—not just satisfaction, but real joy is one of the reasons people work. For most people what they do is one of the things that gives life meaning!

Many forces—including technology, policies, education, global pandemics, and other issues—are affecting the future of work and workers. Workers today are more productive than they've ever been. The impact of technology on work has exponentially increased the rate of production and speed at which business occurs. However, that technology in the workplace that has helped workers become more efficient is the same one that is slowly but surely replacing workers. This chapter focuses mostly on the effect of technology, automation, and AI on the future of work and workers.

A Quick History of Work

Work has existed as long as humans have. We need to work in some form to feed ourselves and care for our offspring, for the survival of the species.

The hunter-gatherer culture, which was often nomadic, was the only way of life for humans until about 12,000 years ago, when archaeological studies show evidence of the emergence of agriculture, referred to as the Neolithic revolution or the first agricultural revolution (National

Geographic, 2021). Human lifestyles began to change as groups formed permanent settlements and tended crops. This marked the transition in human history from small, nomadic bands of hunter-gatherers to larger, agricultural settlements and early civilization. The next agricultural revolution saw the unprecedented increase in agricultural production in Britain due to increases in labor and land productivity between the mid-17th and late 19th centuries.

Then came the Industrial Revolution, which was a transition to new manufacturing processes in Europe and the United States, starting around 1760. This period transformed economies that had been based on agriculture and handicrafts into economies based on large-scale industry, mechanized manufacturing, and the factory system. New machines, new power sources, and new ways of organizing work made existing industries more productive and efficient.

The Industrial Revolution transformed our economy from agriculture to industry. However, advancements in the industry revolved around some form of energy breakthrough.

The first industrial revolution revolved around the discovery of coal (White, 2009). During this period, the discovery of coal and its mass extraction, as well as the development of the steam engine and metal forging, completely changed the way goods were produced and exchanged. Inventions such as spinning machines and looms to make fabric were making their appearance. Canal transportation began replacing wagons and mules for moving around these goods.

The second wave of the Industrial Revolution revolved around the discovery of electricity, gas, and oil. The invention of the combustion engine went hand-in-hand with these fuel sources. Both steel and chemically based products entered the market during this time. Developments in communication technology got a jump-start with the telegraph and later the telephone. Transportation grew by leaps and bounds with the invention of the car and the plane. Mechanical production grew in speed through the advent of mass production.

The third wave of the industrial revolution revolved around nuclear energy, and electronics entered the landscape. Nuclear power began in Europe, and then grew in both Great Britain and the United States. It was

December 20, 1951, when a reactor generated the first electricity from nuclear energy. Enrico Fermi led a group of scientists in initiating the first self-sustaining nuclear chain reaction (MacNeil, 2019).

As of this writing, we are living through the fourth industrial revolution, which centers on the Internet and most recently on renewable energy. We are seeing a huge shift to renewable energy such as solar, wind, and geothermal. However, the momentum actually comes from the acceleration of digital technology energy demands—the old way of generating "unclean" energy is no longer as attractive due to the negative effects on humanity and our planet. The Internet and the digital world have created a need for a real-time connection within more and more components of a production line and increased demands for power generation.

As the development of 5G, the industrial Internet of Things, cloud technology, and artificial intelligence continue, the virtual world is slowly merging with the physical world. Predictive maintenance and real-time data are leading smarter decisions for a myriad of individuals, companies, and governments around the world.

With the exponential nature of development, deployment, and usage of the technologies in the fourth industrial revolution, all aspects of the work and workers will change. However, there are conflicting views on the nature of this change because no one fully knows how it will all shake out just yet, as we sit at the cusp of change.

WHERE WE STAND NOW

Recently, we've witnessed robotics and other forms of "smart automation" advancing at a rate never seen before.

In 2020, the global pandemic had a big impact on the economy and the global workforce. It left millions of people, especially low-pay workers, out of work. However, we also saw the exponential growth of automation and on-demand services. This phenomenon left many experts questioning what the future of work and being a worker will look like.

Workers in automated facilities must now have a greater technological proficiency in order to fulfill their new duties in order to keep their jobs. In fact, the lack of properly trained workers for today's automated factories and manufacturing facilities is one of the few things slowing the progress of automation—a Catch 22! A lack of suitably trained instructors and poorly equipped schools to teach these new vocational skills promises further slowing of the automation process. Nonetheless, it's coming, and it's coming hard.

In 2020, during the coronavirus pandemic, most people were not in a position to meet or go to work in person. Stay-at-home orders then turned the world upside down, transforming kitchens, bedrooms, and home offices of tens of millions of homes into corporate real estate. We saw remote work become the norm. For workers, remote work became the beginning of professional autonomy, permitting greater flexibility to set the working hours and physical conditions that are most comfortable for them and that can lead to greater job and life satisfaction and an improvement in their physical well-being. Less commuting means more time for hobbies and family, as well as lower work-related expenses.

Meanwhile, automation really stepped up and delivered goods and desperately needed services and medicine to citizens. We saw service delivery companies do really well, even though most people were financially struggling. This was the beginning of a new era.

POSITIVE USE CASES OF TECHNOLOGY ON THE FUTURE OF WORK

In the 21st century, you cannot talk about the future of work or workers without talking about technology. This is an exponential force that's set to revolutionize what work looks like and what it means to be a worker. So far, the benefits of automating work have promised and delivered great results, including more efficient use of materials, better product quality, improved safety, and reduced factory lead times.

Today, many of the activities carried out by workers can be automated. Robots are replacing humans in offices and in industrial jobs that are repetitive, hazardous, uncomfortable, or awkward for the people doing them. And automations can be used to cover more hours than humans can work.

This increased productivity leads to economic growth (Stolzoff, 2018). We have seen higher production rates and increased productivity, by AI and automated systems helping businesses to cut down on costs, improve the quality of their products or services, and create better customer profiles. As a result, companies get higher profits, which can be shared among stakeholders as dividends, or reinvested in the business.

According to PwC analysis, automation will contribute up to $15 trillion to global GDP by 2030 (Holmes, 2019). This extra wealth will also generate demand for many other jobs.

The opportunities are endless. In fact, there are many books and other bodies of work dedicated to the benefits of automating work and the workforce in depth—because the upside is great. In this chapter, let's focus a bit more on the unintended and willfully ignored consequences of technology on the future of work.

THE UCOTS OF TECHNOLOGY ON WORK AND WORKERS

The future of work is being shaped by two powerful forces: the growing adoption of artificial intelligence in the workplace and the expansion of the workforce to include both on- and off-balance-sheet remote talent. There are many exponential changes in store for the workplace, the workforce, and the nature of work itself through technology. These changes come with a world of unintended consequences. Let's look at a few examples.

Working from Home

This is not always the best scenario. The COVID-19 pandemic brought lots of changes on a global scale. Many big tech companies rolled out plans to let employees work remotely on a permanent basis.

Remote employment also tends to erode the boundary between work and life. Workplace communication tools invade our personal spaces.

Given the central role work plays in most peoples' social lives, the rise of remote work can lead to a loss of social contact, resulting in loneliness.

And, as most are familiar with by now, there's the ubiquitous phenomenon of tech exhaustion made famous by "Zoom fatigue."

Safety and Security

As work gets more intelligent, it also gets more interconnected, with various systems depending on one another, or at least sharing the same system resources. That makes for a larger attack footprint, and more potentially devastating results from a breach or hack. Hackers have already started targeting state and local government institutions with massive cyberattacks. As noted in other chapters (and it bears repeating), the most notable attack in 2020 in the United States was from the hackers—widely reported as Russian—who compromised high-profile targets like the U.S. Departments of Commerce, Treasury, Homeland Security, and Energy, as well as the system that manages the U.S. nuclear stockpile (Bertrand and Wolff, 2020). All of the attacks appear to stem from one initial source of a compromise at IT infrastructure and network-management firm Solar-Winds. This gave us a small taste of what a large-scale hack of interconnected systems can look like.

Becoming socially, politically, and economically dependent on technology endangers privacy and threatens the possible subjugation of the human race to technology and a catastrophic error in the management of a system that could in turn endanger civilization itself. See Chapter 11 on warfare to consider the things that could go wrong. With technology that has godlike powers, we should not underestimate human stupidity.

We have to be aware of the potential dangers of depending on tech in all aspects of our lives. Large, automated work and worker systems must be held at a higher cybersecurity standard than the average computer network.

Too Much Automation

With automation and smart work, no one is safe from displacement. Even as technology brings benefits to business and society, we need to prepare for major disruptions to work. Automation will displace some workers. A 2018 McKinsey report (Manyika and Sneader, 2018) found that around 15% of the global workforce, or about 400 million workers, could be displaced by automation in the period 2016–2030. This reflects their midpoint scenario in projecting the pace and scope of adoption. Under the fastest scenario they have modeled, that figure rises to 30%, or 800 million workers.

The rollout is happening in phases; the lowest-wage workers will be hit the hardest first, followed by the middle class, then the upper class. Short term, there will be physical worker displacement/migration from smaller cities. Large cities tend to have more managerial and technical professions, which makes for more occupational and skill specialization. Having that advantage over smaller cities will mean that there will be less physical worker displacement in more urbanized areas, meaning that larger cities are less likely to see much worker migration in search for jobs.

However, we will see managerial and technical professionals migrate away from cities into the suburbs and rural towns in search of convenience and bigger real estate properties (Manyika and Sneader, 2018). This is due to the fact that everything is either remote or automated and there is no need to physically reside in crowded cities if a worker is able to fulfill their duties regardless of their geographic location. As a consequence, this will affect both the residential and the commercial real estate market heavily. In the San Francisco Bay area where I live, we saw a small taste of this in the so-called "mass migration of 2020" away from Silicon Valley due to the pandemic. The city had 35,900 people leave during the last three months of 2020, a jump of 61% from the prior year (Avalos, 2021).

As mentioned, automation in the short term will affect low-wage workers in cities big or small. Long term it will affect low-skilled jobs and every other work as we know it. In fact, since many people find life's meaning in what they do, we will get to a point where we question the reason for existence.

For some examples of what I mean, let's take a look at specific industries and contexts.

Transportation

According to data compiled by the U.S. Census Bureau, driving a truck is the most common job in 29 of the 50 states in the United States, employing millions of people (Bui, 2015). An interactive map and timeline created by National Public Radio's Planet Money blog shows the growth in truck driving popularity starting in 1978, when it topped the jobs list in just nine states.

Big tech companies have built a growing fleet of robotic trucks, including UPS, Aurora, Uber, Embark, Locomation, Plus.ai, and even Waymo, the Alphabet spinoff that has long focused on self-driving cars. These and many more companies have invested heavily in automating trucks, taxis, and anything in between. What happens to drivers as their jobs go obsolete?

The United States is just one example; this phenomenon is happening all over the world. This new technological revolution is good news for companies that need to up their production in order to stay competitive in the global markets, but what about the individual workers? When trucks can drive themselves, workers are displaced, just like horses were by the invention of motor vehicles.

"Human inventiveness. . . has still not found a mechanical process to replace horses as the propulsion for vehicles," lamented French newspaper *Le Petit Journal* in December 1893 (*Economist*, 2017). Then humans invented the internal combustion engine, and the number of horses needed was reduced dramatically and eventually they were totally replaced by these engines, which would go on to power industries and change the world. At the current pace I strongly believe that it will not take too long for machines and automation to be part of all aspects of our lives.

This means that for those workers who are already at low- or medium-skill-level jobs, automation of those jobs will likely result in having to find new jobs of even lower quality, with lower pay, fewer benefits, or both. Workers will need to possess skills that are complementary to the new technologies being used to replace them in order to reap any benefits, such as higher wages, that automation will cause.

How are we going to integrate and live with our machine friends that are slowly replacing us? No one fully knows, but they already exist in fields like legal and medicine.

Law

As of this writing there are robot lawyers or robo-lawyer companies offering legal services to clients. These are legal technology applications that can perform tasks typically done by paralegals or young associates at law firms. This makes it very hard for young legal minds straight out of college to gain the necessary experience to join a firm. This is just the beginning; ready or not, robot lawyers are coming to a "cyber-court" near you.

Medicine

Doctors spend 11 years or more of their lives studying to better others' lives. The amount of hard work and training they go through to be accurate in the discharge of their duties is very impressive. In the short term, technologies like AI algorithms are assisting doctors serving as a sharp-eyed partner in tackling problems that doctors cannot detect and solve alone. In the long run, as technology advances and better data and models are created, some areas of the health profession are about to be disrupted, shifting detection of medical conditions from an active to a proactive approach.

The Human Search for Meaning

Automation will be perfected and humans will get everything delivered to them by a click of a button or simply a verbal command. The machine might simply know your needs. There could also be an increased loss of purpose and human search for meaning. What's the purpose of our existence? Human work goes deeper than just a way of getting stuff. Work means more than being an efficient monkey that sits around and gets everything delivered by a robot.

Monopoly Power on Automation Technologies

Large, heavily resourced companies tend to have a monopoly on all the markets. AI technology and automation is characterized by an increase in production, which naturally leads to increase in returns. Large companies can double their production rates and put out two times the original amount of product they once did. This means that large firms will have the advantage of being more scalable than smaller companies will; they'll grow much faster, and eventually those smaller companies will be pushed out of business.

Automating Inequality/Wealth Inequality

As big companies monopolize all markets, this leads to greater wealth inequality, as the few CEOs of successful firms and corporations see their wages skyrocket, while the working class gets fewer and poorer-paying jobs, or no jobs at all.

In addition, the wealthiest among us are the ones investing in, patenting, and owning technology companies. In the transportation sector, the behemoth companies are battling for the ownership of a stake in the industry. Companies like Uber and Google (Waymo) are all in the fight. Even the retail giant Amazon has entered the market with its robotaxi, an electric, fully driverless vehicle that's built for ride hailing. It's a "carriage-style" car, which means that passengers face each other and there's no space for a driver or passenger seat, since there's no steering wheel. It has space for up to four passengers (Palmer, 2020).

Big corporations owning the majority of the automated companies will lead to a scenario where lots of people without the means and the big bucks have zero say in the market and how the industry grows. What's even sadder is that those same people are the drivers and small business owners (such as taxi and Uber drivers) who will lose their jobs to automation. The billionaires who own these companies and others similar to them will reap all the financial benefits and become obscenely wealthier than they are already. And all while the general population gets poorer due to lack of meaningful employment, most of which will have been stolen by automation.

That's what happens when a machine steals your job and you do not have the financial means to own a piece of the pie in the autonomous machine's revolution.

College and Higher Education Changes

Workplace automation will also cause changes in the higher education field. First, there will be an immediate shortage of trained professionals who can use the new technologies, resulting in a greater need for technical and vocational training programs. This may eventually lead to a different view of a college education since a higher education will no longer be as necessary a means to employment or advancement.

We know a lot of jobs will become automated and others will change significantly because of technology, new markets, and industries. In addition, jobs will be created—some of which we cannot even imagine today. In this fast-paced economy, learning should be seen as a lifelong endeavor for individuals at every stage of their career. Higher education and its partners should also be adapting in order to provide the workforce with the foundational competencies and skills they'll need, both now and into the future.

Romance Replaced by Machines

Even the most intimate parts of our lives are getting outsourced to robots.

Sex robots with conversational ability and static silicone bodies are entering the bedroom. A sex robot named Harmony has been marketed as the "first" AI-infused sex robot (Trout, 2018). Harmony and other robots like it can talk, make jokes, blink, and have customizable body parts. They can take and send you a nude selfie when you are on the road. Sex robots are no longer a weird fantasy but a reality. What happens to professional sex workers, a job we traditionally believed could only be fulfilled by humans? Sex robots are another extreme example of technology harnessed for sexual gratification that comes with many ethical questions we do not have time to get into.

Actions Against the UCOTs of Work

As you can gather, there is a potential for a mass job loss due to automation and robotics. While this topic has received significant attention, much of the press focuses on potential problems. However, we also need realistic solutions. The following sections discuss some of the proposed actions.

Universal Basic Income (UBI)

This is a guaranteed, no-strings-attached, recurring payment to every member of a given community or society, sized to meet basic needs. It's universal in nature because it needs to serve all members of society and is enough to cover basic needs. Some state and local government programs in different parts of the world have guaranteed every adult citizen a set amount of money on a regular basis. The goal of this kind of basic income system is to alleviate poverty.

In 2020, Germany began a universal-basic-income trial with 120 people getting $1,400 a month for three years (DeSantis, 2020). In America, there have been many trials by independent companies and cities, with mixed results and outcomes.

In 2019, Silicon Valley incubator Y Combinator dedicated $60 million to a basic-income experiment (Winick, 2018). The program provided unconditional cash transfers to 3,000 participants in two states, including the city of Oakland.

Mayor Libby Schaaf of Oakland pledged to bring a guaranteed income program to the city when she joined Mayors for a Guaranteed Income (MGI) as a founding member in 2020 (Ho, 2021). MGI grew out of the groundbreaking universal income work of Stockton Economic Empowerment Demonstration (SEED), led by former Mayor Michael Tubbs of Stockton, California (McConville, 2021).

The same year, the mayor of San Francisco launched a six-month guaranteed income pilot program that would give 130 local artists affected by the COVID-19 pandemic $1,000 monthly (Sabatini, 2021). It is the latest guaranteed income project to launch in the nation. The model is growing in popularity for its potential to lift people out of a cycle of poverty, address income inequality, and improve health outcomes.

Education

Education and training are currently not set for the speed of change in the modern economy. Schools are still based on a one-time education model, with school providing the foundation for a single lifelong career. With content becoming obsolete faster and with rapidly escalating costs, this system may be unsustainable in the future. To help workers more smoothly transition from one job into another, for example, we need to make education a more nimble, lifelong endeavor. Primary and university education may still have a role in training foundational thinking and general education, but it will be necessary to curtail the rising cost of tuition and to increase accessibility. Massive open online courses (MOOCs) and open-enrollment platforms are early demonstrations of how the future of general education may look: cheap, effective, and flexible.

The learning content of MOOCs has been created by a few high-profile educational institutions, such as Harvard, Stanford, Berkeley, and other top universities. In Europe, it includes the universities of London, Oxford, Munich, and Zurich.

Social Safety Nets to Smooth the Impact of Automation

If predicted job losses due to automation come to fruition, modernizing existing social safety nets must become a priority. While the issue of safety nets quickly becomes politicized, it is worth noting that each prior technological revolution came with corresponding changes to the social contract. As an example, consider the ever-evolving social contract in the United States:

- In 1842 the right to strike (Reddebrek, 2016) arose from the Plug Plot Riots, which started among the miners in Staffordshire, England, and soon spread through Britain, affecting factories, mills in Yorkshire and Lancashire, and coal mines from Dundee to South Wales and Cornwall. Its main purpose was a workers strike for better wages and political reform.

- In 1924 came the abolition of child labor (Yellowitz, 2009). Federal laws regulating and taxing goods produced by underage employees had been declared unconstitutional. These laws were often paired with compulsory education laws, which were designed to keep children in school and out of the paid labor market until a specified age. A constitutional amendment in 1924 gave Congress the power to limit, regulate, and prohibit the labor of persons under 18 years of age.

- In 1935 the right to unionize was granted through the National Labor Relations Act of 1935, also known as the Wagner Act (Doyle, 2020). This is a foundational statute of U.S. labor law that guarantees the right of private sector employees to organize into trade unions, engage in collective bargaining, and take collective action such as strikes.

- In 1940 came the introduction of 40-hour workweek: Congress passed the Fair Labor Standards Act in 1938, which required employers to pay overtime to all employees who worked more than 44 hours in a week. They amended the act two years later to reduce the workweek to 40 hours, and in 1940, the 40-hour workweek became U.S. law (Greene, 2021).

- In 1962, 1974, and 2015 there was the federal program Trade Adjustment Assistance (TAA). This was designed to protect industries and workers from import competition shocks from globalization. The TAA was reestablished under the Trade Adjustment Assistance Reauthorization Act of 2015 (U.S. Department of Labor, 2021), which provides aid to workers who lose their jobs or whose hours of work and wages are reduced as a result of increased imports.

- In 1964, pay discrimination was prohibited. The Civil Rights Act of 1964 prohibited discrimination based on race, religion, color, or national origin in public places, schools, and employment. However, discrimination based on sex was not initially included in the proposed bill and was only added as an amendment in Title VII in an attempt to prevent its passage (U.S. Equal Employment Opportunity Commission, 2021). Pay discrepancies due to gender still have not been fully addressed, with U.S. women making on average 79 cents for every dollar a man makes.

- In 1970, there were health and safety laws. On December 29, 1970, President Richard Nixon signed into law the Williams-Steiger Occupational Safety and Health Act (Glass, 2018), which gave the federal government the authority to set and enforce safety and health standards for most of the country's workers.

- I believe that in the 21st century, AI and automation workers assistance may be necessary to counter the job displacement of these new exponential technologies.

THE FUTURE OF WORK

The world of work is changing. Artificial intelligence, automation, and robotics will make this shift as significant as the mechanization in prior generations of agriculture and manufacturing. Some jobs will be lost, many others will be created, and almost all will change.

Automation, AI, and robotics are moving inexorably forward, and will eventually affect the economies and job markets of all nations. Properly done, with the necessary disruptions to peoples' lives lessened and countered by effective precautionary and immediate aid programs, the possible benefits of technology are astronomical. An increase in productivity and a decrease in labor costs would lead to an economic jump, producing more affordable goods, and a more prosperous society overall (Opentext BC Campus, 2021).

Automation and working from home may last after the pandemic of 2020. Research published by Jose Maria Barrero, Nicholas Bloom, and Steven J. Davis (2021) showed that they surveyed 15,000 Americans over several waves to investigate whether, how, and why working from home will stick after COVID-19. Their survey evidence says that 22% of all full workdays will be supplied from home after the pandemic ends, compared with just 5% before. They also provided evidence on five mechanisms behind this persistent shift to working from home: diminished stigma, better-than-expected experiences working from home, investments in physical and human capital enabling working from home, reluctance to return to pre-pandemic activities, and innovation supporting working from home.

They also examine some implications of a persistent shift in working arrangements. First, high-income workers, especially, will enjoy the perks of working from home. Second, they forecast that the post-pandemic shift to working from home will lower worker spending in major city centers by 5 to 10%. Third, many workers reported being more productive at home than on premises, so post-pandemic work from home plans offer the potential to raise productivity as much as 2.4%.

So, how do you adapt to changes in technology?

Look at the changes positively. Understand that change is inevitable. Get training to stay on top of your game on new technology and sharpen your skills. Take the time to become familiar with the technologies that are coming out.

As a society, the education system and the way we prepare the workforce has to adapt. Retraining and reskilling has to be a priority in the short term and the entire education system will need to be overhauled long term.

Wealth from automation redistribution ideas have to emerge. The use of technology in the workplace has created a polarization of the jobs available. As more and more workers in the middle class find themselves out of work, more new jobs will be created in the low-paying and high-paying labor markets. This forces even more disparity into the division of wealth between the classes. These effects could be countered by a high tax levied on every dollar earned over a certain (usually extremely high) amount. The resulting tax revenues could then be used for unemployment compensation for those workers who have lost their job due to automation, as well as education and training needed by those workers to reenter the "new" workforce.

At this point I know some of you may still be skeptical. And you keep saying to yourself, "Another person crying wolf. When the radio came out, when TV came out—there were guys like you, but we turned out fine." One thing I can say to you is that humans have invented; humans have messed up; and they have reinvented themselves out of a mess. Think about fire extinguishers, speed limits, and stoplights, etc. But we cannot keep innovating our way out of all our mess-ups. With today's exponential tech, we have to get things right the first time. Never in the history of "ever" has humanity had so much technological power over itself, and yet there is no way to ensure we will use it wisely. The way things are going, it does not look good.

With automation, we are driving humanity toward a cliff. Critics may say that this is just fearmongering. As an engineer, I can tell you that it is not. It is called safety engineering. Tuning out the dark side of technology doesn't make it go away. It just makes you falsely blind to the oncoming traffic of its negative effects.

REFERENCES

Avalos, George. (2021). "Exodus: Bay Area migration accelerated in recent months." https://www.mercurynews.com/2021/03/04/covid-economy-bay-area-residents-exit-region-growing-numbers-jobs-tech/#:~:text=San%20Francisco%20experienced%20%E2%80%9Ca%20unique,a%20drop%20of%2025%20percent.

Barrero, Jose Maria, Nicholas Bloom, and Steven J. Davis. (2021). "Why Working from Home Will Stick." http://dx.doi.org/10.2139/ssrn.3741644

Bertrand, Natasha, and Eric Wolff. (2020). "Nuclear weapons agency breached amid massive cyber onslaught." https://www.politico.com/news/2020/12/17/nuclear-agency-hacked-officials-inform-congress-447855

Bui, Quoctrung. (2015). "Map: The Most Common Job in Every State." https://www.npr.org/sections/money/2015/02/05/382664837/map-the-most-common-job-in-every-state

DeSantis, Rachel. (2020). "Universal Income Trial Giving Select Citizens $1,400 Per Month Begins in Germany." https://people.com/human-interest/universal-income-trial-giving-select-citizens-1400-per-month-begins-in-germany/

Doyle, Alison. (2020). "The Wagner Act of 1935 (National Labor Relations Act)." https://www.thebalancecareers.com/the-wagner-act-of-1935-national-labor-relations-act-2060509

Economist. (2017). "The death of the internal combustion engine." https://www.economist.com/leaders/2017/08/12/the-death-of-the-internal-combustion-engine

Glass, Andrew. (2018). "Nixon signs workplace safety bill, Dec. 29, 1970." https://www.politico.com/story/2018/12/29/this-day-in-politics-dec-29-1970-1074961

Greene, Jessica (2021). "Is 40 hours a week too much? Here's what history and science say." https://www.atspoke.com/blog/hr/40-hour-work-week/#:~:text=In%20

1938%2C%20Congress%20passed%20the,hour%20workweek%20became%20U.S.%20law

Ho, Vivian. (2021). "Oakland to launch one of the largest US universal basic income programs yet." https://www.theguardian.com/us-news/2021/mar/23/oakland-california-universal-basic-income-program

Holmes, Frank. (2019). "AI Will Add $15 Trillion to the World Economy by 2030." https://www.forbes.com/sites/greatspeculations/2019/02/25/ai-will-add-15-trillion-to-the-world-economy-by-2030/?sh=34560ad21852

Liles, Honah. (2020). "Can Money Buy Happiness? Research Says: Yes, up to a Point." https://www.insider.com/can-money-buy-happiness

Luscombe, Belinda. (2010). "Do We Need $75,000 a Year to Be Happy?" http://content.time.com/time/magazine/article/0,9171,2019628,00.html

MacNeil, Jessica. (2019). "1st breeder reactor generates electricity, December 20, 1951." https://www.edn.com/1st-breeder-reactor-generates-electricity-december-20-1951/

Manyika, James, and Kevin Sneader. (2018). "AI, automation, and the future of work: Ten things to solve for." https://www.mckinsey.com/featured-insights/future-of-work/ai-automation-and-the-future-of-work-ten-things-to-solve-for

McConville, Saadia. (2021). "Guaranteed Income Increases Employment, Improves Financial and Physical Health." https://www.stocktondemonstration.org/press-landing/guaranteed-income-increases-employment-improves-financial-and-physical-health

National Geographic. (2021). "The Development of Agriculture" https://www.nationalgeographic.org/article/development-agriculture/

Opentext BC Campus, (2021). "20.2 Labor Productivity and Economic Growth." https://opentextbc.ca/principlesofeconomics/chapter/20-2-labor-productivity-and-economic-growth/

Palmer, Annie. (2020). "Amazon Zoox unveils self-driving robotaxi." https://www.cnbc.com/2020/12/14/amazons-self-driving-company-zoox-unveils-autonomous-robotaxi.html

Reddebrek. (2016). "The general strike of 1842." https://libcom.org/history/general-strike-1842

Sabatini, Joshua. (2021). "SF launches guaranteed income pilot program for 130 artists." https://www.sfexaminer.com/news/sf-launches-guaranteed-income-pilot-program-for-130-artists/

Stolzoff, Simone. (2018). "By 2025, machines will do more work than humans." https://qz.com/1391116/machines-will-do-more-work-than-humans-by-2025-wef-predicts/

Trout, C. (2018). "There's a new sex robot in town." https://www.engadget.com/2018-01-10-there-s-a-new-sex-robot-in-town-say-hello-to-solana.html

U.S. Department of Labor. (2021). "TAA Law." https://www.dol.gov/agencies/eta/tradeact/laws

U.S. Equal Employment Opportunity Commission. (2021). "Title VII of the Civil Rights Act of 1964." https://www.eeoc.gov/statutes/title-vii-civil-rights-act-1964

White, Matthew. (2009). "The Industrial Revolution." https://www.bl.uk/georgian-britain/articles/the-industrial-revolution#

Winick, Erin. (2018). "Y Combinator's $60 million basic-income experiment will begin next year." https://www.technologyreview.com/2018/08/28/140557/y--combinators-60-million-basic-income-experiment-will-begin-next-year/

Yellowitz, I. (2009). "Child Labor." http://www.history.com/topics/child-labor

CHAPTER 12

Climate: Are Humans the New "Weapons of Mass Destruction"?

Are you tired of hearing about climate change? Are you interested in the topic but increasingly feel jaded and helpless? Is it a question of chronic political fatigue? Or are our brains simply not wired to think long-term?

To understand more about climate change, we need to think about the *fight-flight-freeze response* in reaction to perceived threats, such as oncoming traffic or a growling dog. Physiological changes—like rapid heart rate, muscle movements, and reduced perception of pain—kick in to quickly defend against a perceived threat. The response is primitive and happens automatically. Sometimes, though, we perceive threat or harm when in reality things are fine. And other times we have a false sense of security when things are not fine.

Fight or flight is most effective when the perceived threat is visible and immediate. It creates that sense of urgency to respond instantly. But humans have a tendency to put off threats that don't seem urgent. They may put off going for a checkup or an oral hygiene visit. Deep down they know if they don't do it, there might be danger down the road, but they have a false sense of security and belief that "there is time."

When it comes to climate change, the human race is experiencing a delayed fight-flight-freeze (FFF) reaction. Those who care are exhausted with the magnitude of it all and the feeling of helplessness. Others either don't understand the science behind it or believe some political misinformation, or the media has made them so desensitized that they have no idea what to believe. Furthermore, it's inconvenient if climate change is real because it means we need to change, and change is hard. So we opt to delay our FFF.

Climate change doesn't care whether we believe in it. It is making itself known with ever increasing intensity and destruction. If we want a livable planet, we need to snap out of our "delayed FFF" and do something—now.

This chapter explores the role of technology in climate change. What are some of the unintended consequences? What solutions already exist? And what are some breakthroughs to help solve the challenges of climate change?

WHAT IS CLIMATE CHANGE?

Simply put, climate change describes a change in the average conditions—such as temperature and rainfall—in a region over a long period of time. Global climate change refers to the average long-term changes over the entire Earth. The Earth's average temperature is about 15°C/59°F. There are natural fluctuations, but scientists say temperatures are now rising faster than at any other time. *Industrialization, human activities, and the rise of exponential technology have a huge hand in that* (American Chemical Society, 2021).

The temperature rise is linked to the *greenhouse effect*, which describes how the Earth's atmosphere traps some of the Sun's energy. Since the industrial revolution, levels of CO_2 (a greenhouse gas) have risen more than 30% (Lindsey, 2020). The concentration of CO_2 in the atmosphere is higher than at any time in at least 800,000 years (Lopez, 2019). Other greenhouse gases are also released through human activities, but they are less abundant than carbon dioxide (Environmental Protection Agency, 2021).

What is the evidence for warming? According to the World Meteorological Organization (WMO), the world is about 1 degree Celsius (1°C = 33.8°F) warmer than before widespread industrialization. The five-year span of 2015–2019 was the warmest on record, with temperatures trending in the upward trajectory (World Meteorological Organization, 2019). Across the globe, the average sea level increased by 3.6 millimeters per year between 2005 and 2015 (Lindsey, 2021), mostly due to a combination of meltwater from glaciers and ice sheets and thermal expansion of seawater as it warms.

What evidence do we have that human activities are the main contributors to climate change?

There is a lot of scientific evidence to prove that there is less solar heat escaping to space (the greenhouse effect). If all solar heat energy emitted from the surface passed through the atmosphere directly into space, Earth's average surface temperature would be tens of degrees colder than today. Greenhouse gases make the surface much warmer because they absorb and emit heat energy in all directions (including downward). Scientists have determined that, when all human and natural factors are considered, Earth's climate balance has been altered toward warming, with the biggest contributor being increases in CO_2 (Royal Society, 2021).

There is a shrinking thermosphere. This layer above the Earth blocks harmful ultraviolet rays. It expands and contracts regularly due to the Sun's activities. The Sun undergoes a magnetic metamorphosis every 11 years, when it flips its magnetic poles. Within each solar cycle, the frequency of sunspots and flares ebbs and flows in response to the changing magnetic field. The Earth's thermosphere is particularly sensitive to these variations in solar activity (Geophysical Research Letters, 2019).

There is more fossil fuel carbon in the corals, the air, and in the trees. Our ever-increasing demand for fossil fuels is changing the carbon cycle, with far-reaching climate change consequences.

There is less oxygen in the air and water; ocean patterns are warming. One study found that over the past 800,000 years the amount of oxygen in the atmosphere has decreased by 0.7% and continues to decline (Nace, 2016). Warmer ocean water holds less oxygen and is more buoyant than cooler water. This leads to reduced mixing of oxygenated water near the surface with deeper waters, which naturally contain less oxygen. Warmer water also raises the oxygen demand from living organisms.

The nights are warming faster than the days and the winter is warming faster than the summer. The study shows this "warming asymmetry" has been driven primarily by changing levels of cloud cover. Increased cloud cover cools the surface during the day and retains the warmth during the night, leading to greater nighttime warming (University of Exeter, 2020).

We burn fossil fuels to power our technologies. All these issues point to a combination of advanced technology and human activities as the culprit.

A Quick History of the Climate Change Movement

In the 1820s, French mathematician and physicist Joseph Fourier proposed that energy reaching the planet as sunlight must be balanced by energy returning to space since heated surfaces emit radiation (Lynch, 2019). But some of that energy, he reasoned, must be held within the atmosphere. He proposed that Earth's atmosphere acts as a greenhouse would: energy enters and is trapped inside, resulting in the *greenhouse effect*.

This analogy stuck, and some 40 years later, Irish scientist John Tyndall explored exactly what "greenhouse gases" were most likely to play a role in absorbing sunlight. Tyndall's laboratory tests showed that coal gas (containing CO_2, methane, and volatile hydrocarbons) was especially effective at absorbing energy (Graham, 1999). He eventually demonstrated that CO_2 alone acted like sponge in the way it could absorb multiple wavelengths of sunlight.

By the 1930s, at least one scientist claimed that carbon emissions might already be having a warming effect. British engineer Guy Stewart Callendar noted that the United States and North Atlantic region had warmed significantly on the heels of the industrial revolution. Callendar's calculations suggested that a doubling of CO_2 in Earth's atmosphere could warm Earth by 2°C (3.6°F) (Rescue That Frog, 2021). He continued to argue into the 1960s that a greenhouse-like warming of the planet was under way.

Fast-forward to the early 1980s, which marked a sharp increase in global temperatures. Many experts point to 1988 as a critical turning point when watershed events placed global warming in the spotlight. The summer of 1988 was the hottest on record (although many have been hotter since then). That year also saw widespread drought and wildfires in the United States and other regions (*Los Angeles Times*, 1989).

Scientists sounding the alarm began to see the media and the public paying closer attention. NASA scientist James Hansen delivered testimony and presented models to Congress in June 1988, saying he was "99 percent sure" that global warming was upon us (Demeritt, 2001). Government leaders began discussions to prevent the direst predicted outcomes. The first global agreement to reduce greenhouse gases, the Kyoto Protocol, was adopted in 1997 (United Nations Climate Change, 2021) and called for reducing the emission of six greenhouse gases in 41 countries plus the European Union to 5.2% below 1990 levels during the target period of 2008 to 2012.

In March 2001, President George W. Bush announced the United States would not implement the Kyoto Protocol, saying it was "fatally flawed in fundamental ways" and citing concerns that it would hurt the U.S. economy. That same year, the IPCC's third report on climate change stated that global warming is "very likely," with highly damaging future impacts. Five years later, former Vice President Al Gore weighed in with his film *An Inconvenient Truth*. Gore won the 2007 Nobel Peace Prize for his work on behalf of climate change (Gibbs and Lyall, 2007).

In 2014, the nonprofit Project Drawdown was created to help the world reach *drawdown*, the point when levels of greenhouse gases start to steadily decline, thereby stopping catastrophic climate change. Project Drawdown provided a detailed roadmap for what needs to be done in each industry (Project Drawdown, 2021).

In 2015, under President Obama, the United States signed another milestone treaty, the Paris Climate Agreement (White House Archives, 2016), in which 200 countries pledged to set targets for their own greenhouse gas cuts. The backbone of the agreement was a declaration to prevent a global temperature rise of 2°C (3.6°F). Many experts considered this to be a critical limit, which, if surpassed will lead to increasing risk of more deadly heat waves, droughts, storms, and rising global sea levels.

Unfortunately, President Trump in 2016 withdrew the United States from the Paris treaty, citing "onerous restrictions" imposed by the accord, which "punishes the United States" (McGrath, 2020).

In August 2018, Swedish teenager and climate activist Greta Thunberg began protesting in front of the Swedish Parliament with a sign: "School Strike for Climate." Within a few month, her actions mobilized over 17,000 students in 24 countries to participate in climate strikes. By March 2019, Thunberg was nominated for a Nobel Peace Prize. She participated in the United Nations Climate Summit in New York City in August 2019, famously taking a boat across the Atlantic instead of flying, to reduce her carbon footprint.

The UN Climate Action Summit reinforced that "1.5°C is the socially, economically, politically and scientifically safe limit to global warming by the end of this century," and set a deadline for achieving net zero emissions to 2050.

Hours after he was sworn in on January 20, 2021, President Biden signed an executive order beginning the 30-day process for the United States to reenter the Paris Climate Agreement (Cho, 2021). The country officially rejoined the landmark international accord to limit global warming.

These are just a few of the many initiatives that have come a long way with varying degrees of success to address climate change. In the following section, we dive deeper into the negative effect of technology on climate change.

THE UNINTENDED CONSEQUENCES OF TECHNOLOGY ON THE CLIMATE

The scientific evidence of the changing climate can be linked to the increase in consumption, which has directly led to more fossil fuels being burned. Electricity and heat production are the largest contributors to global emissions, followed by transport, manufacturing and construction (largely cement and similar materials), and agriculture.

The digital technology industry is one of the least sustainable and most environmentally damaging industrial sectors in the modern world (ICTworks, 2020). When it comes to unintended and willfully ignored consequences, there are four areas to pay attention to here:

- Technologies with direct impact on the environment such as electricity demands and infrastructure upgrades.

- Technology's exploitation of people and the environment, due to the need for rare minerals, which leads to damaging mining methods and waste spillages.

- Technology drives electricity demands for manufacturing and usage of devices.

- Redundancy and unsustainability are built into the digital technology business model: the replacement rather than repair culture, the never-ending upgrades, and the growing electronic waste problem. (See Chapter 13, which covers e-waste.)

How to Mitigate the UCOTs of Technology on Climate Change

Mitigating climate change involves reducing the flow of heat-trapping greenhouse gases into the atmosphere, either by reducing sources of these gases (such as burning fossil fuels) or enhancing the "sinks" that accumulate and store these gases (such as the oceans, forests, and soil). The ultimate goal is to avoid significant human interference and stabilize greenhouse gas levels in a time frame sufficient to allow ecosystems to adapt naturally. This section discusses some ideas for how we can do this.

Clean Energy

Possibly the most obvious solution is the transition to a clean energy economy. On-shore wind turbines and utility-scale solar photovoltaics are listed as the top two solutions (Project Drawdown, 2018). The affordability of installing new wind and solar now exceeds coal production, making it the optimal choice (Gearino, 2019). As the demand for carbon-free energy sources grows, the International Renewable Energy Agency estimates that 80% of the global electricity supply will come from renewables in 2050 (International Renewable Energy Agency, 2021). In order for renewables to be successful on a wide scale, battery technology is crucial for storage of wind and solar, as these sources of electricity can be inconsistent (International Energy Agency, 2020).

There are many companies in the renewable energy sector, such as NextEra, which functions as the largest energy utility (NextEra Energy, 2021) in the United States. Avangrid Renewables (2021), a combination of natural gas and wind, operates in 24 U.S. states. Solstice partners

(Solstice, 2021) focuses on bringing low-cost energy to low-income and marginalized communities.

Electric Vehicles

There was a huge momentum toward a combination of clean energy and electric vehicles. In 2018, the transportation sector in the United States accounted for 28% of greenhouse gas emissions (Environmental Protection Agency, 2018), which presents a major opportunity for transition to reduced air pollution and more efficiency.

Most car companies have made statements about electrifying their fleets. In 2021, General Motors, the largest car manufacturer in the United States, announced they will have an entirely electric fleet by 2035 (Wayland, 2021). Visionaries like Elon Musk pioneered an effort with the combo of his SolarCity Corporation, which develops and sells clean energy, and Tesla Motors, a company accelerating the world's transition to sustainable energy with electric cars, solar, and integrated renewable energy solutions.

In 2021, President Biden unveiled a double attack plan of clean energy combined with electrification, part of a $2.25 trillion infrastructure and stimulus blueprint meant to catalyze investments in a clean energy economy and encourage low-emission technology necessary to constrain global warming. Biden asked Congress to dedicate spending to electric vehicle rebates, charging ports, electric government vehicles, and electric school buses in a quest to drive motorists away from conventional, gasoline-powered automobiles. Some $174 billion in government funding would go to the electric vehicle initiatives, according to a White House fact sheet summarizing the Biden plan (White House, 2021).

Improving Urban Systems

Local metropolises are seeking to support more public transit and alternative methods such as bicycles. Public transit offers an equitable, affordable, and sustainable source of transportation in urban areas (Project Drawdown, 2018). Additionally, *smart cities* are urban areas that use different types of electronic methods and sensors to collect data to manage assets, resources, and services efficiently, such as an initiative to improve transportation patterns through monitoring, evaluations, and data-informed decisions to reduce vehicle emissions. By leveraging technology based on the Internet of Things (IoT) and integrating the online population into new systems that make a city work, smart cities have emerged all around the world., including Singapore, Dubai, Oslo, Copenhagen, Boston, Amsterdam, London, and many more (Kosowatz, 2020).

Air Travel

Air travel is expected to triple from 2015 levels by 2045 (Bugault and Holger, 2021), presenting a pressing concern over emissions from the second largest emitter in transportation behind cars. Airlines are being pushed to transition to Sustainable Aviation Fuels (SAFs), such as biomass (Bugault and Holger, 2021). New innovation around producing fuel from other sources like renewable energy, through a process of electrolysis, could increase alternative energy available on a wider scale for airplanes.

Regenerative Agriculture

Another promising method is using farming practices such as *cover crops*, which are planted to cover the soil rather than for harvesting. Cover crops manage soil erosion, soil fertility, soil quality, water, weeds, pests, diseases, biodiversity, and wildlife in an agroecosystem, and are used to implement diverse crop rotations, limiting the use of chemicals and tilling; area-focused grazing can create healthy soil that will retain nutrients and carbon over long periods of time. Many innovative companies are taking this approach, such as Indigo Agriculture, a company that produces seeds that increase soil health. Their Terra-Ton project incentivizes farmers to sequester carbon through adoption of regenerative agriculture practices (Indigo Ag, 2021).

Accelerated Carbon Sequestration

One of the few solutions that focuses on removing greenhouse gases from the atmosphere rather than reducing emissions is *carbon sequestration*, the long-term removal, capture, or sequestration of CO_2 from the atmosphere to mitigate or reverse global warming. Regenerative agriculture, grazing, reforestation, and ecosystem management have the potential to naturally bury carbon from the air into the soil through plant processes.

As a Leader, What Can You Do About Climate Change?

One of the biggest challenges is that the troubles of today are a consequence of the actions in the past. The actions of today have their effects in the future. That time lag creates a conundrum of lack of urgency and a question of who to hold accountable.

Technology companies that may be heavy polluters love to idolize success and ignore failures, driving humanity toward a path of self-destruction. Future generations are voiceless; they don't vote or participate in markets, so tackling future problems seems too distant and "delayed FFF" feels manageable now.

But climate change is urgent. The negative effects are about to get very real unless we do something about it very quickly. Reports each year are increasingly worse than the year before (Forster and Le Quéré, 2020). These predictions should prompt all scientists, politicians, corporate leaders, and average citizens to think of solutions to this global environmental catastrophe.

We have seen everything from banning plastic straws to eliminating reliance on fossil fuels as proposed solutions. We've also seen the rise of many greener alternatives to products that have been harming the environment. And yet despite decades of greener practices, climate change is still getting worse (United Nations, 2019), because our exponential use of technology has exacerbated the rate at which we are producing greenhouse gases. What can we do to mitigate the negative consequences?

The Five Cures for Climate Change

We need to focus on all five of the issues discussed here to cure climate change for good:

- Stop plankton decline.
- Limit fossil fuel use.
- Stop forest clear-cutting.

- Promote the diversity of trees and plant life.
- Limit the CO_2 in the atmosphere.

Protect the Plankton

Plankton in the ocean provide a crucial source of food to aquatic organisms of all sizes. One of the most essential parts of the marine food chain is *phytoplankton*. These small but mighty single-celled organisms are responsible for half of the ocean's oxygen supply (Woods Hole Oceanographic Institution, 2021). Warmer oceans spell trouble for phytoplankton. We've seen a 40% decrease in phytoplankton since the 1950s (Morello, 2010). Since phytoplankton are the main food source for many marine animals, the decline affects the entire oceanic system. Beyond affecting fisheries and marine economies for humans, the decrease in phytoplankton will also trap more carbon dioxide in the atmosphere.

The proposals for saving plankton are complex and may have unintended consequences. Ideas range from using geoengineering to artificially cool the planet, to seeding the ocean to stimulate phytoplankton growth, to using pipes to simulate the churning large fish and whales used to be responsible for before their own numbers started dying out (The Week, 2021). Concerns include the risk of acidifying the ocean, and the unpredictability of introducing new organisms and minerals during seeding and altering the ecosystem in other unknown ways. Yet if something isn't done soon, the plankton may die out.

One of the things we can do immediately is require governments to share data on plankton research. By working together, scientists will have a much clearer understanding of how to save the plankton and maintain harmony in the oceans that we all depend on.

Stop Taking Fossil Fuels out of the Ground

Drilling, fracking, and mining needed to power our addiction to technology are negatively impacting the planet in so many ways that we're not even aware of all the unintended consequences. Until recently, seismologists did not know fracking would result in earthquakes—even in regions where earthquakes should not occur. The lobbying of citizens whose homes were being affected brought the issue to the attention of authorities (Pines, 2014).

The main culprit, however, is the pollution generated by taking fossil fuels out of the ground (Perera, 2018). The release of methane and black carbon, damage from oil spills, disruption of wildlife, increased flooding due to erosion, and the effects of light pollution all have various consequences on the environment.

Concerned citizens are already forcing governments to enact change. Many European countries have banned fracking altogether (Silverstein, 2019) or temporarily halted drilling. After years of pressure from grassroots coalitions, Belize became the first country to reject all offshore oil drilling (Green, 2018). The banding together of average citizens is making change happen. We just need every country to get on board.

Stop Clear-Cutting Forests

Deforestation has a two-fold impact on climate change. Clear-cutting—uniformly cutting down trees in an area—destroys CO_2-absorbing trees and emits large amounts of greenhouse gases. It also destroys ecosystems, leads to erosion and flash flooding, eradicates biodiversity, and pollutes water supplies (Center for Biological Diversity, 2021). Despite the outcry from environmental groups and concerned citizens, global deforestation reached a record 29.7 million hectares—a 51% increase in tree cover loss from the year before (Weisse and Goldman, 2017).

Trees absorb our carbon emissions, making them one of our greatest allies in the fight to halt global warming. The survival of humanity will in large part hinge on the survival of our forests. Since the biggest cause of deforestation is agriculture, one solution is to change global agricultural practices. The lumber industry is another factor and could be replaced by alternatives such as bamboo and hemp.

Plant More Variety of Trees in Larger Numbers

Trees produce oxygen, which we all need to breathe, and they also eat CO_2 for breakfast, which is good for the environment. Trees reduce stormwater runoff, which reduces erosion and pollution in our waterways and may reduce the effects of flooding. And many species of wildlife depend on trees for food, protection, and habitat.

Some people and organizations are taking the matter into their own hands, pioneering reforestation and tree planting projects. The story of Antonio Vicente went viral in 2017 after it was discovered that he had single-handedly replanted 50,000 trees on his 31-hectare property (Spooky, 2017).

Another effort is Africa's Great Green Wall, an epic ambition to grow an 8,000-kilometer natural wonder of the world across the entire width of Africa. A decade in and roughly 15% under way, the initiative is already bringing life back to Africa's degraded landscapes at an unprecedented scale, providing food security, jobs, and a reason to stay for the millions who live along its path. It promises to be a compelling solution to the many urgent threats facing not only the African continent but the global community as a whole—notably climate change, drought, famine, conflict, and migration. Once complete, the Great Green Wall will be the largest living structure on the planet, three times the size of the Great Barrier Reef (Great Green Wall, 2021).

Why not get technology involved? For example, a UK-based company backed by drone manufacturer Parrot came up with a way to plant up to 100,000 trees a day, quickly and cheaply. And trees can be planted by drones in areas that are difficult to access or otherwise unviable.

It's simple math. We are chopping down about 15 billion trees a year and planting about 9 billion, a net loss of 6 billion trees a year. Planting trees by hand is slow and expensive, so we need an industrial-scale solution (Edmond, 2017). Sadly, tree planting work suffers from a major mismatch between ambition and effort. Furthermore, there's so much CO_2 in the atmosphere that planting trees can't be the only solution; we need to work on all five efforts concurrently.

Stop Pumping CO_2 into the Atmosphere

A report from the Intergovernmental Panel on Climate Change (IPCC)—created to provide policy makers with regular scientific assessments, implications, and potential future risks—determined that, to prevent 1.5°C of warming, we need to reduce global emissions by 45% from 2010 levels by 2030 and 100% by 2050 (Intergovernmental Panel on Climate Change, 2018).

Additionally, in his book *How to Avoid a Climate Disaster,* Bill Gates says that there are two numbers that may frame the future of the world's climate: 51 billion tons of greenhouse gasses are added to the atmosphere each year, and zero is the number of tons we need to get to by 2050 in order to avert a climate crisis (Gates, 2021). The Gates Foundation has been investing heavily in the search for an energy miracle to support 9 billion people in a zero-carbon world (Bennet, 2015).

The CO_2 reduction needed is so dramatic that many are rightfully concerned that it will not be politically or economically possible. Governments and corporations have vested financial interests in maintaining the use of fossil fuels and other practices that pump CO_2 into the atmosphere. While some countries experienced a decline in their contribution to energy-related CO_2 emissions, the overall global increase proves that all countries need to collectively reduce emissions in order to cure climate change. Part of that effort is to wean the world off fossil fuels.

Renewable energy sources such as wind and solar must replace fossil fuels by at least 70% to 80% by 2050 (Union of Concerned Scientists, 2017). Wind and solar energy corporations already understand the economic benefits, but without government support from around the world, fossil fuel companies will continue to hinder any progress.

Ironically, fossil fuel companies are some of the largest funders of clean energy efforts. It may be for PR purposes, or maybe they are realizing that there is a business opportunity in the clean energy space, or maybe they finally also realized the negative impact and assault their work is having on humanity and our planet. Whatever the case may be, we need all hands on deck.

Take CO_2 out of the Atmosphere

In 2016, CO_2 levels in the atmosphere surpassed the symbolic 400 parts per million threshold (Jones, 2017). The long-term effects of this increase are devastating, including record heat waves, wildfires, flash floods, and air pollution. It's no longer enough to stop producing CO_2; it must be sucked out of the atmosphere as well.

Making *direct air capture* affordable may be the key but requires advancements in technology. The CO_2 captured by the process can then be permanently stored in deep geological formations or used in the production of fuels, chemicals, building materials, and other products. While it's not without possible unintended consequences, technology such as lab-made minerals that turn carbon dioxide into magnetite and direct air capture facilities are already under way.

Greenhouse emissions removal company Opus 12 uses technology to bolt onto any source of CO_2 emissions and transform that CO_2 into chemical products. The company promises to reduce the carbon footprint of the world's heaviest emitters, while creating a new revenue stream from what is discarded today as a waste product (Opus 12, 2021).

In 2021, President Biden's $2-trillion-plus infrastructure plan proposed an expansion of a tax credit that supports the underground storage of carbon dioxide, popular with both environmentalists and oil companies. According to the White House summary (White House, 2021), Biden's plan would revamp the carbon-capture tax credit so it benefits retrofits of existing power plants, technology directly capturing greenhouse gas emissions from the air, and hard-to-decarbonize industrial sectors, such as steel and cement making.

Of course, there is always a timeless, more natural approach. Planting trees is affordable, accessible, and any unintended consequences would be minimal. Plus, it has the added benefits of combating deforestation and compensating for declining plankton.

What Can You Do to Help?

Business leaders and a global citizens can pressure government agencies and corporate influencers to implement these cures for climate change. Environmental organizations, nonprofits, grassroots coalitions, local communities, and conscientious corporations all need to continue forcing the issue for an immediate change.

The real change needs to come from big governments, big money, and big corporations. The collective influence of united citizens can accelerate the move to a more sustainable world. Use the power of your dollars. Vote for people who take climate change seriously. Plant a tree or two, or sponsor a tree with a nonprofit that will plant it on your behalf.

Some detractors say switching to clean energy is a job killer. Do you know what else is a job killer? A planet that can't support life.

References

American Chemical Society. (2021). "What are the greenhouse gas changes since the Industrial Revolution?" https://www.acs.org/content/acs/en/climatescience/greenhousegases/industrialrevolution.html

Ategeka, Christopher. (2018). "6 Medicines That Can Cure Climate Change—If We Take Them in Time." https://thriveglobal.com/stories/6-medicines-that-can-cure-climate-change-if-we-do-them-in-time/

Avangrid. (2021). "A leading sustainable energy company." https://www.avangrid.com/wps/portal/avangrid/aboutus

BBC. (2020). "What is climate change? A really simple guide." https://www.bbc.com/news/science-environment-24021772

Bennet, James. (2015). "We Need an Energy Miracle." https://www.theatlantic.com/magazine/archive/2015/11/we-need-an-energy-miracle/407881/

Bugault, Olivia, and Dieter Holger. (2021). "Airlines Push to Reduce Carbon Footprint with Greener Fuels." https://www.wsj.com/articles/airlines-push-to-reduce-carbon-footprint-with-greener-fuels-11612893657

Center for Biological Diversity. (2021). "Clearcutting and Climate Change." https://www.biologicaldiversity.org/programs/public_lands/forests/clearcutting_and_climate_change/

Cho, Renee. (2021). "The U.S. Is Back in the Paris Agreement. Now What?" https://news.climate.columbia.edu/2021/02/04/u-s-rejoins-paris-agreement/

Crawford, Elisabeth. (2021). "Svante Arrhenius—The Swedish chemist." https://www.britannica.com/biography/Svante-Arrhenius

Demeritt, David. (2001). "The Construction of Global Warming and the Politics of Science." http://citeseerx.ist.psu.edu/viewdoc/download?doi=10.1.1.195.6444&rep=rep1&type=pdf

Edmond, Charlotte. (2017). "These drones can plant 100,000 trees a day." https://www.weforum.org/agenda/2017/06/drones-plant-100000-trees-a-day/

Energy Agency. (2020). "A rapid rise in battery innovation is playing a key role in clean energy transitions."https://www.iea.org/news/a-rapid-rise-in-battery-innovation-is-playing-a-key-role-in-clean-energy-transitions

Environmental Protection Agency. (2018). "Sources of Greenhouse Gas Emissions." https://www.epa.gov/ghgemissions/sources-greenhouse-gas-emissions

Environmental Protection Agency. (2021). "Climate Change Indicators: Atmospheric Concentrations of Greenhouse Gases." https://www.epa.gov/climate-indicators/climate-change-indicators-atmospheric-concentrations-greenhouse-gases

Environmental Protection Agency Journal. (1989). "Environmental protection." https://books.google.com/books

Forster, Piers, and Corinne Le Quéré. (2020). "Climate change is getting worse but it is no worse than we predicted." https://www.theccc.org.uk/2020/05/04/climate-change-is-getting-worse-but-it-is-no-worse-than-we-predicted/

Gates, Bill. (2021). *How to Avoid a Climate Disaster*, p. 3. Alfred A. Knopf.

Gearino, Dan. (2019). "New Wind and Solar Power Is Cheaper Than Existing Coal in Much of the U.S., Analysis Finds." https://insideclimatenews.org/news/25032019/coal-energy-costs-analysis-wind-solar-power-cheaper-ohio-valley-southeast-colorado/

Geophysical Research Letters. (2019). "The Thermosphere Responds to a Weaker Than Normal Solar Cycle." https://eos.org/research-spotlights/the-thermosphere-responds-to-a-weaker-than-normal-solar-cycle

Gibbs, Walter, and Sarah Lyall. (2007). "Gore Shares Peace Prize for Climate Change Work." https://www.nytimes.com/2007/10/13/world/13nobel.html

Graham, Steve. (1999). "John Tyndall (1820-1893)." https://earthobservatory.nasa.gov/features/Tyndall

Great Green Wall. (2021). "Growing a World Wonder." https://www.greatgreen-wall.org/about-great-green-wall

Green, Graeme. (2018). "Belize bans oil activity to protect its barrier reef." https://www.theguardian.com/travel/2018/jan/14/belize-bans-oil-activity-to-protect-reef-diving-tourism-belize-barrier-reef

Harvey, Chelsea. (2018). "Cleaning Up Air Pollution May Strengthen Global Warming." https://www.scientificamerican.com/article/cleaning-up-air-pollution-may-strengthen-global-warming/

ICTworks. (2020). "Digital Technologies Are Part of the Climate Change Problem." https://www.ictworks.org/digital-technologies-climate-change-problem/

Indigo Ag. (2021). "What if a healthy planet began with a healthy farm?" https://www.indigoag.com/

Intergovernmental Panel on Climate Change. (2018). "Global Warming of 1.5°C." https://www.ipcc.ch/sr15/chapter/spm/

Intergovernmental Panel on Climate Change. (2021). "History of the IPCC." https://www.ipcc.ch/about/history/#:~:text=The%20Intergovernmental%20Panel%20on%20Climate%20Change%20(IPCC)%20was%20established%20by,UN%20General%20Assembly%20in%201988.

International Renewable Energy Agency. (2021). "Renewable Energy: A key climate solution." https://www.irena.org/climatechange/Renewable-Energy-Key-climate-solution#:~:text=Renewables%20could%20supply%20four%2Dfifths,key%20part%20of%20the%20mix

Jones, Nicola. (2017). "How the World Passed a Carbon Threshold and Why It Matters." https://e360.yale.edu/features/how-the-world-passed-a-carbon-threshold-400ppm-and-why-it-matters

Kosowatz, John. (2020). "Top 10 Growing Smart Cities." https://www.asme.org/topics-resources/content/top-10-growing-smart-cities

Lindsey, Rebecca. (2020). "Climate Change: Atmospheric Carbon Dioxide." https://www.climate.gov/news-features/understanding-climate/climate-change-atmospheric-carbon-dioxide

Lindsey, Rebecca. (2021). "Climate Change: Global Sea Level." https://www.climate.gov/news-features/understanding-climate/climate-change-global-sea-level

Lopez, Edward. (2019). "Climate Change." https://atlascorps.org/climate-change/#:~:text=Most%20man%2Dmade%20emissions%20of,cutting%20down%20carbon%2Dabsorbing%20forests.&text=Since%20the%20industrial%20revolution%20began,have%20risen%20more%20than%20140%25

Los Angeles Times. (1989). "1988 Was Hottest Year on Record as Global Warming Trend Continues." https://www.latimes.com/archives/

Lynch, Peter. (2019). "How Joseph Fourier discovered the greenhouse effect." https://www.irishtimes.com/news/science/how-joseph-fourier-discovered-the-greenhouse-effect-1.3824189

McGrath, Matt. (2020). "Climate change: US formally withdraws from Paris agreement." https://www.bbc.com/news/science-environment-54797743

Morello, Lauren. (2010). "Phytoplankton Population Drops 40 Percent Since 1950." https://www.scientificamerican.com/article/phytoplankton-population/#:~:text=Researchers%20at%20Canada's%20Dalhousie%20University,surface%20temperatures%20are%20to%20blame

Nace, Trevor. (2016). "Earth's Oxygen Levels Are Declining." https://www.forbes.com/sites/trevornace/2016/09/27/earths-oxygen-levels-declining-scientists/?sh=7da1a1147e4d

NextEra Energy. (2021). "Producer of wind and solar energy." https://www.nexteraenergy.com/

Opus 12. (2021). "We have developed a device that recycles CO_2 into chemicals and fuels." https://www.opus-12.com/technology

Perera, F. (2018). "Pollution from Fossil-Fuel Combustion Is the Leading Environmental Threat to Global Pediatric Health and Equity: Solutions Exist." https://www.ncbi.nlm.nih.gov/pmc/articles/PMC5800116/

Pines, Elizabeth. (2014). "The Business of Fracking and Corporate Power." https://marcellus.cas.lehigh.edu/sites/marcellus.cas2.lehigh.edu/files/LizPines_0.pdf

Project Drawdown. (2018). "Project Drawdown global efforts to address climate change." https://drawdown.org/solutions/table-of-solutions

Project Drawdown. (2021). "Solutions." https://drawdown.org/solutions

Rescue That Frog. (2021). "Scientific evidence of global climate change: A brief history." http://www.rescuethatfrog.com/history-of-evidence/

Riebeek, Holli. (2011). "The Carbon Cycle." https://earthobservatory.nasa.gov/features/CarbonCycle

Royal Society. (2021). "The Basics of Climate Change." https://royalsociety.org/topics-policy/projects/climate-change-evidence-causes/basics-of-climate-change/

Silverstein, Ken. (2019). "Will the UK's Temporary Ban on Natural Gas Fracking Impact U.S. Policy?"https://www.forbes.com/sites/kensilverstein/2019/11/17/will-the-uks-temporary-ban-on-natural-gas-fracking-impact-us-policy/?sh=7345d2225b5b

Solstice. (2021). "Affordable clean energy for all." https://solstice.us/

Spooky. (2017). "Brazilian Man Spends 40 Years Bringing a Forest Back to Life." https://www.odditycentral.com/news/brazilian-man-spends-40-years-bringing-a-forest-back-to-life.html

TED Conferences. (2020). "We Can Change Climate Change." https://countdown.ted.com/

Union of Concerned Scientists. (2017). "Benefits of Renewable Energy Use." https://www.ucsusa.org/resources/benefits-renewable-energy-use

United Nations. (2019). "Only 11 Years Left to Prevent Irreversible Damage from Climate Change, Speakers Warn during General Assembly High-Level Meeting." https://www.un.org/press/en/2019/ga12131.doc.htm

United Nations Climate Change. (2021). "What is the Kyoto Protocol?" https://unfccc.int/kyoto_protocol#:~:text=The%20Kyoto%20Protocol%20was%20adopted,Parties%20to%20the%20Kyoto%20Protocol

University of Exeter. (2020). "Nights warming faster than days across much of the planet." https://www.sciencedaily.com/releases/2020/09/200930194912.htm#:~:text=The%20study%20shows%20this%20%22warming,to%20greater%20night%2Dtime%20warming.

Wayland, Michael. (2021). "General Motors plans to exclusively offer electric vehicles by 2035." https://www.cnbc.com/2021/01/28/general-motors-plans-to-exclusively-offer-electric-vehicles-by-2035.html

Week, The. (2021). "Should scientists artificially cool the planet to stave off climate catastrophe?" https://theweek.com/articles/953090/should-scientists-artificially-cool-planet-stave-climate-catastrophe

Weisse, Mikaela, and Elizabeth Goldman. (2017). "Global Tree Cover Loss Rose 51 Percent in 2016." https://www.wri.org/blog/2017/10/global-tree-cover-loss-rose-51-percent-2016

White House. (2021). "The American rescue plan act of 2021." https://www.whitehouse.gov/briefing-room/statements-releases/2021/03/31/fact-sheet-the-american-jobs-plan/

White House Archives. (2016). "President Obama: The United States Formally Enters the Paris Agreement." https://obamawhitehouse.archives.gov/blog/2016/09/03/president-Obama-United-states-formally-enters-Paris-agreement

Woods Hole Oceanographic Institution. (2021). "Phytoplankton." https://www.whoi.edu/know-your-ocean/ocean-topics/ocean-life/phytoplankton/#:~:text=Phytoplankton%20are%20some%20of%20Earth's,most%20other%20ocean%20life%20possible

World Meteorological Organization. (2019). "Urgency of climate action highlighted for U.N. summit preparatory meeting." https://public.wmo.int/en/media/press-release/urgency-of-climate-action-highlighted-un-summit-preparatory-meeting

CHAPTER 13

Ethics: Are Universal Ethical Principles Possible in Technology?

The year 2020 was a particularly interesting time to be thinking about ethics in technology. I think it's safe to assume we all ended 2020 at least a little different than we entered it. The pandemic left a lasting impact on all of our lives, just as older generations were forever changed by world wars. Life will never be the same for people who lost a loved one. The year made it clear how polarized society has become and how set so many people seem to be in their ways, values, and beliefs. Paradoxically, ethics and values seemed to be shifting in many different ways.

A cocktail of technology, fables, misinformation, and herd mentality is playing a huge role in the exponential change in our understanding of right and wrong. It starts with the little things: white lies that become big lies, that are recorded as data, that are then encoded as algorithms. They turn into strong, powerful software programs, powered by faulty data, and they control our lives. As we have explored in this book, such lies have many real-world negative consequences.

Let's take the COVID-19 vaccine roll out as an example. When goods are scarce, people sometimes behave badly. When the right thing to do is also the hardest, people sometimes adjust their ethics for temporary convenience. This was on full display during COVID-19 vaccine distribution. The attempt to do it in an equitable, ethical, trustworthy, prioritized manner faced a few ethical conundrums. Many people's ethics were tested. Since COVID-19 vaccines were scarce, many people who wanted the shots couldn't get them, either because they were not yet eligible, according to priorities set by their state or county, or because there weren't any available appointments. People were "becoming" waiters, farmers, teachers, or asthmatics overnight just to get the shot. One may say this is benign and didn't harm anyone directly (although it delayed vaccine availability to some who were legitimately eligible). But this is how it starts: with small things. Then come the big ethically questionable behaviors.

WHAT ARE ETHICS?

Ethics are the moral principles that govern a person's behavior and actions. It is a branch of philosophy that involves systematizing, defending, and recommending concepts of right and wrong behavior that prescribe what humans ought to do—usually in terms of rights, obligations, benefits to society, fairness, or specific virtues.

Ethics are derived from the ethos of that person or group. *Ethos* is an ancient Greek word meaning "character" and is used to describe the guiding beliefs, values, and ideals that characterize a person, group, community, or nation. Ethics are important because they provide structure and stability for society.

As our lives become more and more dependent on algorithms to make daily decisions, we need to examine how universal ethical principles can be applied to technology. We need to apply ethical thinking to the practical concerns of a technology before, during, and after its creation.

As we have explored in previous chapters, the new technologies give us much more power to knowingly or unknowingly act on living and nonliving things on the Earth and beyond, which means that we have to make choices we didn't have to make before. According to the Peter Parker principle—so-named because it was popularized by Spider-Man comic creator Stan Lee—"With great power comes great responsibility."

Some ethical considerations in technology include personal privacy, access rights, harmful actions like cyberattacks and cyber-terrorism, patent infringements, copyright issues, trade secrets, liability, piracy, and many more.

As technology gets better, faster, and more efficient, we must be careful not to mistake efficiency for morality. We have become so powerful that we now have the ability to innovate ourselves into extinction.

In our increasingly polarized world of *echo chambers*, ethics are being tested. Echo chambers are situations in which beliefs are amplified or reinforced by communication and repetition inside a closed system and insulated from rebuttal.

Laws may be easy to implement when there is a clear right and wrong, but ethics are very hard to legislate unless they break the law. In today's world, technology is now universal but ethics are not. How do you handle a technology that has the ability to harm everyone the same, but the ethics of developing, deploying, and using it are not universal? We need to explore these questions as a whole.

What Ethics Are Not

Ethics are not the same as *feelings*. Our feelings are not always accurate indicators of something being unethical (e.g., taking a long lunch or spending too much personal time on social media while on the clock at work). We all develop defense mechanisms to protect ourselves, to avoid feeling bad about a particular unethical act. Some people may actually feel good about behaving unethically. Also, another person can hurt our feelings without actually doing something unethical.

Ethics are not the same as *religion*. Most religions champion high ethical standards, but not everyone is religious. Even religious people behave unethically and many atheists have high standards of ethics. Ethics apply to everyone.

Ethics are not necessarily synonymous with the *law*. There will be instances in which ethical behavior and the law are the same (e.g., in the cases of murder, discrimination, and fraud). Such instances are illustrative of a good legal system. There will, however, be times when the law takes a different path than ethics—the result being ethical corruption that serves the interests only of an individual or a small group. In addition, sometimes the law has not caught up with a new ethical issue that is plaguing society. Passing laws takes time, and that process is often a reaction to breaches in ethics.

Ethics are not about following *cultural norms*. Following cultural norms works only for ethical cultures. Although most cultures probably like to see themselves as ethical, all societies have been and will be plagued by unethical or questionable norms.

Ethics are not synonymous with *science*. Science cannot tell us what to do. Science provides us with insights and facts, but ethics provides the reasons and the guidance for what we should do.

Ethics are not the same as *values*. Values are the degree of importance of some thing or action, with the aim of determining what actions are best or which way is best to live for an individual or a group. Although values are essential to ethics, the two are not synonymous.

It is important to look at what ethics are *not* in order to fully understand and deal with the challenges that we face while attempting to create ethical technologies.

Ethical Challenges of Technology in a Global Context

With the advent of technology, which affects everyone in the world, the attempt to find a consistent, moral framework that describes the right thing to do in a given situation and with some finite number of rules that fit together nicely together is turning out to be more of a challenge than anyone anticipated. Here is why.

Ethics Are Subjective

Subjective ethics is when one's personal taste, emotional state, culture, and contextual situation causes one person to reach a different moral conclusion in a situation than another person, even given the same moral problem and the same set of facts. What's considered ethical in the United States, for example, may not be ethical in China or South Africa and vice versa. One country may consider mass surveillance on its citizens ethical and allowed, while the other may frown upon this practice.

Ethics Change Depending on One's Loyalties and Hierarchy of Values

For example, some countries practicing "do not kill" as an ethical value might still execute criminals, go to war, or allow its citizens to defend property with lethal force. Superficially, the ethics appear the same (in this case, "do not kill"), but the way they are interpreted is different.

The principle that comes to mind about this is the Euthyphro dilemma, also called the trolley problem. This is a thought experiment about a fictional scenario in which an onlooker has the choice to save five people in danger of being hit by a trolley, by diverting the trolley to kill just one person. The term is often used more loosely with regard to any choice that seemingly has a trade-off between what is good and which sacrifices are "acceptable," if any.

Add exponential technology to the mix, and matters get complex very quickly!

Ethics Evolve Over Time

We no longer diagnose gay people with mental disorders or women with hysteria. We don't think epilepsy is caused by the devil anymore. Ethics evolve and there are some merits to that. Here are some examples.

Slavery: For thousands of years, slavery and involuntary servitude was considered ethical in many parts of the world. Regardless of their location or job, slaves were property and could be brutalized, raped, and murdered with impunity. Ethics evolved, and the slave's predicament changed as well.

In another example, for a depressingly long period of U.S. history, the native people of North America were regarded as being too savage to understand how to properly raise their own children (Blais-Billie, 2014), even though they had done so perfectly well for quite some time before the first Europeans showed up to tell them they were doing everything wrong. Consequently, Native American children were more or less regarded as property of the state and taken away by the government until the 1970s. The government could swoop into any Native American household at any time and whisk the children away to a "safer" environment ("safer" is a term here meaning "white"). Thanks to the power of evolving ethics, at the time of this writing, slavery and snatching children are illegal and unethical in the majority of the world.

Smoking indoors: Back in the day, you could light up a cigarette pretty much anywhere—at a friend's house, in restaurants, in the workplace, in an elevator, even in planes. Thanks to the power of evolving ethics and scientific studies about the dangers of second-hand smoke, this has changed.

Eugenics: This is the process of breeding certain people out of the gene pool, lest they pollute society with their horrid diversity. It was a popular and well-received idea in the early part of the 20th century and a favorite of Hitler (and Charles Lindbergh). This was done via castrations and sterilizations. Its proponents claimed that the practice could create a world in which genetic disease would be a thing of the past. As an example, in the United States, people who were deemed mentally ill and disabled were involuntarily sterilized, and the practice went on until 1972 (University of Vermont, 2021).

I could go on and on with more examples like lynching, gay marriage, and other elements of our society that have benefited greatly from the evolving nature of ethics.

When judging your ancestors, do it with lots of understanding. If you lived during their time, you would probably do many things "wrong" as well. You are a different iteration of what they believed, and technology has played a huge role in educating you. The same way that the technology superpowers are able to change society for the better, it's also a breeding ground for many unethical norms and behaviors.

Most of the terrible practices mentioned above took place when communication and socialization was mostly analogue. Fast-forward to the 21st century, where shopping, school, mail, work, meetings, recreational activities, news, sex, you name it, are all online, fueled by an enormous amount of data input from flawed humans. Ethics, and what's right or wrong, are bound to be tested.

THE UNINTENDED CONSEQUENCES OF UNETHICAL PRACTICES IN TECHNOLOGY

Most of us would rather work for a company that does the right thing and most customers would rather do business with a company that does the right thing. So why do the same people who want good ethical behavior followed elsewhere make unethical choices? Is it the seduction of "do as I say, not as I do"? This section covers some examples of unintended consequences of unethical practices in technology.

Financial Cost

Unethical behavior can be expensive. A perfect example of this is the alleged violations by a number of large banks related to mortgage loan origination, servicing, and foreclosure practices that led to the 2008 market crash. Even if you do not consider the huge settlements they paid, all banks had to increase their compliance budgets to comply with new regulations from the Consumer Financial Protection Bureau (McNeill, 2014).

This is just one example of unethical behavior in one specific industry. However, unethical practices span almost all the technology sectors and may include ethical dilemmas like profit maximization at all costs, health issues on humanity and the planet, intellectual property theft, creating killer technology to destroy human life, and many more. The cost of unethical behavior is staggering. This may include loss of physical assets, loss of customers, loss of employees, loss of reputation, legal costs, loss of investor confidence, regulatory intrusion, and bankruptcy costs.

Furthermore, unethical business behavior has an adverse impact on sales, stock prices, productivity, performance of highly skilled employees, efficiency, communication, and employee retention and recruiting, plus the risks from scandal and employee fraud.

Making ethical decisions requires sensitivity to the ethical implications of problems and situations. It also requires practice. Individuals, governments, and companies alike need a process for how to navigate the world in an ethical way. Having a framework for ethical decision-making is essential, because it's not always black and white. Running ethical businesses is the most cost-effective way for any tech company to operate.

Loss of Life

One of the unintended and sometimes intended unethical uses of some technologies is the loss of life. In many cases use of surveillance technology, for instance, is literally a matter of life and death. News media cycles are full of examples, but I will spare you the gruesome details on this subject.

ETHICAL CONCERNS RELATED TO TECHNOLOGY

It's not your imagination: you're correct in thinking that every week there's a new scandal about ethics and the tech industry. Even as the tech industry is trying to establish concrete practices and institutions around ethics, hard lessons are being learned about the wide gap between the practices of "doing ethics" and what people think of as "ethical." Here are some examples.

Democratized Technology

Gene editing: Is it ethical to eliminate species? Is it ethical to design a baby with features and qualities to your liking?

3D printing (additive manufacturing): This is the process whereby a physical object is constructed using a 3D computer model and a standard machine that extrudes material to build the object, often layer by layer. These machines are extremely affordable for small-batch productions relative to the manufacturing equipment we've relied on until now. Flexibility in 3D printing was designed into their architectures from the beginning. 3D printers are designed to enable someone to make almost any design a reality. Today, 3D-printable items already range from the mundane, like plastic toys, to the life-changing, like affordable housing. The first airplane with a 3D-printed parts took flight in 2014. And the world's first 3D-printed heart was announced in April 2019.

Simply put, 3D printing is democratizing the production of anything. On its face, this is amazing. Imagine completely eliminating the organ-transplant waiting list. The superpowers allowing us to bypass the controls that have existed for generations in supply chains are also potentially dangerous if gone unchecked.

Is it ethical to 3D print a human (although not possible at the moment, we are on our way), as opposed to going through the traditional birth process? Is it ethical to 3D print a gun? The model for the Liberator, a 3D-printable plastic gun, was downloaded more than 100,000 times before a federal judge blocked the posting of 3D gun blueprints online (Hafner, 2018).

Tech Surveillance as a Revenue Model

In 2021, personal information on more than 533 million users spanning 106 countries was breached on Facebook (Peters, 2021).

Another incident happened in 2018 with Facebook and the Cambridge Analytica data scandal (Confessore, 2018). Like most large technology conglomerates, Facebook collects a lot of personal data. Technology conglomerates use this personal data to determine which ads a user should be targeted with. Facebook's algorithms are so advanced that they can predict almost everything about you—what recipe you want to try out in your new air fryer, whether or not you're in a relationship, even if you haven't shared this information publicly, or what you should get your dad for his birthday. Although it's no secret that Facebook collects a lot of personal data, Facebook's most serious ethical lapses in judgment have involved its handling of this data and how (or if) other large companies are able to access this data (Wessel and Helmer, 2020).

YouTube's recommendation algorithm promotes conspiracy theory videos as a way to boost ad revenue, which misinform users in a harmful way (Cuthbertson, 2020).

A wide variety of ethical issues still remain with smart-wearable glasses. Ethical issues identified by experts (Hofmann, 2017) are related to privacy, safety, justice, change in human agency, accountability, responsibility, social interaction, power, and ideology.

The Future of Ethical Technologies

The reality is that most tech companies practice *market fundamentalism*, also known as free market. This is a term applied to a strong belief in the ability of unregulated laissez-faire or free-market capitalist policies to solve most economic and social problems. It is often used as a pejorative by critics. Although tech companies don't choose profit over social good in every instance, it is the case that for the organizational resources necessary for morality to win out, they need to be justified in market-friendly terms. When push comes to shove, profit usually wins.

In addition, most tech companies practice *technological solutionism.* The idea that all problems have tractable technical fixes has been reinforced by the rewards the industry has reaped for producing technology that they believe does solve problems. Even if the negative effects are glaring in everyone's eyes, they would justify it with "it's all in service for a greater good."

Another reality is that most technology companies would like to build predictable processes and outcomes that serve the bottom line. Always evaluating how much "ethics" adds to the cost of doing business? They need lots of external pressures to respond to ethical considerations (Moss and Metcalf, 2019).

The third reality is that until recently, the education system was busy cranking out programmers to build technology companies but did not spend enough time looking at the ethical considerations. Today, there is some momentum in universities around the world to develop courses that bridge technology and ethics. For example, at Harvard University (Karoff, 2019), some of the ethical problems that courses are tackling include these: Are software developers morally obligated to design for inclusion? Should social media companies suppress the spread of fake news on their platforms? Should search engines be transparent about how they rank results? Should we think about electronic privacy as a right?

Establishing an ethics curriculum in schools or policies in companies is critical for creating an ethical technology. The contents of the policy should be specific to the values, goals, and culture of the institution or companies in different communities. One size does not fit all.

Are universal ethical principles in technology possible? The answer is no. Nor should universality be the goal. Ethics are culturally dependent; thus, expecting them to all be the same is setting yourself up for failure.

As a leader and a human being, think hard about the ethical implications of what you bring into this world. What are you building? Who plans to use it? What can it potentially be used for—intended and unintended? What are some of the worst-case scenarios if bad actors get their hands on it? What fail-safes can you put into place to mitigate or expose that? Will the systems you work for or create be used to hurt, control, or profile others?

If you were born in another country, would you feel differently about your contribution to this system? What effects on the planet will your project have? Is your system susceptible to bias?

With each cultural shift and technological advancement, we are constantly being forced to reevaluate our ethics and policies, traverse new possibilities, and deal with unintended consequences. Knowing too well that our world is interconnected and interdependent, let's strive together for a better world and for each other.

There is a lot that individuals can do—locally, nationally, internationally—to proactively and reactively mitigate the unintended consequences of technology. In order to get there, we need a reset. A reboot. A restart.

In the next and final chapter, we will look at what a technology restart might look like.

REFERENCES

Blais-Billie, Braudie. (2014). "10 Things You Don't Know About Native Americans." https://lenapeprograms.info/teacher-parent-resources/stereotypes-debunked/

Confessore, Nicholas. (2018). "Cambridge Analytica and Facebook: The Scandal and the Fallout So Far." https://www.nytimes.com/2018/04/04/us/politics/cambridge-analytica-scandal-fallout.html

Cuthbertson, Anthony. (2020). "YouTube Bias Exposed By 'TheirTube' Project That Shows How Platform Looks to Conspiracy Theorists." https://www.independent.co.uk/life-style/gadgets-and-tech/news/youtube-bias-algorithm-theirtube-mozilla-conspiracy-theory-videos-a9624936.html

Hafner, Josh. (2018). "Make an AR-15 at home: 3D printed 'downloadable guns.'" https://www.usatoday.com/story/tech/nation-now/2018/07/23/3-d-printing-guns-downloadable-gun-legal-august-1/820032002/

Hofmann, Björn. (2017). 'Smart-Glasses: Exposing and Elucidating the Ethical Issues." https://www.researchgate.net/publication/305470106_Smart-Glasses_Exposing_and_Elucidating_the_Ethical_Issues#:~:text=A%20wide%20variety%20of%20ethical,social%20interaction%2C%20power%20and%20ideology.

Karoff, Paul. (2019). "Harvard initiative seen as a national model." https://news.harvard.edu/gazette/story/2019/01/harvard-works-to-embed-ethics-in-computer-science-curriculum/

McNeill, Stuart. (2014). "The cost of unethical behavior." https://assets.corporatecompliance.org/Portals/1/PDF/Resources/ethikos/past-issues/2014/scce-2014-03-ethikos-mcneill.pdf

Moss, Emanuel, and Jacob Metcalf. (2019). "The Ethical Dilemma at the Heart of Big Tech Companies." https://hbr.org/2019/11/the-ethical-dilemma-at-the-heart-of-big-tech-companies

Peters, Jay. (2021). "Personal data of 533 million Facebook users leaks online." https://www.theverge.com/2021/4/4/22366822/facebook-personal-data-533-million-leaks-online-email-phone-numbers

University of Vermont. (2021). "Virginia Eugenics." https://www.uvm.edu/~lkaelber/eugenics/VA/VA.html

Wessel, Max, and Nicole Helmer. (2020). "A Crisis of Ethics in Technology Innovation." https://sloanreview.mit.edu/article/a-crisis-of-ethics-in-technology-innovation/

CHAPTER 14

Restart: The Most Powerful Vote We Have: The Ballot, Money, or Attention?

The COVID-19 pandemic has provided a unique opportunity to think about the kind of future we want. The way things are going, this "computer called life" we are currently running nonstop needs a restart! If we are to have even a chance at saving our species and our planet, technology development, deployment, and usage all need a restart.

It's very easy to feel powerless in the face of the many never-ending streams of unintended consequences of technology, but you are not powerless. We all have a role to play. Our power and influence are in our "vote." Allow me to explain. There are three types of votes:

- Voting with our attention

- Voting at the ballot box

- Voting by spending money (otherwise known as spending power)

Most human beings have at least one of these three ABM (attention/ballot box/money) powers.

VOTING WITH OUR ATTENTION

If I ask you to think of the most valuable commodity that you have, chances are good that attention isn't the first thing that would come to mind. But to companies all around the world, there's nothing more valuable than the customers' attention. They spend millions of dollars trying to capture our attention. Technology has evolved to take advantage of us and it does it surreptitiously, tapping into many aspects of our human psychology. But it's created something even more sinister in its wake: an environment of perpetual digital distraction.

In the attention economy, attention is not only a resource but a currency. Users (formerly known as humans) pay for a service with their attention. Today, the dynamics of the attention economy incentivize companies to draw users in to spend more and more time on apps and websites.

The attention economy is a resource that cannot be bought by money, as users pay for the service or information they receive online by giving their attention. Social networking sites such as Facebook, Instagram, Twitter, and TikTok are a few of the many platforms out there fueling the attention economy. Worldwide, 3.96 billion people use social media, according to platform reports on the current number of active users. That's 58.11% of the world's population (Dean, 2021).

When we choose to spend time on an app or website, in essence we are voting for it. Giving it our time, we are implicitly or explicitly saying it's good. Companies mine this attention many ways, one of which is by charging ad rates based on how many users/visitors they can claim.

Sharing a site or an app with our friends and inviting them to join is like guiding someone to the polling station to vote. The more voters an app gets, the more popularity it has. The more popularity, the more the company makes money through ads. The more it makes money, the more it's incentivized to keep you hooked longer, but also to entice you to invite more friends. The loop never ends.

It's all about the money. Advertising is what makes these huge platforms their billions. Your viewing history is tracked for the sole purpose of showing you tailored content, whether it's the news that Facebook shows you or the ads that appear on Instagram. By using information like the time we spend on a site or our click-through rate, these companies can control us, and the more we participate, the more powerful their control.

As consumers, you can choose to look away. Take your attention elsewhere. You can also press them to do better for our well-being and for the betterment of humanity and our planet. If you don't like how things are going, press the restart button. We can vote with our feet and switch to alternative products that support humanity.

Vote with your attention!

VOTING AT THE BALLOT BOX

This is the type of voting that we associate with the word "vote." Voting at the ballot box means you get a say in who is running your government, or which laws or propositions are passed. Democracies elect office holders by voting. Citizens vote for leaders to represent them and their ideas, and the leaders support the citizens' interests. These elected leaders represent the community and make laws that run it. Your vote has power. It's a formal indication of a choice between two or more candidates or courses of certain action. When you vote, it gives you (the good guy or gal) the right and power to make the right choice by voting other good humans into office.

Sometimes, eligible voters chose not to vote, a procedure referred to as *abstention*. This may happen either when an eligible participant does not go to vote (on the designated election day/time) or is present during the vote but does not cast a ballot. When you abstain, you allow choices about you and your community to be made by others.

For the longest time as an adult, I never voted. Not because I was a terrible citizen, but because life dealt me cards that put me in a position to be ineligible in the United States, where I lived. I was born and raised in rural Uganda. When I turned 18, it was in the middle of an election cycle. At 21, I moved to the United States to go to school in search of a better life for me and my family. In the United States, I was old enough to vote, but since I was not a U.S. citizen, I was ineligible. Up until I was eligible to take part in a democratic process, I always envied people who have the power to choose the politicians and the laws that represent their views.

I am blown away by people who are eligible and able but chose not to vote because they think it does not matter. If you don't like how things are going, vote with your feet. Go to the polling stations and vote for the politicians who are going to vote on and create laws that represent you and your interests. Perhaps those laws will protect citizens against the many unintended consequences of technology.

Vote at the ballot box!

VOTING BY SPENDING MONEY

My son and I occasionally go to our favorite burger joint for a bite. I always tell him that by going to this place, in essence we are voting with our dollars. Which we are!

Every time you buy something, you are voting with your wallet. This type of voting is one of the most powerful. If you have money to spend, you have power. It shows companies what you like and dislike, by choosing where to shop and what to buy. As a customer, if you don't like a certain product, you vote with your wallet by not buying it. Terrible products and businesses that can't sell products eventually go under. The ones that sell products not only survive, they thrive. Technology companies are not any different. A cocktail of exponential technologies and capitalism is going to create lots of good and can create harm on steroids.

Part I of this book is about how we got into this mess. Chapter 1 is about capitalism. Voting with your pocketbooks is what drives capitalism. The free-market model has managed to generate a triple crisis for capitalism: it is financially unstable, environmentally unsustainable, and politically unpopular. If we are to have a shot at saving our species and our planet, capitalism has to change.

A better economy is possible. But we need to reimagine capitalism to do it. There are reasons to believe that a better economic system is possible—and that it could be just around the corner. As the initial shock of the COVID-19 crisis receded, we saw a glimpse of what was possible. Tech CEOs made declarations toward stakeholder capitalism: 181 CEOs, including the likes of Apple's Tim Cook, Salesforce's Marc Benioff, and JP Morgan's Jamie Dimon, signed a letter espousing stakeholder capitalism (Ward, 2020), the belief that companies exist to benefit not just their shareholders, but their workers, customers, and the environment. We need this shift in the outcomes of capitalism to start acting on the public good and the well-being of all, instead of just a few.

Rather than chasing short-term profits or narrow self-interest, companies could pursue the well-being of all people and the entire planet. This does not require a 180-degree turn; corporations don't have to stop pursuing profits for their shareholders. They only need to shift to a longer-term perspective of their organization and its mission, looking beyond the next quarter or fiscal year to the next decade and generation (Schwab, 2020).

There is a huge distance between declarations and deeds—between translating words into actions on the ground into the lives of people and for a better planet.

Vote with your wallet. Let companies know that workers need to get equal pay for equal work. This it's good for the individual worker but it's also good for the company, because it helps attract and retain the very best, diverse workforce and top talent.

With your wallet, vote for companies that take care of their customers. Companies consider product safety, data privacy, and fair pricing—all things most humans deem important.

With your wallet, vote for companies that respect and protect our environment. The technology industry has a disproportionately detrimental impact on the environment, as we have discussed in the book.

Vote for companies that respect and support local communities where they operate. Companies and their leaders are in a unique position to affect the economic opportunities and livelihood of their local communities, further helping the people who work for them or the communities where they reside.

With the power of your wallet, vote! You have a huge role to play in shifting the direction of capitalism. To silence greed, we must raise the voices of equality.

If you don't like how things are going, press the restart button. Vote with your feet and buy products from companies that support humanity.

Vote with your wallet!

Final Thoughts

My fellow global citizens, the biggest power we have to make sure species and our human race does not go extinct is the power of our vote. The politicians you vote for matter. The way you spend your money matters. The bank you store your money in matters. The app you download and the ads you click on matter.

My hope is that you will harness your voice and your vote—reflecting on all that you've witnessed and hungered for, all that you know to be true—and use it to create more equity, more justice, and more joy in the world.

As we develop, deploy, and use exponential technologies, we need to be thinking about their unintended negative consequences. My ultimate hope is that we deploy technologies that bring about what my friend author Lynne Twist calls an "environmentally sustainable, spiritually fulfilling, socially just human presence" that puts people and the planet above profits.

Be sure to vote wisely! That's the restart we need, for the survival of our humanity. Our planet depends on it.

References

Dean, Brian. (2021). "Social Network Usage & Growth Statistics: How Many People Use Social Media in 2021?" https://backlinko.com/social-media-users

Schwab, Klaus. (2020). "A Better Economy Is Possible. But We Need to Reimagine Capitalism to Do It." https://time.com/collection/great-reset/5900748/klaus-schwab-capitalism/

Ward, Marguerite. (2020). "181 CEOs of companies like Apple and Walmart committed to stakeholder capitalism." https://www.businessinsider.com/business-roundtable-survey-stakeholder-capitalism-apple-jpmorgan-walmart-shareholders-2020-8

ACKNOWLEDGMENTS

First and foremost, I would like to thank my family for their patience and love: Caroline (this journey of life is better with you), Matt (keep shining, son), Grandma Elnora (the foundation), Mom Martha (the rock), and Dad Michael (the anchor), Carol Adams (the wind beneath my wings), and Ben Isoke (the Instigator). There would be no Chris Ategeka without you all. Thank you!

To my siblings, Tristan and Chelsi, Hillary and Martin, Patrick, Margret, Deo, and Rachel.

To my in-laws, Susan and Jim—and Anna, Eric, Caterina, Beau, Marian, Elis, and Misha.

I could not ask for a more loving and supportive family.

I would like to thank all those who helped me on this book journey. Those who helped me write and those who helped me delete—and also those who supported in many different ways.

To Brian Neill and my publisher Wiley, who reached out and offered me the opportunity and guided me through the long process of writing a book—and also the entire team at Wiley for all their creativity, hard work, and support.

To my managing editor, Deb Schindlar, thank you for steering the ship.

To my developmental editor, Kezia Endsley, who devoted much time and effort to correcting my mistakes and enabling me to see things from new perspectives. Thank you for editing the manuscript as well as shepherding this book from draft to reality.

To my copy editor, Amy Handy, thank you for your hard work and for helping with the final draft.

To my friend Gary Liu, thank you for your contributions on 5G, sir!

To my research team, Aaron Xi and Claire Brady, thank you for helping with the research on some of the amazing people and organizations out there in the world working hard on the solutions to the UCOTs.

To Gemma Bulos and the Kravis Lab for Social Impact over at Claremont Mckenna College for the support and galvanizing the research team.

To Parul, Matt, and the community at the London Writers' Salon. Thank you so much for the feedback, for creating such an amazing writer's community, and for holding the Zoom space for accountability and support.

Thanks to those who gave feedback to all or part of this writing process: The Tribe: Aisha, Peter, Lauren, Jen, Kimberly, and Tabitha; my CG group: Natalie, Cassie, Seth, Fatimah, James, Jess T. Juliana, Ashok, and Jess S. Thanks for the spiritual support and for cover-page feedback. Your support made this book so much better.

To my devoted team at UCOT, who have worked tirelessly for many years to support our mission and also inspired the writing of this book.

To the supporters of my work at UCOT over the years: Michael and Martha Helms, George Anwar, Kristen Sadler, Meena Palaniappan, Suvi Sharma, 1440 Multiversity, and the Knight Foundation. Thank you!

To my extended network: UC Berkeley, TED and TED Fellows, YGL and the World Economic Forum; Echoing Green (Cheryl and team), Ashoka, Harambe Entrepreneur Alliance (Mr. Okendo), SOCAP, Opportunity Collaboration (Topher and Jorian, Ron and Marlys, and Ron and Marty); Conveners (Avary and SaraJoy); Planet Home (Antony and Gabrielle); Hatch (Yarrow); Forbes 30 under 30; Katapult (Ida and Katie); Skoll World Forum, Reality Israel, the Muhammad Ali Center, Cordes Foundation, the BIG Ideas at CAL (Phillip and the team), Judith Lee Stronach Baccalaureate Prize (Prof. Raymond Lifchez + Mary C.), Modernist (Steve Chen and the crew), and many more. Thank you!

I could not ask for better warriors and fellow travelers in this human experience here on spaceship Earth.

And finally, to all my readers, for their interest, time, and comments.

Mwebale Muno! (*Rutooro—my mother tongue—for "Immense Gratitude."*)

ABOUT THE AUTHOR

Chris Ategeka is an engineer, entrepreneur, and philanthropist. Born and raised in rural Uganda, Ategeka has overcome extreme hardship and committed himself to give back to his homeland and to the world. Chris is the founder and serves as CEO of UCOT, a company with a unique model creating solutions to unintended and willfully ignored consequences of technology.

Before that, he was the founder and board chair at Health Access Corps, which focuses on strengthening healthcare systems in Africa using local talent to combat the extreme shortage of healthcare services in underserved regions. He is also the founding partner at Startup Playbook VC, which is a pre-seed fund that provides the "friends and family" round of financing to support software startup companies run by women and other entrepreneurs who have been traditionally underrepresented in the venture capital market.

Chris has won many international honors for his work. He was named to *Forbes* magazine's "30 Under 30" list, an Echoing Green Fellow, Ashoka Fellow, TED Fellow, World Economic Forum as a Young Global Leader, and most recently was honored at his alma mater by Chancellor Carol Christ and the UC Berkeley Foundation Board of Trustees with a 2021 Mark Bingham Award for excellence in achievement by a young alumnus in the last 10 years. Chris acquired his education from the University of California, Berkeley, where he graduated with a bachelor of science and a master of science in mechanical engineering.

INDEX

C

Ca$hvertising (Whitman), 106
California Consumer Privacy Act
    (CCPA), 52
Callendar, Guy Stewart, 222
Cambridge Analytica, 72, 247
Canada, on gene editing, 131
Cancel culture, 104–105
Capitalism, 3–18
    advantages of, 7
    alternatives to, 6–7
    conscious capitalism, 16
    defined, 3
    future of, 15–16
    history of, 3–6
    mitigating UCOTs and reimagining,
        12–15
    negative consequences of, 8–12 (*See
        also* UCOTs)
    See also Economic issues; Tech-states
Capitol riots (January 6, 2021), 28, 51,
    70, 167, 170
Carbon
    carbon dioxide (CO_2), defined, 220
    carbon sequestration, 227, 228, 231–232
    emission regulation vs. capitalism,
        12–13
    See also Climate change;
        Energy sources
Cartagena Protocol on Biosafety, 133
Causation, 48
Cell phones. *See* 5G; Smartphones
Charpentier, Emmanuelle, 123
China
    5G security concerns, 146–147,
        150, 151, 153
    Hong Kong political crisis and, 102
    telecom dominance of, 145–147
    U.S. economic conflict with, 178–179
Cigarettes, 163, 244
CISCO, 144
Citizen's Assembly, 115
Civil Rights Act (1964), 212
Climate change, 219–238

climate change, defined, 220–221
    energy consumption and,
        90–91, 148, 152
    fight-flight-freeze (FFF) reaction to,
        219–220, 228
    5G technology and, 148, 151–153
    forest clear-cutting and, 225, 227, 228,
        230, 231, 233
    fossil fuels and, 13, 221, 224,
        225, 228–230
    greenhouse effect and, 13, 220–223,
        225–228, 230, 232–234
    history of, 222–224
    plankton/phytoplanton and,
        228–229, 233
    taking action against, 228–234
    UCOT examples of, 224–225
    UCOT mitigation of, 225–227
Clinton, Hillary, 187–189
Cloud data storage/computing, 40,
    56, 139, 201
Coded Bias (Netflix), 67
Code-division multiple access (CDMA),
    143–144, 148
Coherence theory of truth, 157
CoinDesk, 163
"Cold war" (military applications of
    5G), 142–143
Comet Ping Pong pizzeria, 166–167
Comprehensive National Cybersecurity
    Initiative, 192
"Computing Machinery and
    Intelligence" (Turing), 63
Conditioning, 99–100. *See also*
    Social media
Confirmation bias, 46, 159, 168–169
Confounding variables, 48–49
Connected devices, 138–139, 140–141
Conscious capitalism, 16
Conspiracy theories. *See* Truth and
    willful ignorance
Consulting Association, 26
Consumer Financial Protection
    Bureau, 245

Truth in advertising law (FTC), 57–58
Tubbs, Michael, 210
Turing, Alan, 63
24/6 (Shlain), 116
Twitter, 103–104, 112, 162–163
Tyndall, John, 222

U
Uber, 53, 208–209
UCOTS (unintended consequences of technology)
  defined, 3
  reimagining capitalism for mitigation of, 12–15
  tech-states and mitigation of, 31–33
  UCOT examples and capitalism in technology sector, 8–12
  "voting" as restart for technology, 251–256
  See also individual technology and trend topics
Uganda, on social media, 24
Ulbricht, Ross William, 89–90
Ultra-High Definition (UHD), 139
Underfitting, 48
United Kingdom, Minister for Loneliness in, 111
United Nations, 78–79, 224
United States
  China and economic conflict with, 178–179
  military applications of 5G, 142–143
  monopoly power of tech-states in, 30
  telecom dominance lost by, 143–147
  See also Regulation; individual names of agencies; individual names of leaders; individual names of legislation
Unite in the UK, 26
Universal basic income (UBI), 210
U.S. Air Force, 166
U.S. Census, 40, 206
U.S. Department of Homeland Security, 192
U.S. Department of Justice, 184

U.S. Department of State, 180
U.S. Fair Lending regulations, 76
Userbase
  data created by Internet users, 41
  individual level reset of big data, 56, 58–59
  social media users, defined, 103 (*See also* Social media)
  tech-states and dehumanizing of customers, 24
  of tech-states vs. population of nation-states, 23–24
  tech-state treatment of, 26
  worldwide social media userbase, 252
User experience (UX), 117
"Us vs. them" mentality, 108

V
Vaccines, 125–126, 165, 239–240
Values vs. ethics, 242
Verizon, 143–145
Vicente, Antonio, 231
Virus (computer), 183
"Voting" as restart for technology, 251–256
Voting laws, AI and, 71–72
Vs (Volume, Velocity, Variety) of big data, 41–42

W
Wagner Act (1935), 212
Walmart, 15
Warfare. *See* Cyber warfare
Water system, attack on, 187
Wealth inequality
  access rights and, 240
  AI and, 71
  inherited wealth and, 10–11
  stakeholder capitalism vs. shareholder capitalism, 14
  tech-states' political power and, 27
  universal basic income (UBI), 210
  work and automation issues, 205, 206, 208–209, 214